IN SEARCH OF AMERICA'S FUTURE

A Story That Will Change Your Life

Steven A. Cunningham
P. Leigh Thomason

The authors have no affiliation with any
political party or political organization.

Sound Advice Productions, LLC
Atlanta, Georgia

Published by Sound Advice Productions, LLC,
Atlanta, Georgia

Cover and inside illustration by Michele Phillips,
www.michelecreates.com

Back cover photo by Kayla L. Smith
kaylal.smithphotography@yahoo.com

Publishing support provided by Booklogix Publishing services,
Alpharetta, Georgia

Government, Political, Economy

ISBN 978-1-61005-005-0

For more information:
Sound Advice Productions, LLC
PO Box 2263
Dawsonville, GA 30534
www.insearchofamericasfuture.com

To

AINSLEY

and all the children of America

may their future be as bright as her beautiful smile!

Dr. Lee,
Thank you so much for
being so supportive and caring.
I cherish the memories of
the birth of my son Dillon and
your support and kind words
after his death. His Daughter
Ainsley is a very special gift
to the world. Take care and
Thank you!
Teresa Thomason

DEDICATION

'Show Us the Way to Go Home'

This book is dedicated to the millions of hard-working Americans who believe in the American way of life, but also believe that the American way of life is being undone by those who use and abuse our political and economic system to their benefit and our detriment.

This book is also dedicated to the Greatest Generation, to whom all of us today owe a debt of extreme gratitude for preserving and enhancing the American way of life -- a way paved by them with great sacrifice, even of life. They showed us the way to prosperity, peace of mind and freedom from oppression. Although we may have lost the way and are wandering in an economic and political wilderness largely of our own making, we do know the way to go home, thanks to the Greatest Generation and to the Founding Fathers. Together they left us wonderful and reliable maps to the success of a nation and a people, and we have to dust off those maps and retrace the route they laid out long ago and not so long ago to true democracy and true capitalism. We have to get off the dead-end and deadly-end paths we have been traveling these past years. Backtracking to find our way again will not be easy, but the longer we wait, the more difficult it will be.

And so we also dedicate this book to today's pathfinders, the modern-day pioneers of the almost lost and increasingly obscure American Way who are fiercely committed to guiding the rest of us out of the morass -- by rebuilding roads which have fallen into states of disrepair, building new roads around and through treacherous terrain, and providing safe passage for travelers against the political and financial robbers and highwaymen who today freely prey on the unwary and the unprepared.

The path we have been following has been leading us to become the "Divided States of America." The right way, the one less traveled, will restore us to greatness and bring us together again as the "United States of America." To all of you who are willing to put your shoulder to the wheel of renewed progress and reclaim our proud heritage of "America the Great," this book's for you.

ACKNOWLEDGMENTS

'With a Little Help from Our Friends'

Throughout the years, we have asked, with an increasing sense of frustration, why we, the American citizens, allow a handful of elected officials to make laws which take away our freedoms. And we wonder why we, the American citizens, allow a handful of elected officials to spend money they do not have on programs we do not need and then demand we pay for their bad decisions without fear of accountability or retribution.

Think about it. Somewhere along the way, Congress convinced itself that it possessed the right to indebt us without first seeking our permission. It may not be the taxation without representation the Founding Fathers considered so abhorrent, but it is taxation without authorization, which we find equally atrocious. Congress simply assumed it had carte blanche to tax and spend and tax some more and spend some more when we failed to take back control of federal spending, when we allowed Congress after Congress and Administration after Administration to increase the size of the bureaucracy exponentially, increase the magnitude of the public debt by orders of magnitude and restrict accessibility to the privileged few. We watched, mesmerized and amazed, as if viewing some visually disturbing circus sideshow, but unfortunately this was the real deal (worse, the raw deal).

Now, facing times of political turmoil and economic duress not seen since the dark days of the Great Depression, we again have an opportunity to do something about Congress and the process which allows it to function totally removed from the people who sanction its existence. No, more than an opportunity to make a change, we have an *obligation* to do so -- an obligation to ourselves and to future generations.

To all who gave us ideas for the book and the plan and encouraged us to write this book, we greatly appreciate your input, especially David H. Russell, Jean P. Thomason, Teresa Thomason,

Matthew Stucki, Austin Cunningham, Betty Cunningham, Steve Swartz, Dr. William Keating, David A. Fox, Esq., Hollis Hooks and his family, Johnnie Hall, David Hill and the employees at the Kroger-Suwanee Starbucks, Suwanee, GA, who so graciously plied Steve with 4-shot café lattes and loads of helpful encouragement.

And we extend a very special thanks to Mr. H. Ross Perot for being the torch bearer for the kind of fundamental change in government we are calling for. He provided us the necessary inspiration to take a chance and take a stand in the hope of making a difference in the public discourse. In 1992 in his book *United We Stand*, Mr. Perot insisted we could to do better as a nation for ourselves and our children by holding politicians and their allies and "hangers on" accountable. He challenged and implored us to take our nation back from the politicians who had taken control, reminding us that the people are the true and rightful owners of this great land. It is a small book, but it had a big impact on us. And now, 18 years later, the call is the same, but the plea is even more urgent and the times even more desperate. We failed to take up the gauntlet then, but failure to do so again is not a viable option, not if we want a future worthy of one of the greatest nations in history. This time around we must heed the clarion call to take our nation back from the lawmakers, lobbyists, political parties, corporate elitists and the talking heads and spin masters who enable and entrench the powers that be.

We hope this book and especially the plan we propose will provide readers with insight into where we have been, how we got there and how we got here, and how we can build a better future. That last one may seem daunting, but not in comparison to the crises faced by the Greatest Generation and the Founding Fathers. We take great comfort and courage in our knowledge that we have in our national DNA the genetic code to confront and conquer today's daunting array of problems. It's time to get down to business!

TABLE OF CONTENTS

INTRODUCTION

'What You Don't Know Can Hurt You'

*"There are two mistakes one can make along the road to truth --
not going all the way and not starting."*
- **The Buddha**

*"I am a firm believer in the people. If given the truth, they can be
depended upon to meet any national crisis. The great point is to
bring them the real facts."*
- **Abraham Lincoln**

Most of us are quite familiar with the age-old ***Humpty Dumpty***
nursery rhyme:

> *Humpty Dumpty sat on a wall,*
> *Humpty Dumpty had a great fall,*
> *All the King's horses and all the King's men*
> *Couldn't put Humpty together again!*

Now, you are probably saying to yourself, what on earth does a
200 year old nursery rhyme have to do with America's future?
Well, we believe there are hidden truths regarding the demise of
one Humpty Dumpty that may hold important lessons for us and
the state of our current political and economic system.

For example, why was the wall built in the first place? Was it
erected in order to separate the seat of government from the
people? Or maybe to protect the King from his subjects who were
feeling oppressed and growing quite unhappy with the
government?

And who built the wall? Did the King use conscripted labor?
Or did he use contract laborers provided by the nobility and pay
them exorbitant fees from the Royal Treasury which was funded
by taxing the people? Either way, the subjects of the realm would
not have been pleased.

I

And was the wall a big wall? Judging from the results of Mr. Dumpty's spectacular fall, it must be assumed the wall was quite high and therefore a relatively imposing (and hence expensive) structure. Plus there had to be some considerable costs associated with maintaining such a structure.

And who was Humpty Dumpty anyway? More likely than not, he was a government official. Otherwise, he would not have been allowed to be on top of the wall.

And how did H.D. get up to the top of the wall in the first place? He surely had to have assistance to get up there and we can only assume that the assistance was provided by the King, since his men and horses apparently tried desperately to aid him after his fall.

And why was Humpty Dumpty on the wall to begin with? Could it be he was assigned to that post so he could look down upon the people and report to the King any instances of disrespect or rumblings of discontent he might happen to observe? And maybe he was charged with the duty of pointing out troublemakers to governmental agents on the ground.

And why, as depicted in most of the illustrations, was Mr. Dumpty so large? Could it be that he had grown fat off the taxpayers of the kingdom? Could he have become bloated with greed?

And here we get to a sticky point in the story of Mr. Humpty Dumpty. Did he really fall from the wall or was he pushed off by some of the people who had grown weary of his profligate behavior and gluttony? Maybe some folks were not willing to sit idly by while H.D. lorded it over them day after day from his lofty perch, just sitting way up there above them, gorging himself on their hard-earned wages and giving them nothing in return but the "pleasure" of his "large and in charge" presence.

There are reports, after all, of protestors, just prior to his fall, carrying signs which read "Dump the Hump" and "Tear down the

Wall" and "Dumpty is a Bad Yoke." Other demonstrators were overheard shouting, "This Wall Must Fall" and "Dump Dumpty."

Or maybe H.D. wasn't shoved, but really did just fall, but only because he had grown so huge that he had become unsteady and lost his balance.

All we know for sure is that fall he did and it was a devastating fall at that since he obviously shattered into so many pieces that he could not be reconstructed, despite the best efforts of all the King's men and all the King's horses. It would come as no surprise to us if those men and horses were not intentionally delayed in their travel to the scene of the "accident" by some obstructionist subjects who were frankly glad to see the end of such a notoriously "bad egg."

And who's to say that anyone, other than the King and his lords, really wanted Humpty Dumpty to be put back together. If you ask the common folks, they would most likely tell you that the tale of Humpty Dumpty actually had a happy ending because the last thing they wanted to see was Humpty Dumpty back on that wall monitoring them and making their lives miserable.

We think the parallels to what's going on with our Humpty Dumpty (the current state of the system today) are startling and we believe this book will prove our point.

Unless we take corrective action soon to reverse the stranglehold that our two-party political system has on us, our great nation will fall from economic and societal stability and our hope will be shattered -- maybe beyond restoration. Today we are a country of many controlled by a few. In fact Congress, with its Wall Street allies, has fashioned a monopoly (a "wall") of power and influence that adversely affects and restricts all of us.

Today, as many as 35 or maybe even 40 million Americans can no longer meaningfully participate in a system in stark contrast to just 3 years earlier, because of the greed of Wall Street and the protection provided by lawmakers and regulatory agencies that allowed the pernicious greed to run rampant and roughshod over us. To make matters worse, our own Federal Reserve (one of the biggest Humpty Dumptys in the land) played a major role in allowing, often facilitating, the "greeding frenzy." Even today, the Fed continues to allow Wall Street to make billions using our money without compensation, but obligates us to be personally liable, without our consent, for trillions of dollars in national debt that may eventually lead to a period of debilitating inflation. The Fed hopes that inflating (or hyper-inflating) the money supply will lead to corporate profits and eventually jobs. It hasn't worked so far, not at all. And history shows us that failure of the Fed to turn off the easy money spigot in time will inevitably create huge inflationary pressures. It's not a matter of *if*, but *when*. Then we could find ourselves in the worst of worlds: high unemployment and rampant inflation. But the Fed, like all the other potentates of power, adheres to the convoluted philosophy of *"never do today what you can put off until tomorrow."* Time and action for all of the power peddlers are measured in terms of election cycles and with mid-term elections coming up, we will be subjected to a flurry of activity by the politicians and their lackeys, designed with one purpose and one purpose only: how to do just enough to placate the voters to get elected one more time. Then it will be back to "business as usual" -- but only if we let them implement their disingenuous strategy once again.

Sadly, there is no difference in the aspirations of the current party to stay in power than the party so feverishly attempting to return to power. And that is one of the fundamental tenets of this book. The primary objective of both political parties, the Democrats and the Republicans is, and for the most part always has been, to be the party in power. The next best thing is to be the party seeking to get back into power. The two-party system may in fact be the worst Humpty Dumpty of all, the one most in need of a fall. It is a system operated by many corrupt and corruptible lawmakers and yet we allow it to continue its rock solid hold on the reins of government election after election, believing in the electoral mystics who claim to know, by divine political communion, that the party seeking to regain power will be different and will work for real change. Never mind that the last time that party was in power, it made the same promise in order to get back into power, but did not and never really intended to walk its talk. Why will this time be different? It won't and that's the point.

One look at the current state of affairs will prove the point. In the past ten years, we have incurred more national debt than in the previous two centuries and two decades combined. Obviously, the periodically prognosticated change has not happened and will not happen unless we, the electorate, decide to make real and lasting change to the current system of politics. We need a system that works for us, not one that looks down upon us with varying degrees of disdain and disregard from the top of some wall. We must implement a new system whereby we control the lawmakers instead of the lawmakers controlling us. We must have a system that makes lawmakers and their cohorts accountable and responsible to the citizenry. We must bring the "Humpty Dumpty" down to earth, bring them outside the wall of insulation and isolation which has been built around Washington.

Think about this: during the past three years, at least 35 million Americans can no longer either afford or qualify to buy a home. Over 20 million homes have already been foreclosed or will likely be foreclosed over the next two years. That is one in five homes lost to foreclosure, a record that we can only hope stands forever. In addition, 30 million Americans are either unemployed or underemployed and millions have lost their savings and pensions (more than $5 trillion worth). And do not be fooled into believing the recent run-ups in the stock market point to an "all clear" sign because the real financial forecast is anything but. The Fed and the financial institutions have manipulated the run-ups to make us believe that the worst is over, to make us feel better about our prospects and restore confidence in the economy. This effort to instill false confidence may work to some degree for people with jobs, but it is seen for what it is by those struggling to make ends meet on a daily basis -- a meaningless charade. In truth, the only way that our economic way of life will improve is with real job growth and real wage growth and neither is happening now or is likely to happen with the current regime.

Who is to blame? Ultimately we are if we don't stop the madness that we are being forced to endure as we discuss in detail in the following 19 chapters of this book and adopt radical changes as we propose in the final chapter. We saw an e-mail posting on *The Cafferty File* on *CNN* by a 27-year old and he had this to say:

> *"I hate to write this, because it applies to my parents, too, but the Baby Boomer generation has rested on its laurels. They did not build at all on the legacy left them by the Greatest Generation. In fact, they have pretty much squandered it and left us with little or nothing. Unfortunately, they have made something of a mess of things in America and seem to be bent on leaving it for me and my generation to find a way to clean up."*

This view, we believe, is widely shared by the so-called Generation Y and most likely Generation X young folks also. And why shouldn't they feel this way? They should be angry and frustrated with us. We have not done right by them and by future generations and we are asking them to pay for our excesses and our devil-may-care attitude. Honestly, the only saving grace in this state of mind we have caused to develop is that it is not too late for our generation to get moving and honor the legacy that was built with the blood, sweat and tears of the Greatest Generation. But time is truly of the essence and we cannot waste another minute doing nothing. We have to decide here and now if this generation is destined for *greatness* or destined for *lateness* -- as in waiting too late to take a stand and make a difference.

Mr. "twenty-something," we hear you loud and clear and we get it, at least we think we do. And so, in an effort to find a path to a better future for all of us and our progeny, we have developed a 20-point plan for extensively overhauling the system which we have entitled *A Plan for a Better America.* It is our **Call for Action.** It is outlined in the final chapter, but we would ask that you not skip ahead but instead first read the preceding chapters which explore the "systemic" problems which our *Plan* seeks to solve.

We believe our *Plan* provides the foundation to start us on a road to real recovery. We recognize we are well beyond band-aids and antibiotic ointments. We need radical reconstructive surgery. And we realize the federal government is not the answer to our societal or economic woes; it is ourselves, it is "power to the people" that will provide the nation with healing power. In this regard, nothing has really changed since the founding of this great land when Thomas Jefferson spoke these words: "I predict future happiness for Americans if they can prevent the government from wasting the labors of the people under the pretense of taking care of them."

We sincerely hope and we truly believe our *Plan* does provide a blueprint for a better future, a better America, a better system. Let us put our children's and grandchildren's future first and foremost and rebuild a system that works for the people for a change!

CHAPTER 1

DESPAIR
'Down But Not Out'

"I must lose myself in action, lest I wither in despair."
- Alfred Lord Tennyson

"But what we call our despair is often only the eagerness of unfed hope."
- George Eliot

It is the year 2010 and we find ourselves frustrated to the point of despair over the direction in which our political leaders are leading us (leading us astray, to put it mildly), so much so that, to preserve our sanity, we must discover why the larger "we," the citizenry, blindly allow ourselves to be herded down a path to economic and social defilement and decay. So, as ones who never desired or sought to be actively involved in understanding the larger issue of politics, for the first time we begin to reflect seriously on what is going on around us. This reflection has led us to begin to pen some random and not-so-random thoughts on the eye-catching headlines and news items of the day.

One cannot turn on the radio, television or computer without being barraged by some talking heads (spin doctors) sermonizing about how the economy is beginning to improve at long last and that the Administration is cautiously optimistic (now there's a hackneyed phrase), believing its actions have served to place us on the ever elusive "road to recovery" -- which will take us to the "economic promised land" (promised by them, of course) where we can revel in sustained economic growth and leave in our rear view mirrors the worst economic downturn since the Great Depression. If not this financial post-apocalyptic talk, we are instead harangued by the "other side," the doomsday prophets, who proclaim that the worst is yet to come and the current powers that be have really done nothing more than apply iodine and band-aids to mortal economic wounds. For the first group, the patient (the American economy) is out of intensive care, for the latter, it should be receiving last rites.

As the day progresses, our despair worsens and we find ourselves filled with doubt as to the Administration's new pronouncements (if not rosy, at least a healthy shade of pink) and the other side's assessment that this same Administration's tax and spend policies are bankrupting our country and running the ship of state aground. Then, we are hit with that strong sensation of déjà vu from the prior eight years of the same denouncements from the Democrats railing against and wailing about the then Bush administration. The inescapable conclusion: no matter the issues, no matter the date, no matter the players, the role of the politicos remains the same -- stir the pot, constantly stay in "attack mode," get re-elected, game on and "we're in it to win it". Then we begin to consider the seriousness of this so-called "game":

❖ 31 million Americans are unemployed or underemployed (one in every five workers)

❖ one in four homeowners is in danger of losing his or her home to foreclosure

❖ more than 6 million American property owners have already lost their homes to foreclosure and 8 million homeowners are in foreclosure or about to be

❖ 6,000 Americans are filing for bankruptcy every day (more than four every minute)

❖ a staggering $55 trillion from pensions and savings has been wiped out over the past three years

❖ the percentage of American workers with less than $10,000 for retirement hit 43% this year, a 10% increase from 2009

❖ the percentage of workers with less than $1,000 for retirement reached 27% this year

❖ our health care costs are now the highest in the world (more than $8,000 for every man, woman and child in the country), but the quality of our health care has fallen far below the top

❖ wealth inequality in the United States is now the highest on record, with the top 10% of the population earning more than 50% of total income and the top 1% owning 40% of the nation's wealth, more than the bottom 90% combined

❖ today, despite the new health care legislation, 47 million Americans, including almost 9 million children, have no health insurance

❖ 40 million people in America are living in poverty, including 14 million children

❖ over 49 million people in this great nation. live in households that cannot afford the food they need to eat -- over 14% of all adults and 23% of all children

❖ more than 27 million people in this country face hunger and malnutrition on a daily basis

❖ our Gulf Coast is being ravaged by oil from the worst environmental disaster in our nation's history

There is something rotten in the State (and States) of America and the stench is growing worse by the day.

Yet the profits of the Wall Street banks last year topped $55 billion, more than triple the previous record, and bonuses exceeded $20 billion, the second highest on record (it helps to write those numbers out with all their zeros to better appreciate their magnitude -- $55,000,000,000 and $20,000,000,000, respectively). Goldman Sachs, the leader of the pack (sometimes referred to as the "Godfather of Wall Street" or better yet, the "Puppet Master") reported record profits of $13.4 billion last year, almost $5 billion in the fourth quarter alone. And it's off to the races again this year, reporting a 91% increase in first quarter profits at $3.46 billion.

Yes, the money merchants have barely skipped a beat. The number 2 bank (also a Wall Street "Puppet Master" in its own right), JP Morgan Chase, reported a hefty first quarter 2010 of $3.3 billion, but was bested by another of the Wall Street contenders for the heavyweight crown, Citigroup, coming in with first quarter profits of $4.4 billion -- our response is the same as the quip of former tennis star John McEnroe when confronted with a ghastly call by a linesman or umpire: *"you CANNOT be serious!"* And these billions of dollars for the very same people who were, far and away, the greatest single contributor to the financial crisis, which some claimed almost brought down the world's economies in one fell swoop.

You would certainly think that, in the hopeful twilight of the "great crisis", the banks at the very heart of the crisis would have been subjected to some "downsizing" and adopted greater risk containment policies and procedures. Sadly, such an expectation would be entirely too much to ask of a culture so steeped in greed and hubris. Quite to the contrary, according to noted economist Simon Johnson, in a PBS interview with veteran journalist Bill Moyers, which aired on PBS on April 18, 2010:

> *"The big banks became stronger as a result of the bailout. That may seem extraordinary, but it's really true. They're turning that increased economic clout into more political power. And they're using that political power to go out and take the same sort of risks that got us into disaster in September 2008."*

Johnson is certainly no lightweight when it comes to credentials and credibility. He is Professor of Entrepreneurship at MIT's Sloan School of Management and formerly was Professor of Economics at Duke University's Fuqua School of Business and the Chief Economist of the International Monetary Fund. He holds a Ph.D. in economics from MIT, an M.A. from the University of Manchester, and his B.A. is from the University of Oxford.

Mr. Johnson, appearing with colleague James Kwak (the two co-authored and released in March a critically acclaimed book entitled ***13 Bankers: The Wall Street Takeover and the Next Financial Meltdown***, a blistering blow-by-blow indictment of Wall Street's role in the financial crisis) claimed that the six largest banks (Goldman Sachs, Morgan Stanley, JPMorgan Chase, Citigroup, Bank of America, and Wells Fargo) are today a true oligarchy (which they define as *"political power based on economic power"*). As Kwak explained:

> *"They have assets equivalent to over 60% of our gross national product; and to put this in perspective, in the mid-1990s, these six banks or their predecessors, since there have been a lot of mergers, had less than 20%. Their assets were less than 20% of the gross national product."*

You know what they say about absolute power corrupting absolutely. Well, the oligarchical power wielded by the *"six sisters"* may set us up for another fiasco because, as Mr. Johnson further observed:

> *"They can distort the system. They can change the rules of the game to favor themselves. And, unfortunately, the way it works in modern finance is, when the rules favor you, you go out and you take a lot of risk. And you blow up from time to time, because it's not your problem. When it blows up, it's the taxpayer and it's the government that has to sort it out."*

We have a saying down South that "pigs get fat (or fed) and hogs get slaughtered." But this obviously does not apply to Wall Street. In their world, pigs get fat (and fed) and hogs get, well, fatter, but certainly not butchered. The Wall Street pigs are more like the ones in George Orwell's 1945 classic novel, ***Animal Farm***, who took over the farm, threw out the farmer, and established a totalitarian regime. These (not so) little piggies went to market, all right, but they ended up running it and eating all the roast beef and leaving us with none – but, unlike the nursery rhyme, they cried "we, we, we" instead of "wee, wee, wee" all the way home.

And following right behind the investment bankers on the crisis causation totem pole are the hedge fund managers, who worked hand-in-glove with many of the Wall Street bankers to facilitate the buying and selling of high-risk, highly leveraged, opaque securities, like credit default swaps, collateralized debt obligations, collateralized mortgage obligations, and arbitrage instruments. Yet they too are back and back with a vengeance -- last year, the top 25 hedge fund managers earned a record $25 billion (that's $25,000,000,000 or $1 billion on average each).

To borrow from a popular 1982 country western song by Jerry Reed, "they got the gold mine and we got the shaft." What drives the bankers and hedge fund managers? You know the answer to that question. It is greed, pure and simple (well, maybe not so "pure"). In their minds, capitalism equates to and is powered by greed. Their mantra is the same one espoused 23 years ago by Gordon Gekko in the film *Wall Street*: *"Greed is good. Greed is right. Greed works."* And it works even better when the mistakes stemming from unchecked greed get bailed out by the American taxpayer, when they can say with impunity "what's mine is mine and what's yours is mine."

The Wall Street game is a zero sum game-by definition, that's a "winner take all" game in which one party necessarily wins and the other party loses (in this case, the financial institutions won and the taxpayers lost). Desmond Lachman, a fellow at the American Enterprise Institute, former chief emerging market strategist at Salomon Smith Barney and deputy director of the International Monetary Fund's Policy and Review Department, agrees:

> *"Much like the oligarchs did in Russia, a small group of traders and executives at onetime venerable institutions have brought the United States and global financial systems to their knees with their reckless risk-taking -- with other people's money -- for their personal gain."*

We have all been fed a steady diet of "what's good for Wall Street is good for Main Street." But, honestly, how can that be when the top 1% of families in America own almost 50% of the stocks and bonds and the richest 20% of Americans own 85% of all of the stocks and bonds? The middle class (Main Street) actually has very little wealth in the stock market, so it is not the case that Wall Street runs parallel with Main Street. We will say this, however: Wall Street is a nicely paved boulevard these days and Main Street is a rutted dirt road in some places and a pothole-filled, "under construction", one-lane road in other stretches. Of course, there are also many sections of Main Street which are toll roads, but, guess what, the toll booths are owned and operated by Wall Street.

How was Wall Street able to turn the "bigger they are, the harder they fall" idiom into the "too big to fail" idiocy? How did "survival of the fittest" become, for Wall Street, "survival of the fattest"? How was Wall Street able to transform the free market into a fee market? One need only look to the incestuous relationship between Wall Street and Washington, most notably with respect to Goldman Sachs, which deserves much of the credit (pun intended). Consider these facts: Henry Paulson, the principal architect of the infamous TARP (Troubled Asset Relief Program) during his tenure as Treasury Secretary was CEO of Goldman Sachs prior to taking the Treasury job. He in turn appointed former Goldman Sachs Vice President Neel Kashkari to oversee the TARP fund. Tim Geithner, the current Treasury Secretary, has also surrounded himself with Goldman Sachs alumni, including his top aide and Chief of Staff, Mark Patterson, who served as the top Goldman lobbyist. Geithner's time records, obtained by the New York Times, clearly show that he has spent inordinate amounts of time with Lloyd Blankfein, current CEO of Goldman.

Larry Summers, one of President Obama's top economic advisers, received $2.7 million in speaking fees from bailed out banks and other financial institutions, including $135,000 from Goldman Sachs for a half-day visit to the firm. Both Summers and Geithner worked for Robert Rubin, Secretary of the Treasury, during the Clinton Administration, Rubin having spent 26 years with Goldman, rising to the position of Director and Co-Chairman (after the Clinton years, Rubin a cushy spent eight years with Citigroup, during which time he earned more than $126 million, and in 1997, he successfully opposed, along with Alan Greenspan, the proposed regulation of derivatives by the then head of the Commodity Futures Trading Commission Brooksley Born).

Goldman's new head lobbyist was the top aide to Representative Barney Frank, chairman of the House Financial Services Committee. To cap it off, another Goldman top executive, Gary Gensler, was selected to head the Commodity Futures Trading Commission. Nothing like having the foxes guard the henhouses. Talk about Yogi Berra's "déjà vu all over again" -- can't you hear those ghostly cries of "banksters" from the1930s in the aftermath of the Wall Street collapse and the beginning of the Great Depression? We sure can and it sends chills down our spines. One wonders if the Goldman connection is about altruism or protection! Nevertheless, Goldman needs to be wary that the hand that keeps it in business does not come back in the form of a fist, because politicians, and especially a political party, when threatened with losing power, will jettison a favored donor or constituent if it appears to do so would be more expedient to save itself. Never forget that the party comes first - relationships are fluid!

After reading about the "kissing cousins" relationship between Wall Street and Washington, we turn on the television and watch and listen to the Fox News commentators tell us that Obama is either a socialist or a communist or both and that we, as a nation, are doomed. We turn over to CNBC to see a marked decline in the value of the dollar as it continues its precipitous descent into an economic dark hole, but wait - a Federal Reserve spokesman just came on to assure everyone that the decline is orderly and is being checked, so, "be happy, don't worry," the Treasury and the Federal Reserve are on the case and united in their support of a strong dollar policy. Not unexpectedly, the chorus of CNBC commentators cheer madly and exhort their viewers to believe all will be well (so long as the stock market keeps on keeping on, that is). Where is that wandering Greek chap, Diogenes, who carried a lantern seeking honesty and truth? He found precious little of it in 4th century B.C. Greece and would find less today in 21st Century America. Most likely, Diogenes would pack his bags and hurriedly move back to Athens in disgust were he to spend any appreciable amount of time in Washington, D.C. or on Wall Street.

As we shake our heads in disbelief to the incredulous Fed Head remarks, we change the channel to CNN and listen to an economic commentator expressing dismay that our national debt will soon reach $14 trillion dollars -- $45,000 of debt for every single one of us Americans! If you want to view the magnitude of our debt in real time, take a few minutes and visit www.usdebtclock.org (believe us, you will find the time both enlightening and frightening). And get this, in the 2011 federal budget released earlier this year, the Administration projects the national debt will soar to $25 trillion by 2020 --that's over $80,000 for every man, woman and child in America. And let's not forget, we are the ones who are ultimately on the hook for every dollar of this gargantuan debt.

Moreover, we begin to think about how much money that represents for stuff we have already purchased. An appropriate analogy would be to think of it as buying items using a credit card and just forgetting about the purchase (out of sight, out of mind) until you receive your credit card statement and wonder if you really needed to make that purchase and whether you can really afford it. Then we begin to wonder if anyone in government can provide us with an itemized breakdown for the $14 trillion (and the operative word here, sadly, may well be "breakdown"). After all, shouldn't we know what we are paying for with all of this debt? Aren't we entitled to a statement showing exactly what we purchased, what we owe, and to whom we owe it? A private creditor would settle for no less, rest assured. Why on earth, then, should we tolerate less from the government?

Now, we realize that this economic morass did not happen overnight, but we still must wonder why we, the citizenry, where the buck truly stops, have allowed politicians to perpetrate this cruel hoax upon us. It is akin to going to the company picnic and having your boss ask you to pay the bill because he (conveniently) left his checkbook at the office. You do not have the cash of course, so you pull out your VISA or some other charge card, hoping it will not be rejected, promising yourself never again to be placed in such a tricky situation. Isn't this precisely what politicians do each year to the taxpayers - they stick us with the bill and promise to repay us at some future date -- with our own money!

We need to think about how the existing system works because it is somewhat like family dynamics, with politicians being the child and the taxpayers the parent. As a rule, children want everything they see and parents desire to accommodate them in a reasonable and responsible manner. Parents invariably desire for their children to have the opportunity for a better life and frequently get caught up in spending and borrowing and borrowing and spending to provide more and more for their children. All too often, it becomes a vicious circle and there may seem to be no easy way out.

As we think about this more, we begin to wonder if the average person on the street, Joe and Jane Q. Public, are truly aware of the calamitous mess that our elected officials have created. They have sailed the Ship of State right into the iceberg and there are far too few lifeboats for us, the passengers. Yet we do have to share much of the blame because we are the ones who voted them into office (albeit with repeated promises of change) election after election. Why we cannot see that the election machinery produces the same product year after year, and a defective product at that, is beyond explanation -- some of you may find yourselves hearing a line from the rock band **The Who** - *"meet the new boss, same as the old boss."*

We then must ask ourselves and each other what our children and our children's children and our children's grandchildren will think of us for allowing a group of elected party members to burden them with a crushing debt, followed by tax hikes, runaway inflation, a reduced standard of living, a marginalized military, and a nation subservient and beholden to foreign countries who hold our debt. In our mind's eye, we glimpse a future broadcast on the History Channel about the rise and fall of the United States, once the greatest economic and military power in the world, but now forced to sit in the back of a bus driven by China, with the front rows reserved for India, Brazil, South Korea, and other former third-world countries who managed to control their debt and become good stewards for their citizenry. Do our ears deceive us or did the announcer just say "shockingly, the United States is now spoken of in the same breath with Zimbabwe, something the top governmental officials and so-called economic experts openly scoffed at just a few years before the debt-triggered collapse"?

Consider the observations this year of Elizabeth Warren, Professor of Law at Harvard Law School and Chair of the Congressional Oversight Panel created to investigate the banking bailout (TARP):

> *"America today has plenty of rich and super-rich. But it has far more families who did all the right things, but who still have no real security. Going to college and finding a good job no longer guarantee economic safety. Paying for a child's education and setting aside enough for a decent retirement have become distant dreams. Tens of millions of once-secure middle class families now live paycheck to paycheck, watching as their debts pile up and worrying about whether a pink slip or a bad diagnosis will send them hurtling over an economic cliff. America without a strong middle class? Unthinkable, but the once-solid foundation is shaking."*

Our fathers used to admonish us thirty or so years ago with: "Watch and see, the rich will get richer and the poor will get poorer." At the time we did not recognize or appreciate their fortune-telling abilities.

But a few months ago, Timothy Smeeding, Professor of Economics and Public Policy at Syracuse University and Director of the Center for Policy Research, noted,

> *"Americans now have the highest income inequality in the rich world and over the past 20-30 years Americans have also experienced the greatest increases in income inequality among all rich nations."*

And so it goes, but instead of working together to try and find long-term solutions to the current financial quagmire, our political leaders instead want to keep pointing fingers and playing the "blame game." Sadly, most of our citizens are divided into polarizing camps supporting one side or the other, desperately wanting to believe that their standard bearers are committed to changing the status quo, even though history shows that it took the spending policies of both political parties many years to build the monumental economic morass of today. In fact, it took 172 years, beginning with the administration of Martin Van Buren, after Andrew Jackson saw to it that the national debt was paid off, for America to bury itself in $14 trillion dollars of debt, but $10 trillion of it has been created since 1992, with almost $3 trillion of the $14+ trillion coming during a little over two years of the Obama presidency (it is this sort of statistic that has some people crying that the Obama Nation is rapidly turning into an "Obamination").

Moreover, bear in mind that this amount does not include the "off the books" liabilities, the so-called unfunded entitlement programs, estimated to exceed $57 trillion dollars (that's $57,000,000,000,000 or $185,000 for every person in America today). Unfunded liabilities represent those that the government accountants cannot yet precisely identify, and include items such as future federal employees' retirement costs, Social Security and Medicare benefits, disability payments, and other future expense which the federal government has promised someone or some group to pay but the actual bill has yet to be presented. But the bills are coming, never doubt that.

And let's not forget about the large number of banks biting the dust in the wake of the "great crisis." Since the start of the financial crisis in 2007, 250 banks have failed, with assets totaling over $600 billion and deposits totaling more than $400 billion. More than 100 banks have been closed just over the first half of this year, almost a 58% increase over the same period last year, placing 2010 on pace to far eclipse last year's140 bank failures which was the most since 1992, the height of the savings and loan crisis. And so the "hits (to the economy, that is) just keep on coming."

Nevertheless, as we continue in our divisive and factious ways, constantly bickering among ourselves and staunchly defending the actions of one political party versus the other, the politicians and political commentators continue to sow and grow the seeds of dissent and mistrust, all while plotting for their own preservation and continued self-dealing.

The anger and righteous indignation so prevalent today is not so different from the political fights of the past. The more we watch and listen to the political discourse and diatribe, the more it appears that the perceived disagreements between the parties and their leaders are orchestrated, much like a televised wrestling match, which we know is a staged event.

As we reflect further on the frustration and despair we face, we think about our Founding Fathers and what they must have experienced at the hands of the British politicians. We have an even greater admiration and deeper appreciation than ever before for their willingness to stand up and stand fast, to the point of risking everything, including their very lives, to the end that their children and future generations would not have to endure political tyranny. We are not saying that we face the same level of political tyranny today, but in a cruel twist of fate, here we are 234 years

13

later, confronted with severe financial and economic tyranny, brought on, in large measure, by the very government forged to preserve and protect us from tyranny in the first place. How ironic is that?

But can we find it in ourselves to fight against this modern-day tyranny with even a semblance of the fervor and dedication exhibited by the Founding Fathers and their followers? We suspect it is in us, but we also suspect it is buried deep down within us and will be difficult to bring to the surface.

One of the central tenets of this book is that concentration of power, whether in government or business, is a danger to us all. Concentration of power means the few control the many and the few will invariably use that power to their benefit and often to the detriment of the many. This has been true throughout history and today is no exception.

We can never forget the first three words of the Constitution are "we the people," not "we the leaders" nor "we the politicians" nor "we the government" nor "we the representatives" nor "we the delegates" nor "we the officials." These three words, 11 simple letters, tell us all we need to know -- that supreme power in this country ultimately and finally resides in *WE THE PEOPLE*, no less so today than in 1787.

So then, *WE THE PEOPLE* must overcome the inundation of indoctrination, reassert ourselves and reclaim control of our national destiny. We must no longer allow ourselves to be convinced that a $14 trillion national debt is not a national disgrace, but rather a necessary, only "temporary" evil that will work out, in the long run, for us and posterity. The truth alone won't set us free. It's a start, but it has to be coupled with action.

We are of the opinion that an attitude of "letting George do it" (a popular colloquialism in the 1940s for passing the buck) is no longer acceptable. We are "George" and he is we. We cannot go around wringing our hands and wailing "woe is me." That's not going to get the job done. We cannot lament how we would like to change America but we don't know what to do, so we'll just leave it up to the few. The few must become the many and we must get off our collective duffs and act with a sense of urgency. Otherwise, we will surely be branded the generation that became "We The Sheeple" instead of reclaiming our national birthright as "We The People" -- and that's not the way we want to be remembered in future editions of American history books.

Now many will say in response to our claims: "Wait a minute. What you say may be true, but we are still far better off than almost everybody else in the world and so stop your complaining!" That's a misguided adaptation of the proverb about crying because you have no shoes until you met someone who had no feet. We admit there are many in the world much worse off than we in America, but that fact should not hinder us from wanting and working to build a better future. Many use that argument as a crutch to justify doing nothing to bring about change. If our forefathers and foremothers had decided to adopt that "it's just our lot in life" attitude of acceptance of the status quo, where would we be today? Much worse off than we are now, without a doubt.

Many who practiced racial discrimination after the Civil War and well into the 20th century (and some continuing the practice into the twenty-first century) used a similar brand of fallacious reasoning to support their untenable positions. They contended that African-Americans in this country really had no cause to complain about discriminatory attitudes and activities since they were so much better off than back when they were subjected to slavery. Subconsciously for some and all too consciously for others, was a feeling that blacks (they would say "coloreds" or worse) should simply "grin and bear it" and be thankful they were no longer considered chattel property and forced to pick cotton in the brutal summer heat of Dixie from dawn to dusk. Obviously, that kind of reasoning is not acceptable, not now, not then, not ever. And neither is the analogous reasoning that we are doing better than our neighbors in the world so we should be content.

And some will resort to the "wave the flag" in your face approach and will proclaim (with varying degrees of hostility), "if you boys don't like it here in the good old USA, you are welcome to pack your bags and move out and see how you like it somewhere else!" This is the same chant of *"America - love it or leave it"* we heard over and over back in the Vietnam War protest days and it holds no more water now than it did then. In reality, this argument represents a form of counterfeit and disingenuous patriotism. True patriots (like the original ones who took the British to task and forged this nation) consider it their right and, more importantly, their obligation to implement change when change is needed to make the system of government more responsive and more responsible. True patriots march to a different refrain: *"America – love it or lose it."* We do love it and we don't want to lose it. That's why we wrote this book in the first place. So what else can we say? Only this: *We can do better. We must do better. We will do better.*

CHAPTER 2

THE LOBBYISTS
'The Fix Is In'

"...winding in and out through the long, devious basement passage, crawling through the corridors, trailing its slimy length from gallery to committee room, at last it lies stretched at full length on the floor of Congress - this dazzling reptile, this huge, scaly serpent of the lobby."
- US Newspaper Columnist on Lobbyists, 1869

"The corporate lobby in Washington is basically designed to stifle all legislative activity on behalf of consumers."
- Ralph Nader

Our imagination leads us to contemplate the many good things that could emerge if we could wave a magic wand and expel all politicians, elected and appointed, at every level of government and replace them with people who care more about the people than their positions in government. As famous French President Charles de Gaulle once quipped, *"I have come to the conclusion that politics is far too serious a matter to be left to the politicians."* Amen to that.

We also contemplate how much government could be transformed (for the better) if the role of lobbyists -- for the most part an insidious and rapacious group of self-serving individuals who will use any device available to influence those who serve in government -- could be eliminated or at the very least substantially diminished. Expenditures to lobby the federal government totaled over $17 million per day in 2008 and $20 million in 2009, for the time Congress was in session. Corporations, both for-profit and not-for-profit, industry and trade associations, labor unions, state and local governments, and other special interest groups reportedly paid more than $3.5 billion to lobby Washington last year.

According to the Executive Director of the Center for Responsive Politics, a 25-year old nonpartisan watchdog group, this conclusion is borne out by the record number of today's Washington lobbyists – about 35,000 (that's 65 lobbyists for every member of Congress), a number which has doubled in just the last ten years.

Sadly, scholars credit the Unites States with giving birth to modern lobbying. Although there is some disagreement, most believe the term "lobbyist" originated at the Willard Hotel in Washington DC, where it was used by Ulysses S. Grant to describe those frequenting the hotel's lobby in order to gain access to the President, often found there enjoying cigars and brandy. Historical records suggest that organized lobbying of American politicians dates back at least as far as the late 18th century, to 1792, just three years after the Constitution was adopted. In the early years, both the press and the public reviled lobbying and viewed it as a disreputable industry. Lobbyists were seen as corrupting Congress and subverting democracy. However, do not forget that the First Amendment to the Constitution, Freedom of Speech, allows citizens of this great land to petition its government, and this includes the right to lobby, and boy the lobbyists have done a whole lot of petitioning over the years.

From the beginning; Congress, the body that protected the lobbyists and helped to ferment their growth, refused to place limitations on their activities because Congressmen were the recipients of the payola supplied by the lobbyists. Thereafter, the role of the "bag man" was born. And so it grew into the mega-industry it has become today, with tentacles reaching into and influencing every level of government, from the mayor and city council to the storied halls of Congress.

A particularly pernicious example of lobbying today is the intense efforts by the health care industry against health care reform. One watchdog group reported recently that the insurance industry and HMOs spent more than $700,000 a day in 2009 to pay 2,000 lobbyists to persuade Congress not to pass health care reform. These groups have spent half a billion dollars over the past two years in political contributions and lobbying expenses to influence public policy and elected officials. Joe Public probably thinks lobbying groups seek to buy votes for their clients, which they do, and we allow these guys to get away with this stuff!

In a similar vein, members of the Senate Banking Committee (chaired by Senator Christopher Dodd, D - Connecticut) who have tasked themselves with changing financial regulatory oversight rules and regulations in order to prevent another credit catastrophe are also recipients this year alone of over $30 million from lobbyists representing the banking industry -- the same group this committee is supposed to be regulating. Since 2000, the banking and financial sector has funneled almost $3 billion directly into the political system in the form of contributions and lobbying expenditures. Now, how is that not a conflict of interest? Many would consider it a form of bribery, legalized perhaps, but bribery nonetheless. Moreover, it is only legal because the very lawmakers who benefit from it made it legal, thereby compounding the conflict. Their rationale is that there will always be lobbying, no matter what anyone says or does, so we should live with it but regulate it. This same flawed reasoning can be used to justify the legalization and "regulation" of any vice known to man, no matter how heinous, including illicit drugs like heroin, crack cocaine, methamphetamines, ecstasy and angel dust, performance-enhancing drugs, prostitution, child pornography, and so on.

And the lobbying drumbeat in Washington persists, sometimes becoming nearly deafening. According to one of the supporters of legislation for greater supervision of financial institutions, Senator Jack Reed (D - Rhode Island), "The same companies that helped cause the financial crisis are now trying to block reform. This cynical attempt by Wall Street lobbyists to kill Wall Street reform before it has a chance to see the light of day must be resoundingly rejected." He is right about the lobbying but his call for rejection of the lobbyist will most likely be ignored.

In 2009, financial industry interests spent $500 million, a record, on Washington lobbying efforts, almost $1 million for every member of Congress. And that money is just for lobbyists' and lawyers' salaries, junkets and dinners, and does not include political donations and issue advertising. Even more impressive, some might say disturbing, is the new lobbying strategy launched by the financial services industry: the banks are keeping a lower lobbying profile today by staying in the background and placing their key corporate customers -- household names of American business, including Apple, Whirlpool, and John Deere -- in front of the campaign. "This is an orchestrated, well-funded effort by the banks to manipulate our legislation and leave no fingerprints," says one congressional staffer involved in drafting financial reform legislation. The staffer, who would speak only on condition of anonymity, gave *Newsweek Magazine* nine pages of proposed changes in the legislation which were intended to protect trading from open scrutiny -- all of it on paper without a letterhead -- that she says came from, drum roll please, Goldman Sachs.

We really had to shake our heads in disgust (and hang them in dismay) when we learned that beneficiaries of the $700 billion bailout spent a total of $114.2 million on lobbying and contributions toward the 2008 election. From TARP, they received $295.2 billion, a return of 258,449%. Those companies must consider their lobbying expenditures to be the wisest (and most lucrative) investments they ever made.

And of course, it is not just during the last year the banking industry has been hard at work with their "bag men" (and women). The financial sector spent a whopping $5.5 billion in political influence-peddling over the past decade as lobbyists worked day and night to win the deregulation that led to the nation's financial collapse, according to a report released last year, entitled *Sold Out:*

How Wall Street and Washington Betrayed America.

Lobbying is one of the few growth industries. In 2008, the Washington Post called lobbying "Washington's biggest business." And Washington, with its 35,000 lobbyists, may well be the "capital" of lobbying, but there are tens if not hundreds of thousands more influence peddlers roaming the halls of state legislatures and bureaucracies and city councils and county commissions. While many of these lobbyists are employed by lobbying and law firms and retain outside clients, others are employed by trade associations, companies, and even state and local governments.

Lobbyists are known as influence peddlers for a very good reason. They ply their trade by using money, big money, as an aphrodisiac to buy influence -- most of all, to buy votes -- votes for the benefit of the lobbyist's clients, but not for the benefit of the electorate. As Ralph Nader observed, *"the corporate lobby in Washington is basically designed to stifle all legislative activity on behalf of consumers."* Think about it, a politician goes off to Washington with a mandate to represent his constituents, yet, more often than not, ends up working for the lobbyists and their "fat cat" clients who provide endless amounts of dollars disguised as contributions needed to keep Mr. or Ms. Formerly Good Intentions in office. How successful have they been? It is estimated that their efforts are largely responsible for favorable legislative and regulatory policies, tax benefits and grants of cash from the federal budget worth about $3 trillion annually to their clientele. I guess you could call that a lot of *"bank for the buck."* That kind of success has led to starting salaries for well-connected Congressional aides topping $300,000 a year.

As many have observed, the primary goal of lawmakers is to stay in office and in order to do so, they have to get reelected, time and again. And elections are expensive propositions, so they need money to get reelected, and the lobbyists are the most reliable source of that money. Of course, it always comes with strings attached -- you scratch my back and I will scratch yours. It is not a pretty picture of our elected officials, to be sure, but power intoxicates and corrupts and money pays for the power and access to the power, and, as we have seen time and time again, there is no shortage of money in Washington. Lobbyists have truckloads of money (in all honesty, we are not surprised they do not drive around in Brink's armored cars to make their deliveries) and stand ready, willing and able to dispense sizable sums to any susceptible politician who needs a "fix." Odd how the good intentions of running for public office far too frequently degenerate into an addiction, an addiction for power and the money needed to maintain that power. Oh and speaking of good intentions, you know what they say about the pavement of the road to Hell -- or, in this case, you might say the same about Capitol Avenue and Pennsylvania Avenue, but, sadly, those good intentions, for the most part, get left outside Congress and the White House on the roads and do not make it inside the hallowed (or is hollowed) halls of those venerable institutions.

Must it be this way? Must our elected officials be captive to lobbyists? Must we allow votes on the laws which govern our very lives to be bought and paid for by special interest groups? Can lobbyists really be reined in? Now, we realize as previously mentioned, that the First Amendment in the Bill of Rights provides for the right to petition the government, but nowhere does it state that the petitioner has the right to buy influence or buy the vote of the elected official.

The plain and unvarnished truth is that lobbyists have no fear of voters and are not answerable to anyone but the politicians -- thus, there is little real accountability except in egregious cases where the lobbyists' actions cross the line into bribery or extortion. To make matters worse, once a politician tires of his political role, he or she is welcomed with open arms (and open pocketbooks) into the lobbying fraternity. In 2005, Public Citizen, a non-partisan, non-profit public interest advocacy organization based in Washington, D.C., published a report entitled *The Journey from Congress to K Street* -- analyzing hundreds of lobbyist registration documents filed in compliance with the Lobbying Disclosure Act and the Foreign Agents Registration Act, among other sources. It found that, from 1998 through 2004, 43% of the 198 members of Congress who left government to join private life registered to lobby. *The Washington Post* described these results as reflecting the *"sea change that has occurred in lawmakers' attitudes toward lobbying in recent years."* The paper noted:

> *"Congressional historians say that lawmakers rarely became lobbyists as recently as two decades ago. They considered the profession to be tainted and unworthy of once-elected officials such as themselves. And lobbying firms and trade groups were leery of hiring former members of Congress because they were reputed to be lazy as lobbyists, unwilling to ask former colleagues for favors."*

However, starting in the late 1980s, the landscape changed dramatically as a confluence of high salaries for lobbyists, an increasing demand for lobbyists, greater turnover in Congress, and a change in the control of the House worked to bring about a change in attitude which made it perfectly acceptable for former elected officials to become lobbyists.

With the development of this revolving door, former lawmakers were eagerly and regularly hired as lobbyists so their new employers could capitalize on the former lawmakers' relationships with their former colleagues as well as other contacts. The Public Citizens report included a case study of one particularly successful lobbyist, Bob Livingston, who stepped down as the House of Representatives Speaker-elect and resigned his seat in 1999 after a sex scandal. In the six years following his resignation, his lobbying group grew into the 12th largest non-law lobbying firm in Washington, earning nearly $40 million by the end of 2004. During roughly the same time period, Livingston, his wife, and his two political action committees (PACs) contributed over $500,000 to the PACs or campaign funds of various candidates.

No discussion of lobbying low lights can be complete without making note of one of the most notorious lobbying transgressions in modern times, the infamous saga of Jack Abramoff and his cohorts. Abramoff launched his lobbying career in 1994 as a Christian Coalition conservative with strong ties to the then new Republican leadership. He had immense ambitions and sought to build the largest lobbying portfolio in town. He opened two restaurants close to the Capitol, bought a fleet of casino boats, produced two Hollywood movies, leased four arena and stadium skyboxes, and dreamed of owning a pro sports team. Washington lawmakers and their aides packed his restaurants and skyboxes and jetted off with him on golf trips to Scotland and the Pacific island of Saipan.

Abramoff hired, for his lobbying team, several Republicans and a few Democrats, most of whom he had wined and dined when they were aides to powerful members of Congress. Team Abramoff included former staffers to Rep. Tom DeLay (R-Texas), then House Majority Leader, as well as to Sen. Conrad Burns (R-Montana), then head of the Senate Appropriations panel's Interior subcommittee; Rep. Robert W. Ney (R-Ohio), then Chairman of the House Administration Committee; Rep. John T. Doolittle (R-California), who had served on the key House committee that oversees American Indian tribes, and Sen. Harry M. Reid (D-Nevada), then Senate Minority Leader. Abramoff had as many as 51 lobbying clients at one time, but the bulk of his lobbying monies came from his representation of American Indian casino gaming interests. Abramoff and his associates collected $85 million from American Indian tribes and, in turn, spread millions around in gifts and contributions to lawmakers and regulators involved with Native American tribal gambling interests. Abramoff pled guilty in federal court in January 2006 to three criminal felony counts relating to the defrauding of several American Indian tribes and corruption of public officials. In September 2008, a Washington federal court found Abramoff guilty of trading expensive gifts, meals and sports trips in exchange for political favors, and he was sentenced to a four-year term in prison to be served concurrently with his previous sentences. He is currently out of "hard time" and in a half-way house, with release now scheduled for December 2010.

The extensive corruption and influence peddling investigation also led to the conviction of two White House officials, U.S. Representative Bob Ney, and nine other lobbyists and Congressional aides, and helped bring about the downfall of Rep. Tom DeLay. Early in the investigation, Abramoff responded to charges of wrongdoing by stating: *"I can't imagine there's anything I did that other lobbyists didn't do and aren't doing today."*

Now that's a scary thought and one for us to commit to memory and use to raise our level of vigilance several notches!

Ever wonder what happened to such once-powerful and prominent lawmakers as Dick Armey, John Ashcroft, Tom Daschle, Tom Foley, Dick Gephardt, Newt Gingrich, Phil Gramm, Dennis Hastert, Bob Livingston, Trent Lott, Bob Packwood, Richard Pombo, Rick Santorum, Bud Shuster, Fred Thompson and John Warner? Instead of returning to the old homestead to dwell among the beloved constituents who sent them to Washington, they moved only a dozen blocks from the Capitol to the K- Street lobbyist corridor where they have cashed in on their congressional experience and connections to draw six-figure or even seven-figure annual salaries for satisfying corporate desires. Indeed, Congress has become a training ground in the development of self-serving lobbyists. Former Congressional members are prized for their insider knowledge and old-boy chumminess that they mastered at taxpayer expense and then sell after leaving Congress to the highest bidder.

Corporations are spending $250 million a month, every month, to maintain their occupying army of hired guns. Why spend so much many would ask? Because it pays off, big time! Consider this example: in 2004, 93 major corporations spent in excess of $283 million dollars on lobbyists to shove a special tax break through Congress. Known as the domestic production deduction, this tax break, according to a 2007 University of Kansas School of Business publication, helped these same 93 corporations save in excess of $6 billion dollars in taxes. A rather significant return on their investment!

David Parsley, Professor of Economics and Finance at Vanderbilt University, did an extensive study in 2008 on whether lobbying produced tangible financial results for companies. His conclusion? Lobbying expenditures yield big returns for companies. Even more telling was his discovery that the bigger the investment (relative to firm size) in lobbying, the greater the return. His study revealed that firms with the highest lobbying activity outperformed both the financial markets and non-lobbying firms by up to 14% in the first year after the lobbying effort and up to 8% over the next three years (and this after taking into account the amount spent on lobbying). His study verified what all of us knew instinctively and intuitively was the case -- investment in Washington pays dividends. And similar studies subsequent to Mr. Parsley's have confirmed his findings.

Consider the following numbers regarding corporations' use of lobbyists: (i) 11,195 -- the number of corporate lobbyists presently plying their nefarious trade day and night in Washington's hallways and back rooms (and the number grows larger every day); (ii) $2.95 billion dollars -- the amount that corporations spent on lobbyists last year; and (iii) $500 million dollars -- the sum that corporate executives and lobbyists have slipped into Washington's many political pockets for the current election cycle, including donations to candidates, leadership political action committees, and political party committees (compare this to the $475 million dollars that was spent for the entire 2008 election cycle).

Two final instances regarding lobbyists further illustrate how their work is beneficial to a few at the expense of the many, sometimes with disastrous consequences. Consider this: even though the Department of Interior had implored Congressional members to add acoustic switches to deep water oil rigs to prevent huge oil spills -- such as the BP mega spill from the rig known as Deepwater Horizon -- BP and other oil companies were able to defeat the inclusion of this acoustic safety switch through an aggressive lobbying campaign which contended the cost of the switch, at $500,000 per rig, was exorbitant and not needed, even though this same safety feature is mandated by many other offshore oil producing countries. Surely the BP executives and safety engineers now realize how very short sighted and self-destructive their lobbying actions were in light of the $20 billion fund BP is now forced to establish to compensate victims of the oil spill, not to mention the additional billions the clean-up will cost.

And let's not forget the agency responsible for regulating offshore drilling for oil and gas -- the Minerals Management Service ("MMS") -- which just happens to be the very same agency that became infamous in 2008 with front-page headlines in national news publications and lead-in "teasers" in television news broadcasts referencing the out of bounds relationship between the Denver office of MMS and the oil and gas industry. You may recall that scandal involved MMS employees accepting football tickets, golf games, meals and ski outings from energy companies. That was nothing compared to the findings of the Interior Department's Inspector General that MMS officials frequently consumed alcohol at industry functions, had used cocaine and marijuana supplied by oil and gas company representatives and had sexual relations with oil and gas company representatives (talk about regulators and the regulated being in bed together). The Bush Administration and Congress indicated that major reforms and a thorough "house cleaning" would be forthcoming and "heads would roll," but as usual, it was a lot of talk and very little action.

Just how little action you ask? Well, according to a new report from the Inspector General released in May of this year (almost two years after the 2008 report), the intimate relationship between MMS and the industry it is supposed to regulate has apparently continued pretty much unabated. This new report cites a variety of violations of federal regulations and ethics rules at the MMS Lake

Charles, Louisiana office (you guessed it, that's the office with primary responsibility for overseeing operations at the rig that led to the BP disaster). The report makes note of a pervasive culture of cronyism between regulators at MMS and the oil and gas industry. According to the report, staff members at the MMS office accepted lunches, trips to the Peach Bowl, hunting and fishing vacations, skeet shooting outings, crawfish boils, tickets to sporting events and many other gifts from industry representatives. One MMS employee inspected a company four times while negotiating for a job there.

That's not change we can believe in and even President Obama had to admit, albeit begrudgingly, there was an all too "cozy relationship" between the Department of Interior and the oil and gas industry on his watch. Apparently someone had to be made a political scapegoat for this "greased palm" relationship and that person was Elizabeth Birnbaum, the MMS head under Obama, who stepped down "voluntarily" in the wake of the revelations about the continuing corruption at her agency, as well as her agency's participation in the initial response (or lack thereof) to the BP spill.

Looking the other way at safety and environmental violations is commonplace among oil and gas inspectors, laxities which may have contributed to the BP oil rig explosion, which, as we all know, claimed 11 rig workers' lives and will likely take decades to clean up. As a matter of fact, it was recently disclosed that MMS specifically exempted BP from filing an environmental impact study on its drilling operations in the Gulf of Mexico, and, worse, its grant to BP of the lease rights at Deepwater Horizon occurred after an intense lobbying effort by BP which convinced the regulators that a major spill was unlikely. The claims by the Administration and BP that the Deepwater Horizon disaster was not foreseeable are just not true. Scientists and environmentalists warned for years that an uncontrollable spill from a deepwater oil rig was not only possible but likely. Moreover, the National Oceanic and Atmospheric Administration (NOAA) sharply criticized the very MMS studies that the President's appointees used to approve the Deepwater Horizon site. The NOAA Administrator sent a memo to the Department of Interior in October 2009 lambasting the MMS assessment of drilling operations. Her memo, along with other warnings of grossly inadequate industry precautions and preparedness for handling a deep water blowout going back to 2004, were all filed under "D" (for "Disregard") or "I" (for "Ignore") or "W" (for "Waste Basket") and forgotten – until today, that is.

In a sadly similar vein to the BP spill is the great tragedy at Massey Energy's Upper Big Branch Coal Mine in West Virginia earlier this year, which resulted in the loss of 29 miners' lives, the worst mine disaster in four decades. Culpability fingers are here too being pointed at the intertwining of industry and government. More than 200 former congressional staff members, federal regulators and lawmakers are employed by the mining industry as lobbyists, consultants or senior executives, including dozens who work for coal companies with the worst safety records in the nation, according to a *Washington Post* analysis. The *Post* further determined the revolving door has also brought industry officials into government as policy aides in Congress or officials of the Mine Safety and Health Administration (MSHA), which enforces coal mine safety standards.

The movement between industry and government far too frequently had led to a regulatory system biased in favor of coal company interests. According to many experts, that "thick as thieves" relationship has put miners at risk and created a flawed enforcement system that probably contributed to the West Virginia catastrophe. Once again the hand holding by industry and government has led to hand wringing by the people.

Never forget that the lobbyist's client is the corporation or other such business group and the target or mark is the lawmaker or regulator. The objective is to pour enough money into the pockets of the lawmaker and the regulator to make sure the corporate client gets the best laws and best regulation that money can buy. The "bag man" calls and the politician falls (into line, that is).

And isn't it a really sad commentary that President Obama ran on an *anti-lobbyist* campaign? You remember how he promised to reign in lobbyists like never before. You don't hear much about that these days though. Quite to the contrary, lobbying has continued to grow bigger than ever since Obama took office – in fact, as we like to say down South, it has grown like kudzu (and it will be just as difficult to contain).

As we conclude our day and take one last gulp of cable television opinion babble, we again listen reluctantly to the neo-cons (neoconservatives) at Fox News tell us how "fair and balanced" their broadcasts are as they rail against Obama and his administration. Instructing their listeners to be wary that Obama is at the least a socialist and probably a communist and that his administration is the bane of the universe, guilty of treason. We tire of the tirades and flip over to MSNBC one last time where its commentators assure us that the country is in good hands thanks to the Democrats. Somehow, though, we have our doubts as to either party's sincerity. It seems that all we really have is a game being played by two opposing groups labeled as political parties; an insidious game at that. The players are disguised as either "Mafia Dons" (politicians) or their "bag men" (lobbyists) and we, the electorate, the unfortunate spectators in this high stakes game, get stuck with the costs of the game, no matter how poor the performance, how detrimental the outcome or how great the cost. Worse yet, we never even receive an invitation to the party!

We wonder why cable networks such as CNBC, C-SPAN or Fox News do not spend time investigating the goings-on of lobbyists and lawmakers. We think most viewers would be interested in knowing about the impact such influence peddling has upon the taxpayer, the inherent conflicts of interest poised by such lobbying efforts, and how legislation is influenced by the actions of the "bag men." Unfortunately for all of us, we do not believe the lobbying industry agrees with our need to know. They much prefer dark rooms with limited "seating" for just a few special "guests."

CHAPTER 3

THE POLITICIANS
'Show Me The Money'

"Politicians have the ability to foretell what is going to happen tomorrow, next week, next month, and next year; and to have the ability afterward to explain why it didn't happen."
- **Sir Winston Churchill**

"In order to become the master, the politician poses as the servant."
- **Charles de Gaulle**

We awake to a new day but time marches on and we find ourselves again drifting back to thoughts from the previous day regarding our future and, more importantly, our children's future. We begin to think about the politicians and the control they exert over us and our lives. And then our thoughts turn to the political parties which exert control over the controllers. Many have come to believe that the term "honest politician" has become an oxymoron, like "good lobbyist." Count us among them.

In our system, there are and have been for the past 150+ years only two real political parties, the Democrats and the Republicans. The older of the two, the Democratic Party, was formed by Thomas Jefferson and James Madison in the 1790s and was then called the Democratic-Republican Party (which is essentially what we have today, when you think about it, there being so little fundamental difference between the two political parties). Earlier this year, Judge Andrew Napolitano, former New Jersey Superior Court judge, graduate of Princeton and Notre Dame Law School, and well-known legal and political commentator on Fox News, hit the nail on the head when he observed:

> *"I believe we have a one party system in this country, called the big-government party. There is a Republican branch that likes war and deficits and assaulting civil liberties. There is a Democratic branch that likes welfare and taxes and assaulting commercial liberties."*

And listen to the words of Theodore Roosevelt, who might just as well have been speaking at a press conference today instead of a century ago when he characterized the Republican and Democratic parties as *"husks, with no real soul within either, divided on artificial lines, boss-ridden and privilege-controlled, each a jumble of incongruous elements, and neither daring to speak out wisely and fearlessly on what should be said on the vital issues of the day."* The increasingly popular stand-up comedian Lewis Black, well-known for his acerbic wit, pungent political satire and impassioned outrage, was a good bit more blunt when he quipped, in his trademark loud and angry stage voice: *"The two-party system in America is a bowl of crap looking at itself in the mirror."* Of course, those of you familiar with Lewis Black know he actually used the more colorful synonym for "crap" -- you know, the one that is usually precedes "happens."

We have to ask ourselves why a multi-party system has failed to take root in this country. The inherent value of a multi-party system was staunchly recognized by our founding fathers. George Washington devoted a major part of his famed farewell address to a strong warning against allowing the political system to fall prey to *"the baneful effects"* of parties. His successor, John Adams, perhaps in a sort of "Nostradamus moment," cautioned that *"a division of the republic into two great parties... is to be dreaded as the greatest political evil under the Constitution."*

And James Madison, the principal author of the Constitution noted: *"when the variety and number of political parties increases, the chance for oppression, factionalism, and no skeptical acceptance of ideas decreases."* Following his admonition, at least five candidates garnered electoral votes in each of the first four presidential elections, a far cry from today.

Since the early days of the Republic, however, support for multiple parties has waned and the two-party system now reigns supreme at virtually every level of government. In fact, to find the last real threat to the two-party domination of presidential politics, one has to go back almost a full century to the election of 1912. In that election, former President Theodore Roosevelt broke from the Republican Party and ran for President as the Progressive (or Bull Moose) party candidate. Running on a strong reform platform that included voting rights for women, an end to child labor, and greater federal regulation of the economy, Roosevelt ran second in the race, beating Republican President William Howard Taft, but losing out to the Democrat, Woodrow Wilson.

Since 1912, only two third party candidates were able to marshal any notable support in presidential contests. In 1968, George Wallace, then governor of Alabama, ran as a third party candidate under the American Independent Party banner and captured 46 electoral votes, along with 10 million popular votes; then, in 1992, Ross Perot ran as an independent, campaigning under the "United We Stand America" banner. He captured almost 19% of the popular vote, which prevented Bill Clinton from claiming a majority of the popular vote.

That being said, over the span of many decades, our nation has seen quite a few attempts by various third party candidates to secure a foothold in American politics. To date, they all have failed, more often than not, miserably. Why? Because the two-party system has evolved into, politically speaking, the ultimate stacked deck. Think of it like this: our electoral system is based, for the most part, on a "winner takes all" approach. We have a system where voters use their single vote to elect a single candidate. Consequently, the political group who controls the turnout typically wins the seat. Moreover, since most voters claim that they are either Republican or Democrat, this leaves little to no opportunity for third party candidates.

Additionally, ballot access laws create a major challenge to third party candidacies. While usually the Democratic and Republican parties easily obtain ballot access in all fifty states in every election, third parties often fail to meet the criteria for ballot access, such as registration fees or, in many states, petition requirements in which a certain number of voters must sign a petition for a third party or independent candidate to gain ballot access. Although Perot appeared on all 50 state ballots as an independent in 1992 and the candidate of the Reform Party in 1996, his efforts were certainly facilitated by his ability, as a billionaire, to provide significant campaign funds from his personal coffers. Patrick Buchanan also appeared on all 50 state ballots in the 2000 election, but largely on the basis of Perot's performance as the Reform Party's candidate four years earlier.

Another obstacle to third parties in presidential elections is the set of rules governing presidential election debates. The first debate between the nominees of the two major parties occurred in 1960. The subsequent three presidential elections did not involve debates. The debates started up again in 1976 and have been held in every presidential election since. Third party or independent candidates have been included in these debates in only two cycles. Ronald Reagan and John Anderson debated in 1980, but incumbent President Carter refused to appear with John Anderson, and so Anderson was excluded from the subsequent debate between Reagan and Carter.

Debates in other state and federal elections often exclude independent and third party candidates, and the Supreme Court has upheld such tactics in several cases. In 1987, the Republican and Democratic parties organized The Commission on Presidential Debates (the "CPD") to establish rules and procedures for presidential debates. Not a hint of a conflict of interest here, certainly. Although independent candidate Perot was included in all three of the debates with Republican George H. W. Bush and Democrat Bill Clinton in 1992, largely at the behest of the Bush campaign (his participation enabling him to climb from 7% before the debates to right at 19% on election day), he was excluded from the 1996 debates despite his strong showing four years prior.

In 2000, the CPD revised the debate access rules to make it even more difficult for third party candidates to gain access by stipulating that, besides being on enough state ballots to win an Electoral College majority, debate participants must clear 15% in pre-debate opinion polls. This rule, had it been in place earlier; would have precluded John Anderson and Ross Perot from participating in the debates.

Walter Cronkite, the legendary broadcast journalist once referred to as the "most trusted man in America," called the CPD-sponsored debates an "unconscionable fraud" on the voting public. The League of Women Voters called them "campaign-trail charades devoid of substance, spontaneity, and honest answers to tough questions." A genuinely nonpartisan, civic organization, The League was proud to sponsor the early presidential debates, but quit in disgust in 1988 after the CPD became the governing body, saying that *the League has no intention of becoming an accessory to the hoodwinking of the American public.*

An additional barrier to third party candidacies is the high cost of running for office, already out of control, yet continuing to escalate. A remarkable example of the high price of success for already well-known third party candidates is the barely successful 2009 reelection campaign of independent Michael Bloomberg for mayor of New York -- he spent an incredible $102 million in this race, or $183 for each vote he received. Campaign spending on the 2008 presidential race topped $2 billion, an all-time record by a wide margin and three times the amount spent in the 2004 election.

Do we, the voting public, now perceive a need for more than two parties? Indeed. Recent public opinion polls have found trust in government at an all time low and that almost two-thirds of Americans would like to see a third party run against Democrats and Republicans. Independents surveyed embraced the idea of third-party candidacies even more warmly. The rise of the Tea Party movement is an example of a growing third-party sentiment. But will it be a lasting example or will it be assimilated by the Republican Party when all is said and done?

Perhaps the prediction earlier this year by Gerald Celente, one of the world's leading authorities on forecasting, analyzing and tracking trends, could actually come to pass -- he has predicted that a third party candidate will be elected President in 2012. Such a result could shake things up a great deal, politically speaking. But to create a lasting change in the political landscape, the third party would need to build a solid grass roots foundation and field viable candidates at all levels of government. If it is viewed as merely the embodiment of one or a few charismatic candidates or one or two issues, it will be marginalized by the two parties and become merely one more transitory stab at change. To borrow from a widely used phrase in connection with the recent financial meltdown, what we now need is "systemic risk" to the two-party system.

But could such a shock to the system become anything more than the proverbial flash in the pan? Could it produce enough voltage to put the two-party system out of "our" misery and produce long-term, radical change to an entrenched and intransigent status quo, born and bred by politicians bent on making it sacrosanct and inviolate? In this regard, we must first examine the Electoral College amendment, the 12th Amendment to our Constitution. For example, let us consider the general election process for president and vice president conducted every four years. Since each state is given a specified number of electoral votes based upon apportionment, then whoever wins the most votes wins the electoral votes. Less populated states, such as Alaska and Delaware, have the fewest electoral votes, whereas states with larger populations, such as California and Texas, have the most. There are 538 possible electoral votes, of which it takes 270 to win the presidency. Strangely, when we vote for a candidate, we also are voting for electors who have pledged their support to the candidate, thereby creating both a direct and indirect system of voting.

The idea to create the Electoral College was novel at the time, brought about because the framers of our Constitution were concerned that less populated states would not be considered as important in matters of governance as their more populated counterparts, and thereby lose political influence. The framers settled on a compromise, a system to resolve their differences, and manufactured a dual election process whereby each state was afforded electors based on population as determined by a national census. Apportionment was the result. Each state was entitled to receive a number of seats for congressional representatives based on the state's population as determined by the census, taken every ten years. For example, if a particular state was apportioned three seats for congressional representatives, then that state was assigned three electoral votes.

The framers initially established in the Constitution Article II, Section I, Clause 2 stipulating the role for electors. In 1804, the Constitution was amended with the addition of the 12th Amendment that made several changes to the way electors voted and those procedures are still in effect today. And in case of a tie in the electoral vote, the election would be moved to the House of Representatives for final determination. The bottom line is that winning the popular vote does not mean winning the election--ask Al Gore.

Now, what does all of this have to do with voters today? Simply this -- the election process greatly favors and facilitates the two party system and greatly disfavors and disenfranchises a multi-party system. Consequently, today, both political parties are so entrenched and wield such power that, in order to change the system to grant third parties an equitable opportunity to effectively participate in the electoral process, only a national ground swell of support demanding fundamental, "systemic" change (there's that word again) by electing candidates who would be magnanimous enough to implement this much needed change.

To say it will not be easy is a gross understatement. The parties are all about self-preservation and self-propagation. So they will take whatever actions they deem necessary to maintain themselves in perpetuity. And they have had centuries of practice. Unquestionably, if we, the electorate, attempt to denude the two parties of power it will be a daunting task fraught with disappointment and pain. They will not give up the throne without a fight!

Now, the hallmark of American business success is competition. Monopolies and oligopolies are anathema to true capitalism but our political process lacks any semblance of competition. There is competition at the fringes between the two parties, but it is sporadic and largely ineffectual to date. And the two parties typically close ranks to perpetuate and defend against any threat to the System (their System, after all). Witness, for example, the aftermath of the Perot candidacy -- Perot campaigned quite successfully on a platform designed to address the then terrible economy, similar to today's, and Perot rapidly gained popularity as a populist who sought to corral a woefully dysfunctional political system, much the same then as now. He made a number of compelling arguments and telling points in the debate, but then both parties turned on him and turned loose their vaunted "dirty tricks" machinery with a vengeance, going so far as to viciously and relentlessly attack his family.

Candidate Perot was so disgusted that he soon dropped out of the race (who can blame him). He later reentered, but his "MIA" status at a critical time in the campaign cost him too much credibility, as he was tagged by the Democrats and Republicans as someone who would quit as soon as the going got tough.

Moreover, Perot's implicit "threat" impelled the parties to act to impair future third party presidential candidacies by, as noted above, joining forces to form the Commission on Presidential Debates. They empowered the CPD to establish rules that would be more onerous for third party participation. And even though Perot laid the groundwork for Republican and later to be House Speaker Newt Gingrich's *Contract with America* -- Gingrich's work being little more than a re-write of Perot's *United We Stand* -- it played a key role in the Republican Party winning a landslide victory in the 1994 mid-term congressional elections. Notwithstanding, Gingrich and the Republican Party got the credit in being the catalyst for political change while independent candidates such as Perot got little except ridicule and scorn. Add in all the other barriers to third parties that the Democrats and Republicans colluded to implement and you have the blueprint for a nice little box that can hold only two parties (the ballot "box," that is). We, as the voting public, have to think and go "outside" this box if we are ever going to make the system responsive and responsible to the people as originally intended and designed.

Think about this. The two-party system is so firmly embedded in our electoral consciousness that we treat as highly positive commissions, boards, and committees being "bipartisan" in composition. All that means of course is that the two parties are represented. Wouldn't we be better off if, in the near future, that term was to be replaced with "tri-partisan" or better yet, "multi-partisan"?

A rather remarkable example of the failure of the two-party system to produce decent candidates for public office is in the race for Chris Dodd's Senate seat in Connecticut. The best the Democrats were able to come up with is State Attorney General Richard Blumenthal, despite his repeatedly distorting (that's a euphemism for lying about) his military service. As for the Republicans, so far the best they could produce is Wrestling Queen Linda McMahon (former CEO of the WWE) whose wrestling antics included kicking a man in the groin, getting slapped across the face by her daughter and sitting in a wheelchair, feigning a coma, while her famous husband cavorted across the screen with a scantily clad, buxom "lady" (her election would put her in position to be a real Republican "ring" leader). Really, now, is that the best the two-party system can produce for the hallowed position of United States Senator? Apparently (and sadly) so.

Never forget that the two parties represent themselves and their own self-interests, not us. They truly operate like members of a mafia family; consequently, we have to look at politicians as *Political Dons* or maybe the *Dons of Washington*. Think about it, they live a life of privilege while we, the electorate, barely scrape by month-to-month and month after month. Do you think they worry about losing their homes, their retirements or savings? Not in this lifetime! Politicians tell us whatever they think we want to hear, all the while lining their pockets with money and grabbing on to as much power as they can coerce and extract from others. Not a pretty picture but the truth. Who created $14 trillion+ of debt plus tens of trillions more in unfunded debt obligations? Who allowed our manufacturing base to be shipped overseas, our currency to be debased, Wall Street to control our very lives, and created a tax system that few understand and most think grossly unfair? None other than politicians -- each a *New Don* (not to be confused with *New Dawn*, that's for darn sure)! And 99% of them represent either the Democratic or Republican Parties.

You would think that the lawmakers would not be so bold as to tolerate blatant conflicts of interest, but not so in the *Alice in Wonderland* world of Capitol Hill. In both houses of Congress, a host of committee chairmen and ranking members have millions of dollars invested in the very business sectors their panels oversee, according to a *Washington Post* analysis of lawmakers' financial disclosure records. This is an important fact because committee chairmen and ranking members have significantly more power than their colleagues to ask questions, hold hearings, launch investigations and push through legislation that in many cases governs the industries in which they hold sizable personal or family investments. Take for example the House Agriculture Committee, which controls farm policies and billions in agricultural subsidies. Its members had farming and agribusiness investments worth five times on average the amount held by other Representatives. Some of the members even had ownership interests in family farming operations which received farm subsidies they got to vote on. If this sounds ridiculous, it is only because it is. Neither of the other two branches of government allows such conflicts of interest. Under current rules, judges must recluse themselves from cases involving a party in which they own stock or have some other financial relationship. Executive branch officials must sell assets in industries they regulate or place them in blind trusts for the duration of their service. But, incredibly, the ethics rules of Congress leave it up to the lawmakers to decide whether their holdings pose a conflict of interest in voting on bills and resolutions.

And honesty is not only lacking for politicians while governing, but its absence is often more pronounced when they are running for office. The election campaigns of most politicians reflect a flagrant disregard for truth and candor, especially their vicious attack ads against opponents filled with innuendo, half-truths and outright lies. The very term *candidacy* is something of a misnomer since there is very little *candid* about it. We understand the importance of preserving the fundamental constitutional right of freedom of speech, but we question whether it should grant politicians free and unfettered license in election campaigns to utterly destroy the reputation of opponents by committing willful and deliberate acts of libel and slander. The campaigns have gotten so terribly nasty (today they are slinging a lot more than muck and mud) that many, probably most, good and decent people will not consider a run for public office. Why should they when they know full well they will be subjected to the worst sort of smear campaigns which may cause untold damage to them and their families?

If you want to answer the question of "how low can you go" in terms of political campaigns, watch the 2010 and the 2012 elections. But take our advice and don't watch or listen unless you have stout intestinal fortitude or at the very least have some wickedly powerful anti-nausea medication handy. In fact, we will bet that the 2010 campaigns, on a scale of 1 to 10 (with 1 representing the cleanest and nicest ads and 10 the nastiest and ugliest) will rate an easy 11.

Finally, we must ask ourselves why we, the electorate, the ones who bear ultimate responsibility for lawmakers' egregious behavior, continue to allow politicians at any level (really every level) to use, abuse and humiliate us? Because they can, they do. But they can only do so, in the final analysis, with our tacit consent. Surely we are not destined to endure endless political masochism. Or are we? We hope not and we trust the next round of elections will force many of the professional politicians to join the ranks of the unemployed -- of course, that will be short-term for most as they are hurriedly inducted into the lobbying profession, proceeding in short order from the elect to the select.

Even if we cannot increase the number of viable parties overnight, we can start by doing our best to turn out the professional party politicians and run ourselves or encourage our friends and neighbors to get involved by running for office, preferably without affiliation to any party. Wouldn't it be nice to have some folks as candidates who are color blind when it comes to politics -- i.e., candidates who do not see Republican *red* or Democrat *blue* or even Nader *green* and certainly do not have to see the *green* and *gold* of the lobbyists?

CHAPTER 4

JOBS
'Help Wanted'

"You take my life when you take the means whereby I live."
- William Shakespeare

"Government at all levels has emerged as our number one growth industry...for the first time in American history -- even in the history of the Western industrialized world -- there are more people working for government at all levels than in manufacturing. Since manufacturing jobs make money while government jobs take money, this has become an equation for economic disaster."
- Martin L. Gross, American political writer

If not already in complete despair, we can readily find that state of mind by tuning in to the evening news, where the commentators are discussing America's abysmal jobs picture. Today's mantra from the media: most economists and government officials think that the unemployment rate, while high, has bottomed out at just under 10% (the Government's "official" count) and will soon begin gradual but definite improvement. The hidden (subliminal) message to us is that we should all just grin and bear it for the time being and be thankful that we are not in worse shape. Apparently buying into this spurious and worse, supercilious attitude, a recent national news broadcaster asked rhetorically (and also rather cavalierly) that, if "only" 1 in 10 is unemployed, doesn't that mean that 9 in 10 are employed, so how bad is that, really? Well, it is plenty bad for the more than 15 million of us who happen to be in that 1 in 10 category. As Harry Truman once noted, "It's a recession when your neighbor loses his job. It is a depression when you lose yours." By that standard, many of us are feeling like we are in a full-blown depression!

In the second place, it is not so onerous for all those commentators and economists and government officials to sit around with their Starbucks cups (always "half-full" and never "half-empty") and decry the high joblessness rate -- while they all have jobs -- and relatively high-paying jobs at that. And let us be honest here, all they really care about is the effect of the unemployment rate on the economy in general and future elections. They have the luxury of staying detached and taking a view of the problem from 30,000 feet. They do not have (or want) to get down in the trenches and witness first-hand the suffering and debilitation that being unemployed for prolonged periods of time causes. Oh, they pay some standard lip service to the painful aspect from time to time, but always from the confines of some comfy studio far away from ground zero -- they would not, after all, want to get too close to the situation, physically or emotionally, because then they might have to touch the pain of the unemployed and underemployed and that experience would be ever so unpleasant and troubling.

Additionally, the real unemployment rate is notably higher than the reported 9.5% or so. The 9.5% or so number is the "official" joblessness rate, as reported by the Bureau of Labor Statistics (known to many as the "BUL S" report). This report is seriously flawed in that it:

(i) uses a survey of households (and only 50,000 at that) rather than actual payroll data, which is far more accurate;

(ii) excludes changes in employment among the nation's 11.2 million farm and self-employed workers, even though these two categories account for more than 7% of the civilian labor force;

(iii) includes Census workers who are only temporary and frequently double and triple counts them; and

(iv) does not take into account the more than 15 million persons who do not have a job but have given up looking for one because they have become discouraged or those who found marginal part-time work but still cannot make ends meet and are still looking for full-time work. If you do the calculation with these adjustments, then the real unemployment rate jumps to 19% (more than 30 million adults or 1 in every 5 workers). This being the case, the economy would need to create over 20 million jobs for us to reach a real unemployment rate of 5%, generally considered "full employment." Since we are barely creating any new jobs right now, the idea of creating 20 million jobs is one whose time has not come and is not on anybody's radar screens. Even the most optimistic economists see only about half that number of jobs being created by the end of 2013. And that is just not acceptable, particularly to those of us trying to get by without a paycheck.

Now, to add insult to injury, the average number of weeks of unemployment for all workers is 30 and climbing, and the number of workers unemployed for six months and longer is over 10 million and climbing. As Ulysses Everett McGill (played by the renowned George Clooney) lamented to his two sidekicks in *O Brother, Where Art Thou? "Damn, Boys. We're in a tight spot."* A sentiment we echo.

Since the start of the Great Recession in December 2007, more than 8 million jobs have been lost (4.2 million last year alone), many of them forever, according to a growing number of economists and labor experts. Moreover, hiring is not picking up to any appreciable degree, contrary to the government's predictions (which are nothing more than a hope and a prayer).

Noted political journalist and author David Corn, in an interview earlier this year, had this to say about our being spoon fed optimistic pabulum even while the economy was crumbling:

> *"Remember one thing, that over the last 20-30 years, people have been told over and over and over again that the economy is doing well. The economy is doing great. The Dow is up. Yet, they themselves, most of them, are not actually making more money. Median wages have hardly gone up at all in the last thirty years. Therefore, you have all these people who are not really making any more money. They're just treading water. And, yet, everywhere they turn, they're being told the economy's doing well. And they start, I think, a lot of people start to blame themselves. They wonder, 'If the economy's doing so well, how come I'm not doing better? It must be me.' And what they don't see is, no, it's not them. It's the way the system works to maintain itself."*

We are reminded of the famous Groucho Marx wisecrack, when caught in the act of adultery: "Who you gonna believe, me or your lying eyes?"

There are many culprits in the unemployment crisis (and it is a crisis, certainly for those who have lost their jobs and in turn lost their homes, their ability to send their kids to college or take the family out to dinner, their creditworthiness, and in far too many cases, their self-worth). The main villain in this tragedy is the financial meltdown, spawned in large measure by pervasive and pernicious financial "excess":

❖ Excess in borrowing which allowed consumer debt to top $2.5 trillion in 2008, almost $1 trillion of which stemmed from high-interest credit card charges and advances (fueled by the issuance of 1.5 billion credit cards to over 170 million Americans, equaling an average of nearly nine credit cards issued per holder).

❖ Excess in mortgage lending, especially the now notorious adjustable rate and subprime categories, which contributed to the financial crisis (home mortgage debt in America increased from an average of 46% of GDP during the 1990s to an unprecedented 73% in 2008, reaching a record $10.5 trillion).

❖ Excess in purchases and guarantees of high risk mortgage-backed securities by the government-sponsored and funded enterprises Fannie Mae and Freddie Mac, which, in accordance with the mandate of the federal government (the Department of Housing and Urban Development) to buy and backstop mortgages in order to "provide affordable housing for low- and moderate-income families in America," owned or guaranteed $5 trillion in mortgage obligations at the time they had to be placed into conservatorship by the Federal Government in September 2008 -- providing still more "growth capital" for the huge housing bubble.

❖ Excess in the Federal Reserve's monetary policies and activities, which, according to one of the foremost Fed insiders, Treasury Secretary Timothy Geithner, were "too loose, too long," inevitably leading to the asset bubble and fostering the unhealthy climate of "money chasing risk" in the form of easy loans and risky investments.

❖ Excess investment in the risky and the largely unregulated financial instruments known as credit derivatives (including the now infamous collateralized debt obligations or CDOs, collateralized bond obligations or CBOs, collateralized mortgage obligations or CMOs and credit default swaps or CDSs) which Warren Buffet referred to as "financial weapons of mass destruction" and which, according to data compiled by **Bloomberg**, have contributed to almost $2 trillion in write-downs at the world's biggest banks, brokers and insurers since the start of 2007 (and which now totals a mind-boggling $650 trillion, or more than 10 times global gross domestic product, according to estimates by the Bank for International Settlements); plus, let us not forget that over $180 million of our dollars, as taxpayers, have been used to bail out AIG due to its inability to honor its many CDS commitments, with Goldman Sachs being the top payee from these funds, receiving an incredible 100 cents on the dollar under its contract with AIG.

❖ Excess use of leverage by the investment banking community which made them much more vulnerable to a financial shock -- consider these facts: the SEC changed the net capital rules in 2004, allowing the 5 biggest investment banks to increase their leverage (debt to net assets) from 12:1 to 40:1, which in turn created an environment which allowed these five firms to take on more than $4 trillion in debt in 2007, about 30% of total nominal GDP for that year.

❖ Excess growth of and reliance by borrowers and institutional investors upon the "shadow banking system," a parallel banking system to traditional banks which allowed highly levered lending and investment institutions and vehicles such as hedge funds, investment banks, conduits, structured investment vehicles commonly known as SIVs (which first came to light in the **Enron** scandal), finance companies, money-market mutual funds, and government sponsored enterprises commonly known as GSE's, such as Fannie Mae and Freddie Mac, and non-bank mortgage companies to perform traditional banking activities without being subject to the protections and safeguards imposed by banking regulations. The shadow banks came to dominate the credit securitization and commercial paper markets and they engaged far more in rank speculation than conventional banking activities and thus became some of the primary participants in the risky credit derivatives market and still hold trillions of dollars of "toxic assets."

❖ Excess reliance by banks on off-balance sheet financing -- in an effort to bypass regulatory restraints and circumvent transparency, many banks utilized the complex financial structures, such as SIVs or conduits, to move enormous amounts of assets and liabilities, including unsold CDOs off their books, enabling them to maintain regulatory minimum capital ratios so they could continue to lend and invest, earning additional fees. In the years leading up to crisis, the top four U.S. depositary banks alone moved more than $5 trillion in assets and liabilities off their balance sheets in this manner, thereby serving to increase leverage and profits during the boom years but increasing losses during the crisis.

❖ Excess reliance on inaccurate and misleading credit ratings -- the credit rating agencies regularly gave investment-grade ratings to mortgage-backed securities based on risky subprime mortgage loans, which enabled these securities to be sold all over the world to investors, thus helping finance the ill-fated housing and credit boom. These rating companies allowed an estimated $3.2 trillion in loans made to homeowners with bad credit and undocumented incomes to be bundled and sold as A- and even AAA- rated securities; the ratings agencies earned 3 times more for rating these instruments than corporate bonds, their traditional business, and the ratings were rife with conflicts of interest, as the agencies were paid huge fees by the investment banks and other firms that packaged and sold the securities to the ill-informed investors. To no one's surprise, numerous Moody's analysts testified before Congress that company executives used fear and intimidation to pressure them into giving falsely rosy ratings to debt instruments, especially mortgage-backed securities and other collateralized debt obligations, ratings which Moody's CEO has characterized as *"deeply disappointing"* (where have we heard that before -- oh, right, our old pal Bernie Madoff used much the same terminology when he delivered his "heartfelt" apology just before he was sentenced to 150 years in prison for bilking billions from his "clients").

❖ Excess predatory lending practices by unscrupulous lenders who approved unsafe and unsound secured loans -- a prime example is the bait-and-switch method employed by

Countrywide, advertising low interest rates for home refinancing, the documentation for which contained page after page of boilerplate "fine print" provisions unintelligible to all layman and most lawyers, which were then swapped for more expensive, higher risk loan products the day of closing (many of which charged greater interest than the amount being paid, creating negative amortization, which the consumer would rarely if ever notice until years after the loan closing.

❖ Excess fees and compensation throughout the mortgage supply chain, from mortgage brokers selling the loans to small- and medium-size mortgage banks that funded the brokers, to the giant investment banks that bundled ("securitized") the loans and sold them in multi-billion dollar tranches to investors; plus the overall incentive compensation structure for the investment banking community at large skewed toward rewarding the assembly and sale of risky financial products, like credit derivatives, rather than the performance of those products and profits to the firms generated over time. President Obama accurately observed in June 2009 that executive compensation "rewarded recklessness rather than reasonability" and yet that very same system remains largely intact today as witnessed by the bonus payments being made to investment bankers, billions with taxpayer dollars from the bailouts.

There is of course another cause of unemployment, which many in government and many segments of private industry would just as soon not talk about and who likes to label those who do talk about it as xenophobic -- foreign outsourcing and in-sourcing practices, which have caused the loss of millions of jobs in this country. Those terms are euphemisms for the exportation of high-paying, more skilled jobs to low-wage foreign countries, and the importation of a less educated, less skilled underclass willing to work for lower wages without benefits. The H1-B visa program has been used to promote in-sourcing, particularly in many high-tech fields, which has worked to level or diminish compensation levels and provide a pool of younger, much cheaper workers so more senior Americans can be "put out to pasture."

The big winners of outsourcing and in-sourcing are the big corporations, while we, the (rapidly shrinking) American middle class are the big losers. Several studies have found that CEOs of the biggest outsourcing companies were paid significantly higher than their counterparts. An additional destructive element to the elimination of jobs as a direct result of these practices run amok is the decline of real wages for the remaining jobs. Consider these two startling and very unsettling statistics: for the first time since the Great Depression, job growth in our country for the last 10 years was negative and median household income fell.

A dated but still relatively timely list of private companies that outsource jobs can be found at:

www.cnn.com/cnn/programs/lou.dobbs.tonight/popups/exporting.america.

You might think that state governments would be opposed to these practices, but think again. More than 40 states are contributing to job destruction by contracting out state-funded work to corporations who then ship the jobs overseas.

One area of American employment hit especially hard by outsourcing is technology. It is estimated that more than 500,000 technology jobs have been outsourced over the past ten years, and, during that same period, 250,000 additional jobs were lost due to outsourcing. According to the U.S. Labor Department and Forrester Research, outsourcing continues to pick up steam even today. They project that over 1,500,000 jobs will move offshore this year. That is bad enough, but by 2015, the number of jobs outsourced from America will exceed 3,300,000.

Moreover, for those of you who have bought into the hype that the "green revolution" will save us on the jobs front, you might want to reconsider. The "green economy" in 2009 accounted for less than one-half of one percent of all U.S. jobs. Moreover, President Obama frequently cited Spain as a country we might want to emulate on green energy policy. We hardly think so. A study by a major university in Madrid found as follows: for every green job created in Spain, another 2.2 jobs in other sectors were destroyed. Another study found that Spain's government spent more than $750,000 to create each new green job. And, as it turns out, more than 80% of the green jobs created here have already been outsourced to foreign workers.

Now, does either political party have a solution to the job crisis? They both say they do, but there is an old saying that "the proof of the pudding is in the taste," and all we are being given and left with on this vitally important matter by both parties is a bad taste. The politicos would rather play the blame game. The current Administration points the finger at the previous Administration and says "We didn't create this mess, we inherited it." The party out of power (now the Republicans, but that will likely change in the future and probably sooner rather than later) points the finger at the party in power and the Administration and says, "The only jobs they are creating are non-productive government jobs and these are being created on the backs of hard-working, gainfully employed American taxpayers." There is never a thought about admitting they are all culpable and all contributed to the quagmire -- is it too much to ask for each official to grab an oar and start pulling together? That would be entirely too constructive for the legions of politicians who have feasted their entire professional lives on a diet of diatribe and denunciation against the other side, seasoned with the salt of self-adulation and the pepper of promises to do a better job when they have amassed more power, becoming truly "large and in charge."

We wish we could say, "Forgive them for they know not what they do," but they know exactly what they are doing and they know it is destructive. As our mothers used to say, "They are just too set in their ways to ever change" (that is the essence of being "hidebound"). And as our fathers used to say, "All politicians have incurable superiority complexes and the only way they can build themselves up is by tearing the other side down." Tragically, the real people being torn down are we, the middle class. Therefore, the beat goes on (the "beat down," that is, of the unemployed and the underemployed).

How hard is it to get people back to work? And rest assured that the economic malaise will not ease much and certainly not end until our people are able get back to work, irrespective of what the politicians and their obsequious "expert" economists might claim about a "jobless recovery." Each newly created real job creates at least five additional jobs. This is known as the employment multiplier effect. Think of it this way: if I give you a dollar and you spend the dollar, my dollar just turned into two dollars and, when you spend that dollar and buy some of this and some of that, then a portion goes to the retailer, some to the wholesaler, and a piece to the manufacturer of the products you bought and, in turn, more dollars are being spent all along the way because of the original dollar that you used in commerce. The same concept holds true when somebody creates a job. The person with the new job is paid and goes out and buys goods and services, and this spending creates other jobs on the supply side and those employees are then able to do the same thing with their disposable dollars. In this way, the sum of the parts creates a greater and growing whole.

Today, it would appear that the Republicans' primary objective is to block substantive attempts by the Democrats to make headway in the job creation department. Why? Because the more they can make voters believe that Democrats' plans will not work to create a meaningful number of new jobs, the better their chances for reclaiming power in Congress in the mid-term elections and the White House in 2012. Never forget, at the end of the day, it is all about the power for the politicos. Greed takes on many forms and the lust for power is one form that can be as potent as, or more potent than, the love of money. And, if the jobless have to play the patsy to facilitate their obstructionist game, well, those are "acceptable casualties" in the Washington wars -- the end justifies the means and all that nonsense.

Now, it takes money to create and cultivate jobs because the newly hired have to be paid and supported and businesses have to have some "staying power" or "lead time" because new hires ordinarily are not immediately productive (i.e., it takes a while before workers can pay for themselves, much less become profitable to the larger enterprise).

Where, then, does the proverbial "little guy" get the money needed to hire and maintain? Borrowing on our homes is no longer an option. Business and personal credit lines have been reduced or eliminated as credit scores have been decimated. For all the ballyhoo about increasing loans to small businesses, SBA loan volume was down over 36% last year and is still in the tank. And all the while, the TARP funded entities are arguing with their government buddies on how much pay and bonuses they should receive. They claim they have to pay big bonuses and offer big compensation packages or they will lose their "talent" to other firms. This same "talent" almost brought the entire financial system down, mind you. What about all the "talent" out there that has no job or has had to take a job well below the skill level just to keep bread on the table and the lights on? I guess they just don't count in the world of "high finance," the world that contributes much of the campaign monies needed to keep the elected in power or get the "wannabe's" into power.

What can be done? First off, the Administration and Congress must act to provide greater tangible incentives to small businesses (independent businesses having fewer than 500 employees) to hire. The Jobs Bill was a start, but it was grossly underwhelming and mostly misdirected. Small businesses employ over half of all private sector employees and are responsible for 64% of all net new jobs over the last 15 years. Raising income and other taxes on small businesses and imposing additional costs for employee health care insurance and other benefits will only serve to encourage them to ramp up foreign outsourcing of work and curtail hiring of American workers -- which is precisely what we are witnessing today. Honestly, the Jobs Bill has not made a dent in the unemployment picture.

In the second place, unless the Administration and Congress step in and require banks and financial institutions to lend to small businesses and entrepreneurs again, unemployment will not decrease and may get worse. Credit is, for better or worse, the lifeblood of small businesses and entrepreneurs who are in turn the lifeblood of job creation. In other words, no credit means no commerce and no commerce means no hiring, simple as that.

In the meantime, the bankers, politicians and outsourcing executives all have nice, cushy jobs while you are left to try to sell or hock any asset you still own to enable you, maybe, to make one more mortgage payment and one more credit card (minimum) payment -- if not, foreclosure attorneys and debt collectors are just around the corner, and maybe a bankruptcy filing.

Nevertheless, do not think that Wall Street by itself destroyed the 15 million jobs lost over the past 3 years, because our Congress shares an equal amount of the blame. Specifically, when Congress allowed Glass-Steagall to be repealed in 1999, the floodgates of greed were opened to their maximum width and Wall Street took advantage of all that Congress gave them - financial deregulation produced obscene profits. The major ingredients for a major financial disaster were, in retrospect, incredibly obvious: an accommodating Fed that allowed interest rates to be kept artificially low for an extended period of time, a Wall Street band of bandits who conspired to cook up incredibly risky investment vehicles, one after another, with the primary goal of fleecing their clients, perilously high leverage ratios to further fuel the risk-taking machinery, and lax (some might say comatose) federal regulators. The result was a toxic brew indeed, proving to be a near fatal dose of economic cyanide for the world's financial system.

Stay tuned as more financial misery is still to follow and much needed jobs are nowhere in sight.

Sleep soundly fellow Americans (at least those of you who have jobs to wake up to)!

CHAPTER 5

DEBT
'Another Day Older and Deeper in Debt'

"I place the public debt as the greatest of the dangers to be feared. And I sincerely believe, with you, that the principle of spending money to be paid by posterity, under the name of funding, is but swindling futurity on a large scale."
- Thomas Jefferson

"I go on the principle that a public debt is a public curse and in a republican government more than in any other."
- James Madison

"Blessed are the young for they shall inherit the national debt."
- Herbert Hoover

Do you ever wonder why politicians believe that it is okay to spend more of your money than they collect from you year after year after year? Or that it is okay to allow our national debt to grow without boundaries or limitation, like kudzu, as we are wont to say down South? Is it because current legislation encourages deficit spending and a largely unaccountable national debt, or is it because of an unassailable two-party political system that is accountable to no one but it?

Article 1, Section 8, Clause 2 of the Constitution grants the United States Congress the power to "borrow money on the credit of the United States." The issue of the federal debt was not addressed again in the framework of the Constitution for almost eighty years, until the addition of the Fourteenth Amendment in

1868. Section 4 of that Amendment provides that the "validity of the public debt of the United States, authorized by law, including debts incurred for the payment of pensions and bounties, for services in suppressing insurrection or rebellion, shall not be questioned." And this clause was added to assure foreign governments who bought our debt to help finance the Civil War would be repaid. Unlike the constitutions of most states, the United States Constitution does not require the Congress to pass a balanced budget. And so, on a national level at least, we have been left with runaway deficit spending, which is getting worse by the second (as a matter of fact, $47,000 per second at the current rate of deficit spending).

Since there is no legislation, rule, or regulation which prohibits deficit spending or the size of the national debt, it is going to continue to grow. However, as Jefferson cautioned, when we do this, we mortgage our future and that of our children and grandchildren. One only has to take a look at the debt clock on www.usdebtclock.org to witness, in real time, the immense size and velocity of growth of our national debt (and it is **our** debt, yours and mine, make no mistake). The total national debt is currently almost $13 trillion, 90% of GDP, $42,000 per person and $120,000 per taxpayer. It is expected to top $14.3 trillion early next year, which would equal almost 100% of our GDP, far and away the highest percentage since World War II. The interest alone on the debt (and this at artificially low interest rates), including the interest on the debt created by the federal government borrowing from the Social Security Trust Fund, is now running at a clip of about $400 billion a year, which is more than 11% of the entire 2010 federal budget. If we were to pay off $1,000,000 of debt each day, it would take us more than 38,000 years to retire $14 trillion in debt.

Last year's budget deficit was an all-time record -- over $1.4 trillion (that's $2.6 million each minute, $160 million each hour, $3.8 billion each day). To pay off just the 2010 deficit, according to the Tax Foundation, would require Congress to increase taxes by 240%. And that would not retire one cent of the overall debt, just one year's deficit. By way of comparison to the gargantuan size of the deficit, Warren Buffet, one of the richest men in the world, has a net worth equal to only 2.6% of a single year's deficit.

Moreover, the deficit last year equaled 10% of the nation's entire GDP, and this year's deficit is on track to soar well above that. Economic experts across-the-board agree that we tread on very treacherous economic terrain when our annual budget deficits exceed 3% of GDP, which, by the way is the level the President promised to reach by the end of his first term in office (in a *"read my lips"* moment) -- he only missed it slightly, by 333%. And the cumulative deficit for the remainder of the decade, according to the Administration's own projections, will take us where "no man (or woman) has gone (or ever wanted to go) before" -- to $25 trillion (and that's if there are no new spending programs, which is highly unlikely).

Recent Congressional Budget Office (CBO) reports underscore the seriousness between spending and revenues. Total revenues covered less than 60% of total spending in 2009, and that ratio is now projected to decline in 2010. With a 40+% shortfall between what the federal government brings in and what is pays out, it is no wonder we are facing record deficits. One CBO report also notes that this year Americans will pay the second lowest; (and it could become the lowest) individual income taxes, as a share of GDP, since 1944. The only year we paid less was last year.

So what are the conclusions of the CBO director about his office's forecasts? Well, he called the budget outlook "dire" and warned that the nation is moving down a path toward growing debt which poses a number of serious "risks" to the economy. He concluded, in a sharply worded overview, that the "outlook for the federal budget is bleak." Tell us something we don't know, Mr. Sherlock Holmes.

It is also worth bearing in mind that these numbers, as bad as they are, do not include the obligations of Fannie Mae and Freddie

Mac, which the federal government has made us, the taxpayer, responsible to pay. At last count, these obligations had soared to an almost incomprehensible $5.5 trillion.

President Obama in his last State of the Union Address pledged to freeze some *"discretionary spending,"* but the savings would be a paltry $250 billion over 10 years. That is a step in the right direction, but to call it a "baby step" is an insult to babies everywhere. And our "spend today, give tomorrow away" Congress approved the administration's proposal to borrow an additional $1.9 trillion to pay the federal government's current bills, an amount that, less than a decade ago, would have funded all operations and programs of the federal government for an entire year.

It took each and every President from George Washington to Jimmy Carter, our 39th president (200 years) to create $1 trillion of national debt. It has taken just 30 years to grow the debt by more than 1,200% (folks, that's an average of 40% per year). And it is surely worth noting that our esteemed Congress never failed to increase the federal borrowing limit during that time, never. So, as we drown in a sea of economic and financial woe, Congress happily throws us an anchor instead of a life preserver. The federal debt is no life jacket, but instead, a straight jacket that will ultimately take away our financial freedom.

This frightening picture becomes absolutely bone-chilling when you add in the unfunded obligations of the federal government for entitlement programs, including Social Security and Medicare. Some estimates place all of these obligations, in the aggregate, at $110 trillion -- $340,000 for every man, woman and child in the country. Can it get much worse? Well of course it can when we have to trust our fate to politicians who follow this rule of political life -- *live for today, for tomorrow you may (politically speaking at least) die.*

Some in the administration and some economists would have us believe that deficits are okay, that, like the poor, they will always be with us and we must learn to live with them -- sort of an "embrace-the-pain" mentality. Nobel Laureate economist Paul Krugman wrote that *"deficits saved the world"* from economic collapse. However, most economists agree that mounting deficits will eventually take a huge toll on our economy. A report released this year that reviewed 200 years of economic data from 44 nations reached an ominous conclusion -- the U.S. debt will undoubtedly lead to slow growth, if not no growth. The study found that, almost without exception, countries as highly indebted as are we grow at sub-par rates. The report, entitled **Growth in a Time of Debt**, written by Carmen Reinhart and Kenneth Rogoth, well-regarded economists from the University of Maryland and Harvard College respectively, found that a nation's growth rate slows precipitously when its debt exceeds 60% of its GDP, and when that ratio exceeds 90%, national economies barely grow or even contract.

As noted above, our national debt is already above 80% of GDP right now, and it is expected to cross the 90% threshold later this year. Ladies and gentlemen, all passengers on this flight of "Debta Airlines" should immediately take their seats and buckle their seat belts. We are heading into some stormy weather and will be experiencing moderate turbulence, but it may well turn severe. Please do not be alarmed if the oxygen masks deploy. Simply put them on and assist children and the elderly with their masks and try to breathe normally. Under no circumstance should you leave your seat until the flight crew advises you that it is safe to do.

Note also that failure to contain the debt will ultimately cause a crippling dollar crisis. In order to continue selling national debt, interest rates will have to increase, thus increasing the costs of borrowing, which in turn will increase the deficits and the vicious cycle never ends. The end result will be a sizable reduction in our standard of living and a downward spiral in the value of the dollar as international creditors are forced to seek safer investments elsewhere. Even Moody's Investors Service, known as a notorious federal government "brown noser," has been forced to admit that the United States has moved "substantially" closer to losing its triple A rating for Treasury bonds. The reason is the budget deficit. Moody's estimates Washington will spend 7% of tax revenues this year in debt service, rising to almost 11% in 2013. And that's the line in the sand, according to Moody's -- anything above 10% and the credit rating will be in real jeopardy. A bond rating reduction would trigger a rise in Treasury bond interest rates that in turn would add to the deficit, and would bring the rating under even more pressure, engendering a vicious circle of rating decreases followed by rate increases.

And, as if this were not enough, consider this sobering statistic: total public and private debt in this country today total more than $50 trillion, or three and a half times annual GDP (the highest in history). What this really tells us is that the great prosperity of the last few decades has been largely an illusion, the result of artificially created credit, much of it through the money printing press known as the Federal Reserve. As Will Rogers, the famous political humorist once quipped, *"The nation is prosperous on the whole, but how much prosperity is there in a hole?"* Sounds funny at first blush, until we realize the joke is on us. So, when you hear someone say she is living on "borrowed" time, she just might be talking about finances, and she just might be speaking for all of us. We have seen the emperor strutting without clothes all right, but we didn't realize until now it is because he can no longer afford to buy any!

The U.S. needs to heed the warning flowing from these countries and the European Union, as the European sovereign debt crisis is beginning to threaten the stability of the Euro and the solidarity of the Union itself. The main culprit in Greece's case - years of massive overspending by the Greek government creating huge deficits. So large were the deficits that, without the $144 billion bailout by the EU, the government of Greece would have been unable to pay its debt obligations. Unfortunately, there are greater similarities between the Greek financial mess and where we seem to be headed at breakneck speed than anyone would like to admit. As a percentage of GDP, Greece's budget deficit is not all that much greater than ours, 13.5% for Greece and over 11.0% for the U.S. But instead of reducing the debt it continues to grow as a percentage of GDP. Greece's uncontrolled debt led to downgrades by the debt rating agencies, which in turn led to ever higher costs of financing (borrowed money) and generated fewer buyers of the debt due to the growing risk of default. Many insiders in the know believe Spain, Portugal, Japan and the United Kingdom are not far behind Greece's systemic failure. Obviously, America is exponentially stronger financially than Greece, but the lesson of Greece is the same: uncontrolled debt and spending leads to catastrophic results. Even the U.S. itself is not too big to fail! In fact, if the U.S. were to require a commensurate bailout to Greece, based on the respective sizes of the GDPs, we would need a staggering $6.4 trillion bailout. That makes TARP look ridiculously tiny in comparison.

And both Japan and Britain, who are saddled with spiraling debt loads similar to our own, are finally taking strong measures to check their out-of-control spending. George Osborne, Britain's new Chancellor of the Exchequer (like our Secretary of the Treasury), warning that financial ruin will be Britain's sure fate without drastic action, has proposed an emergency budget combining deep spending cuts and some tax increases in the most radical fiscal entrenchment in three decades. Japan's new Prime Minister, also warning of financial collapse under an unsustainable sovereign debt load, is proposing similar fiscal austerity measures. So they have finally awakened and smelled the roses. What about us, you say? Aren't we getting with the program? No chance. We apparently would not waken even with a potent dose of *sal volatile* (smelling salts). Washington, as usual, is sitting on its hands while the debt clock time bomb keeps on ticking. In fact, the Administration recently said we will have to keep spending for a while longer. Well, it most likely will not be his problem anyway after 2012, but we are going to have to pay the piper at some point and his bill is going to be way more than we can afford.

So then, since we are ultimately liable for the national debt, shouldn't we have something more to say about it? All we have right now is the voice of the vote, but that is not much good when the politicians are mostly clones of each other who do not have our best interests at heart. So, most times the best we are left with is the lesser of two evils and even then only every few years. And recent electoral history does not give much cause for optimism since more than 90% of incumbents who run for reelection win reelection. But that may change in the next round of elections. One can only hope.

And out of control governmental debt is not limited to the federal level. According to the Center on Budget and Policy Priorities, a nonprofit, non-partisan "think tank" focused on federal and state fiscal policies and programs that affect low- and moderate-income Americans, 48 states now face shortfalls in their budgets for this fiscal year that total almost $200 billion (almost 30% of state budgets) – the largest in history. Projected shortfalls for 2011 total $180 billion and top $120 billion for fiscal 2012.

And the picture gets much worse when state pension obligations are included. Pensions are certainly forms of debt since they must be paid over time, just like bonds. But states conveniently (and purposely) do not disclose the amount they owe retirees when they disclose their bonded indebtedness and state officials have uniformly and steadfastly opposed valuing their pensions at market rates because they know it would put them far behind the financial eight-ball with prospective bondholders. Joshua Rauh, an economist at Northwestern University and Robert Novy-Marx of the University of Chicago recalculated the value of the states' pension obligations in the manner the bond markets value debt and they put the figure at almost $5.2 trillion. After you take away the $1.94 trillion set aside in state pension funds, you are left with a gap of more than $3.2 trillion -- more than three times the debt to all bondholders combined. Raugh also observed that seven states (Illinois, Connecticut, Indiana, New Jersey, Hawaii, Louisiana and Oklahoma) will totally run out of money to pay public pensions by 2020.

The effect of the state indebtedness is beginning to make itself felt in growing and sometimes deep budget cuts. California is a prime example which is in the news regularly. You will recall California has had to resort to paying many vendors with its I.O.U.'s. But California is not alone. In Illinois, the state comptroller general recently said the state was $9 billion behind on paying bills to its vendors, which he claimed was an "ongoing fiscal disaster." Fitch Ratings recently downgraded several categories of the state's debt, citing the amount of accounts payable. Experts have observed that at least ten states are bordering on insolvency -- California, Illinois, Arizona, Florida, Michigan, Nevada, New Jersey, Oregon, Rhode Island and Wisconsin. And 2011 will bring revenue shortfalls as big or bigger than the current ones for many states.

Some states have tried the trick of borrowing from Peter to pay Paul. New Hampshire, for example, was ordered by its Supreme Court to give back $110 million it took from a medical malpractice insurance pool to balance its budget. Colorado's sneaky effort to "borrow" a $500 million surplus from a state workers' compensation insurer that was privatized in 2002 has so far been rebuffed. And many states have balanced their budgets with federal health care dollars that have yet to be appropriated by Congress. Some economists feel the states may soon have a much bigger problem than simply balancing their budgets. If their debt is downgraded and investors become skittish, the resulting credit squeeze could take on shades of Greece, where the financial institutions refused to refinance billions in Greek debt, triggering the panic-driven bailout. Most state officials are convinced they will be bailed out by the federal government if their finances really hit a wall. And we all know they are right, as the President's request to Congress in June for $50 billion in emergency bailout funds for states and communities demonstrates. That amount, our friends, is just the beginning, the tip of a much larger financial iceberg which will cause serious troubles for the "unsinkable" Ship of State as we steer nearer and nearer.

And the municipalities are in no better shape than the states. Some are far worse off. Plus, unlike states, municipalities have the option of declaring bankruptcy under Chapter 9. Former Los Angeles Mayor Richard Riordan contends that the City of Angels will file bankruptcy proceedings by 2014. So may Detroit. In 2008 alone there were 136 defaults on municipal securities -- more than $8 billion. Last year saw $6.4 billion in defaults and this year is on track to meet or exceed that amount.

The overall size of the municipal bond market is in and of itself a cause for serious concern. Municipal securities are a $2.8 trillion market and growing. Many inventors have lined up to buy munis over the past several years, lured by the low default rate (until recently) and the tax free benefits. More than $69 billion flowed into long-term municipal bond mutual funds in 2009, up from only $7.8 billion in 2008 and $10.9 billion in 2010. More than $50 billion is expected for 2010 – assuming of course that the rating agencies continue to turn a blind eye to the risk of default. A major default by a major municipality would change all of that and send potentially devastating shock waves through the market. However, investors are convinced that the good old federal government, the sugar daddy of all sugar daddies, can be counted on to step in if worse comes to worst and backstop municipal debt with federal guaranties.

The more we think about this situation, the more amazed we are that the people have become sideline spectators watching our elected officials play a game of Russian roulette with our economy. And lest you think we are lone voices crying in the prognostication wilderness, according to a recent report from a group of leading economists, financiers, and former federal regulators, a second financial crisis is looming that could make the earlier (current) one look like a walk in the park by comparison. The report warns that America is immersed in a "doomsday cycle" in which banks are using borrowed money to take massive risk, in an attempt to continue to generate huge profits for shareholders and big bonuses to management, all with the implicit assurance that the taxpayers will be there to bail them out again when the risks go wrong. The report blasts Washington, saying: *"Our government leaders have shown little capacity to fix the flaws in our market system."* The study notes that "in 2008-09, we came remarkably close to another Great Depression," and predicts that the next shock waves will cause "a calamitous global collapse" if the financial institutions are not brought to bay. Much like what is occurring today in certain European countries, including Greece, Spain, the United Kingdom, and Portugal, where financial systems are imploding because their governments spent way more than they should have and now it is payback time.

And regarding the report, we share the report's disgust about our lawmakers. Sadly, our elected officials are being paid by us to play the game of Russian roulette that eventually will cause us to take a bullet in the head. For those of you who remember Ross Perot's 1992 presidential run, recall that he addressed this same issue and advocated an electronic town hall approach whereby the citizenry would be permitted to actively participate in approving appropriations or spending bills before enactment. This proposal was not well-received by either party at the time, and was widely ridiculed and Perot himself belittled. However, no one is laughing now at his predictions of spending gone wild if left in the hands of the elected instead of the electorate. If you are interested in the issues that inspired Perot to spend $65 million dollars of his own money in his 1992 bid for president, read his short book/treatise **United We Stand**. We believe you will conclude, as have we, that not much has changed (and certainly not for the better) when it comes to politicians.

No, folks, they do not want us playing in their game. They really do not want us to know the rules of their game. We buy the tickets that allow them to play the game, but they make the rules, they change the rules, and they enforce the rules. We can boo and hiss, but unless we take control of the game, the existing two-party system with its cadre of lawmakers, lobbyists and Wall Street pay masters couldn't care less about our disaffection. They also built the vault that holds the proceeds from the game and they jealously guard the vault and act like the money in the vault is theirs. But it is not, it is ours. And we should be able to have the final say in how it is spent. Until we do, they are going to treat it just like the investment banks treat "OPM" ("Other People's Money") -- if they win with it, they get much of the winnings, but if they lose it, the loss is borne solely by those "other people." From their perspective, it just doesn't get any better than that!

One final thought – we need to see our federal government rebuilt as *The House That Jack Built* – that would be Jack Sprat, of course. Unfortunately, the Houses of Congress and the White House have been built using blueprints for *The House That Mrs. Jack Built.* If you recall the nursery rhyme about the erstwhile Sprats, you will remember that *"Jack would eat no fat and his wife would eat no lean."* Similarly, our federal government has taken its cue from Mrs. Sprat and eschewed Mr. Sprat by never choosing the lean and grandly gorging itself on the fat. Sadly, however, we have all been subjected to the final result as the Sprat couple – with all of our platters licked clean, leaving not a morsel for later on!

CHAPTER 6

TERM LIMITS
'Time Waits for No Man (Except a Congressman)'

*"Term limits would cure both senility and seniority,
both terrible legislative diseases."*
- Harry S. Truman

*"Politicians are like diapers; they must be changed
often and for the same reason."*
- Paul Harvey

We awake to a new day with a bit of optimism, thinking maybe there is a way to make changes to the current two-party system without jettisoning it entirely: limit the amount of time that any elected official may serve, especially members of the United States House of Representatives and Senate. During the early 1990s, advocates of term limits used the legislative initiative and referendum to place congressional term limit proposals on the ballots in 23 states. Voters in every one of these states approved term limits by an average electoral margin of two to one. However, in 1995, in a five to four decision, the United States Supreme Court, in U.S. Term Limits, Inc. v. Thornton, 514 U.S. 779, ruled that states could not impose term limits upon their federal Representatives or Senators, holding that Congressional qualifications for office cannot be stricter than those specified in the Constitution.

The idea of limiting tenure in office is neither new nor revolutionary. In fact, the notion of career politicians (certainly in democracies) who remain in office until he or she has to be carried out "feet first" is of relatively recent origin. In ancient Athens, commonly called the cradle of democracy, the governing council of 500 rotated its entire membership annually. The ancient Roman Republic featured a system of elected magistrates, including tribunes and consuls, who served a single term of one year, with reelection to the same post forbidden for ten years.

Although the framers of the Constitution decided not to include term limits in that hallowed document, they, for the most part, never envisioned the rise of the career politician and perpetuity in office as has developed today. This is not to say that all of the Founding Fathers opposed term limits. To the contrary, three of the most esteemed of the Founding Fathers, George Washington, Benjamin Franklin, and Thomas Jefferson strongly favored the imposition of term limits. Washington backed up his words with his actions (walked the walk, not just talked the talk) by refusing to stand for a third presidential term of office, establishing a precedent that would last for the next 150 years. And, this despite the public clamoring for him to run for a third term. Washington recognized that the country had just fought a war of independence against the tyranny which emanated from the perpetuity inherent in a monarchy and the last thing he wanted to do was have the Presidency take on shades of royalty.

The other Founding Fathers were not overly concerned about a need for term limits because they viewed congressional seats purely as part-time jobs, not professions. James Madison, for example, simply assumed that Representatives would be "called for the most part from pursuits of a private nature and continue in appointment for a short period of office." That assumption, understandable in its day, allowed the framers to believe that Congress would, quite naturally, remain a citizen legislature, without any Constitutional prohibition against those serving in Congress spending their entire adult lives there. The framers and the next few generations never had reason to question this assumption because Congressional service remained the anticipated part-time job for the nation's first century. The early

Congress met for only a matter of months each year. In fact, the early Congresses met mostly during the winter months, when most citizens could afford time away from their normal jobs in the primarily agrarian economy.

A major contributing factor to the popularity of rotation in office during this period was the mistrust of political power so ingrained in the American culture, that, according to one renowned historian (James Young), "even the officeholders themselves perceived their occupations in a disparaging light." Famed early 19th century American author James Fennimore Cooper aptly described the commonly shared view that *"contact with the affairs of state is one of the most corrupting influences to which men are exposed."* An 1822 article in **The Richmond Enquirer** observed that the *"long cherished"* principle of rotation in office had been impressed on the republican mind *"by a kind of intuitive impulse, unassailable to argument or authority."*

It was not until the 20th century that the concept of what we like to call "incumbency perpetuity" became an integral and ultimately inveterate part of the American political culture. Prior to the last half of the 20th century, Congressional turnover was regularly in excess of 50%. During the past 30 years, however, reelection rates have averaged almost 90% (less turnover than with the old Soviet Union's Communist Party Central Committee), creating a condition which has been referred to as "Congressional stagnation," with the main skill honed by elected officials being the "skill" of glad-handing and raising the money needed to ensure reelection. And raising money for campaigns means catering to the special interests, the "bag men," who have the resources to fund reelection campaigns every two or six years.

Additionally, spending year after year in the notorious "Beltway Bubble" isolates Congress from the real world and their constituents (unless you want to call lobbyists and their corporate clients the "constituents"). One way to pop the pernicious Beltway Bubble mentality would be to impose term limits so that Representatives and Senators would have to leave the cozy confines of Congress after a reasonable period of time and return to their communities of us ordinary folks and live with the laws they helped fashion.

There is no doubt that the electorate favors term limits. Polls show that Americans support Congressional term limits by margins of three and four to one. So then, how can we limit the number of years that an elected official may serve in office? We did it with respect to the Presidency after President Franklin Delano Roosevelt successfully shattered the informal tradition of two-term limits by running for and being elected to a third and then fourth term (although he died in office after serving less than three months of his fourth term). Roosevelt's impaired physical health (and many say mental health) during the latter part of his third term and certainly his highly abbreviated fourth term gave rise to a successful move in Congress to formalize the former two-term tradition. Thus was born the Twenty-Second Amendment to the Constitution which was ratified in 1951. Why should the same kind of restrictions not be placed upon Representatives and Senators?

There have been efforts to bring this change about. Congressional term limits were a prominent feature in the Republican Party's proposed **Citizen Legislature Act**, as a fundamental part of the *Contract with America*, in the 1994 election campaign and may well have been a significant contributing factor in the successful "Republican Revolution" as the Republicans wrested control of the House of Representatives from the Democratic Party for the first time since 1952. The Republican leadership brought to the floor of the House a constitutional amendment that would limit House members to six two-year terms and members of the Senate to two six-year terms. However, this rate of rotation was too slow for the populist backers of term limits, including U.S. Term Limits, the largest and most vocal of the private organizations advocating term limits (who wanted House members to be limited to three two-year terms). None of the House proposals could muster the two-thirds majority required to pass a constitutional amendment.

Recently, however, a handful of Republican Senators, led by Senator Jim DeMint of South Carolina, are proposing a constitutional amendment whereby service in the Senate be limited to twelve years and service in the House would be limited to six years. According to DeMint:

> *"Americans know real change in Washington will never happen until we end the era of permanent politicians. As long as members have the chance to spend their lives in Washington, their interests will always skew toward spending taxpayer dollars to buy off special interests, covering over corruption in the bureaucracy, fundraising, relationship building among lobbyists, and trading favor for pork -- in short, amassing their own power."*

Truer words have rarely been spoken, particularly in Washington's political circles. The chance of getting two-thirds of the members of either house to back this measure is slim to none (and, as the saying goes, "Slim just left town"). President Eisenhower drew this same conclusion in the 1950s when he observed that a constitutional amendment for Congressional term limits could never achieve the blessing of Congress, but rather could only be initiated by the states.

That is precisely the stance taken by Dr. Larry Sabato, Professor of Politics at the University of Virginia and director of that institution's renowned Center for Politics. In 2007, Professor Sabato revived the debate over term limits by arguing in his book, **A More Perfect Constitution,** that the success and popularity of term limits at the state level (there are term limits for 15 state legislatures, city councils and/or mayors in eight of the ten largest cities, and 36 governorships) suggests that they should be adopted at the federal level as well. He specifically advocates Congressional term limits and proposed holding a national constitutional convention to effectuate such an amendment, observing that Congress would be highly unlikely to propose and adopt any amendment that served to limit its own power.

We heartily concur with Professor Sabato and we have little doubt that the amendment would be approved by the necessary number of states. However, it would be better and more expeditious for our elected Congressional officials to approve such an action, yet this will not happen until we replace the existing self-serving bunch with members that understand that they are citizens first, officials second, and that they represent our interests, not their own. Too many have confused being "the elected" with being "the elect" (as in, being of the nobility, the elite, the aristocracy, the best, the chosen few). Theirs is not a position of entitlement or a lifetime appointment. Rather, members need to recognize it for what it is -- a privilege and an honor -- a privilege and an honor to serve the interests of their friends, neighbors, and fellow citizens for a limited period of time and then allow another worthy citizen to do the same.

Furthermore, the current policies which afford elected officials lifetime retirement and health benefits, even after minimum service, should not be continued, unless the elected member, due to prior qualified service, satisfies all the standards required for retirement and health benefits as formulated under the Civil Service Retirement System for federal employees. Just because someone is elected to Congress does not mean that individual should be entitled to receive monetary and other benefits for themselves and their spouses during their remaining lifetimes. Again, it is a privilege to serve their constituency, not an opportunity to fleece the constituency.

You will not hear much about term limits from the parties themselves because it is in both parties' best interests on this issue to maintain the status quo. And you will not hear much about it from the talking heads in the media because they do not perceive it as an issue which has any chance of success and, if neither party really supports it, it must not be truly "newsworthy." So that leaves it to us to make it happen. And it will only happen if, at the grassroots level, advocacy becomes so large, so organized and so vocal that it cannot be safely ignored, even by the entrenched powers.

We would be remiss in this chapter to fail to make note of the need to impose term limits on Supreme Court Justices. An insightful albeit brief article decrying life tenure for Supreme Court Justices (***Life Tenure is Too Long for Supreme Court Justices***) was published in ***The Atlantic Magazine*** in 2005. The author, Stuart Taylor, an accomplished legal journalist, discusses eight cogent reasons for amending the Constitution to impose a staggered 18-year term limit on all future Supreme Court Justices. Taylor's proposal is in line with one put forth by an ideologically diverse group of 45 of the nation's leading legal scholars, led by Paul Carrington and Roger Cramton, professors and former deans of the Duke and Cornell Law Schools, respectively, Carrington a Democrat and Cramton a Republican). The eight points are summarized below:

❖ **Decrepitude**. Some Justices have remained on the Court until mentally impaired or at least well past their primes (a problem that will surely increase as advances in medical technology and genetics work to prolong life past the point of mental competence (witness William Douglas who served a record 37 years on the High Court and was barely functional during his last 10 months of office, after suffering a debilitating stroke in 1975, and Justices Hugo Black and Thurgood Marshall who were but shadows of themselves years before retiring at age 85 and 87, respectively).

❖ **Intellectual Autopilot.** Health issues aside, the rigid mind-set that frequently goes hand in glove with advancing age diminishes the open-mindedness that is critical to the exercise of good judgment. Many of the older Justices, in particular, seem to rely much more heavily on their law clerks for their opinions while they go on mental autopilot.

❖ **Complacency and Arrogance**. If power corrupts, surely then life-tenured power must exercise an even more potent (and deadly) corrupting influence.

❖ **Unaccountability.** By making new appointments less frequent, longer tenure has lessened the ability of presidents and senators to provide the only form of democratic accountability that is consistent with judicial independence. The average time between appointments has almost doubled from 1.7 years before 1970 to 3.2 years since.

❖ **Randomness.** Filling Supreme Court vacancies is a cardinal presidential power; however, life tenure leaves each President's allotment to chance, skewed by individual justices' efforts to hang on to thwart the ambitions of presidents they dislike (Richard Nixon chose four justices in his first term, while Jimmy Carter chose none).

❖ **Uglier confirmation battles.** Slower turnover has raised the stakes on each new appointment so high as to make confirmation battles even more intense and vicious.

❖ **Erosion of Decisional Legitimacy.** Quasi-monarchical judicial tenure makes it less likely that turnover will lead to reconsideration of erroneous or unpopular constitutional rulings. This feeds doubt about the legitimacy of those rulings among voters and elected officials who may feel disenfranchised.

❖ **Diminished productivity.** The justices have reduced their number of full opinions each year by half (about 75) over the past two decades and most are delegating more and more of their work to their 20-something law clerks. The clerks do almost all of the opinion drafting and screening-out of the 99% of all petitions that the justices dismiss without comment. In truth, how much fresh thinking and enthusiasm for long hours of long work on frequently tedious issues can we honestly expect form octogenarians and septuagenarians who have already spent 20 or 30 years on the job?

Additionally, according to a 2006 article by Northwestern University law professors Steven Calabresi and James Lindgren, the average tenure in office for a Supreme Court Justice was 12.2 years for those retiring between 1941 and 1970. Between 1970 and

2005, however, it more than doubled to 26.1 years and the average age of a justice upon leaving office rose by more than a decade, from 67.6 years to 78.7 years.

We believe it is safe to conclude that the problems posed by life tenure for the Supreme Court Justices will only get worse over time.

Washington politics thrives on "repeat business." We believe it is time to put an end to the seemingly endless "repeat business" (or recidivist politics) of federal lawmakers and judges by subjecting them to a form of "forced retirement" through the imposition of term limits. Only then can we begin to prevent the continued entrenchment of power that so pervades Washington and the federal judiciary.

CHAPTER 7

TAX POLICY
'A Government that Robs Peter to Pay Paul Can Always Count on Paul'

"If, from the more wretched parts of the old world, we look at those which are in an advanced stage of improvement, we still find the greedy hand of government thrusting itself into every corner and crevice of industry, and grasping the spoil of the multitude. Invention is continually exercised, to furnish new pretenses for revenues and taxation. It watches prosperity as its prey and permits none to escape without tribute."
- Thomas Paine

"We contend that for a nation to tax itself into prosperity is like a man standing in a bucket and trying to lift himself up by the handle."
- Sir Winston Churchill

"The income tax is a slave tax – inherently incompatible with freedom. Abolishing it is therefore not just economically feasible; it is a moral imperative if we are to meet our obligation to bequeath liberty to future generations. It is time that we insist on a tax policy for grown-ups, and that means abolishing the income tax and replacing it with a tax structure whose first premise is the capacity of American citizens to make their own economic decisions responsibly."
- Dr. Alan Keyes, conservative political activist

Now, listening to a discussion on CNBC regarding federal tax policy, we are perplexed on the one hand, and dismayed on the other, as to why so many learned individuals extol the merits of our tax policy. Seriously, now, how is it that intelligent people can contend that the shameless use of our national tax policy to advance social engineering agendas is good or even acceptable in a democracy?

It is undeniable (and tragic in many respects) that Congress and presidential administrations utilize tax policy as a mechanism to promote their social engineering objectives, most notably the redistribution of wealth, but also the encouragement of certain forms of industry over others (e.g., some alternative energy industries, such as wind and solar, are given highly preferential tax treatment over others, such as nuclear), the punishment of bad habits (e.g., taxing cigarettes and alcohol), and the promotion of certain aspects of human behavior over others (e.g., home owners are given substantial tax breaks not enjoyed by renters). Ultimately, of course, as the first and possibly most famous of the Supreme Court Chief Justices, John Marshall, noted almost 200 years ago, *"The power to tax is the power to destroy."* Don't we know it!

Let us first examine in simple terms the philosophical nature of wealth redistribution. One could argue that the tax code attempts to incorporate egalitarianism such that the economic inequality between the classes can be reduced or eliminated. In other words, take from the wealthy and give to the poor. And this would be in keeping with beliefs expounded by many in Washington that, in order to keep the masses from revolting, the federal government must give at least an appearance that it is expropriating property from the rich for the benefit of the lower (less well-off) classes. And in order to better facilitate this subterfuge, the lawmakers fashioned a tax code so convoluted and complex that only skilled technicians, such as CPAs and tax attorneys, were (and are) able to master tax filings and defend taxpayers if and when audited or challenged by the IRS. In this way, the wealthy (who can afford the most knowledgeable and sophisticated tax advice and tax planning) are able to minimize the amount of taxes they are required to pay, and the poor are "none the wiser" since they have to pay little or nothing in income taxes, so why should they bother questioning the way the system is "accessed" by wealthier taxpayers. This is borne out by a recent report from the IRS estimating that almost half (47%) of all American households will pay no income tax for 2009.

Well, then, are the more affluent truly able to avail themselves of the so-called "tax loopholes" or is that just libertarian folklore? Consider this: in March of this year, *Forbes Magazine* published the amounts the top U.S. corporations paid in taxes last year. *"Perhaps most egregious,"* **Forbes** noted, is General Electric, which *"generated $10.3 billion in pretax income, but ended up owing nothing to Uncle Sam, but instead, recorded a tax benefit of $1.1 billion."* Similarly, Big Oil giant Exxon Mobil, which last year reported a record $45.2 billion profit, paid nothing to the IRS. Some might say that "evens things out" for the lower and upper classes. We guess that is another way of saying the middle class is left holding the bag, AGAIN!

Come tax time, we are faced with one of the most daunting documents ever contrived by the mind of man: the U.S. tax code. The code contains more than five million words, about seven times the length of the Bible and more than the entire Encyclopedia Britannica. The size has more than tripled in the past 30 years. According to the Government Printing Office, the tax code and the associated regulations issued by the Treasury Department total 20 volumes containing 16,845 pages. There are more than 600 income tax forms. General Electric's annual tax returns exceed an astounding 2,400 pages, for which GE spends millions of dollars each year to have prepared (of course it pays off since last year, as noted above, GE paid a big fat zero in federal income taxes). Fifteen years ago, Mobil Oil Company (now Exxon Mobil) was spending more than $10 million a year and had the equivalent of 57 full-time workers to figure out its taxes. The company is undoubtedly spending at least double that amount today (but, again, money well spent since last year it also paid nothing to the IRS, despite making over $45 billion in profits). If you can afford to work the tax system, the tax system will work for you.

The CCH Standard Federal Tax Reporter, a leading publication for tax professionals that summarizes administrative guidance and judicial decisions issued under each section of the Internal Revenue Code, now comprises 25 volumes and takes up nine feet of shelf space. Some believe that the Internal Revenue Code is proof positive of the validity of the theory that the universe will continue to expand *ad infinitum*, as the code continues to expand by roughly 1000 words every day (with 500 changes adopted last year alone). President Obama's budget for fiscal year 2011 includes a whole panoply of new (but not improved) tax measures which, if adopted, will add hundreds, probably thousands, of pages to an already grossly distended tax code.

Today taxpayers and businesses spend 7.6 billion hours each year complying with the filing requirements laid down by Congress and the IRS. If tax compliance were an industry, it would be one of the largest in the country. To consume 7.6 billion hours, such a "tax compliance industry" would require the equivalent of 3.8 million full-time workers. The cost of complying with individual and corporate tax requirements is estimated at $193 billion -- a staggering 14% of total income tax receipts -- according to the 2008 Annual Report to Congress by the National Taxpayer Advocate. This same report found that more than 80% of individual taxpayers find the process of filing tax returns so difficult, they pay for assistance. Approximately 60% of American taxpayers pay preparers to do the job, and 20% purchase tax software to help them prepare their returns. This Report concluded, in part:

> *"Most importantly, the complexity of the tax code leads to perverse results. On the one hand, taxpayers who honestly seek to comply with the law often make inadvertent errors, causing them either to overpay, or to become subject to IRS*

*enforcement actions for mistaken underpayments. On the
other hand, sophisticated taxpayers often find loopholes that
enable them to reduce or eliminate their taxes."*

Their solution? A radical overhaul of the entire tax code to
make it simpler and less burdensome, so that "most taxpayers can
prepare their own returns and compute their tax liabilities on a
single form." Tax simplification measures have been consistently
and vigorously opposed by the likes of H & R Block (a $4 billion
company with 12,500 retail tax offices in the Unites States) and
vast legions of tax attorneys and tax accountants. Small wonder
when you consider the vast sums of money they rake in on tax
returns and tax planning.

A simplified tax code would also obviate the need for the
ludicrously high funding requirements of the IRS, the largest
federal bureaucracy, with well over 100,000 employees and a
proposed budget this year exceeding $12 billion. Incredibly, the
IRS has more employees than the Environmental Protection
Agency, the Occupational Safety and Health Administration, the
Federal Bureau of Investigation, the Drug Enforcement Agency,
the Food and Drug Administration, and the Bureau of Alcohol
Tobacco and Firearms - combined.

Most taxpayers do not really see the need to get embroiled in
tax policy arguments because most of the tax code does not pertain
to wage earners with limited assets. Rather, the code is directed at
taxpayers who have enough taxable income and assets to be able to
avail themselves of the myriad of deductions, exemptions, credits,
and deferrals provided for in the code (often buried in the "fine
print" which accounts for much of the code's language). In truth,
the code has been designed by Congress to hoodwink the low-
income taxpayer.

Let us briefly explain: assume a taxpayer's federal taxable
income is $40,000 derived from wages of $57,500 and assume
further that this taxpayer is married with three children. He or she
did not itemize deductions, and so, he or she ends up paying

$4,399 in Social Security and Medicare tax and another $3,000 - $5,200 in income taxes, depending upon tax credits. This equates to 24% of the hypothetical taxpayer's taxable income. Now, then, let's compare this result to one for a taxpayer who earns $500,000 a year, but, by accessing deductions for mortgage interest, business losses, business expenses, donations of appreciated property to qualified charities, sale of property to qualified charities for less than fair market value, energy-saving home improvement expenditures, fair rental property deductions, etc., resulting in the reduction of his or her gross adjusted income to $150,000. Remember, FICA taxes apply only to the first $106,800 of earned income or $8,170 in our example. After utilizing the exemptions for two adults and three children, taxable income is reduced to $132,500 and, after subtracting $25,000 of available tax credits in our example, the taxable income is reduced to $107,500, resulting in federal income taxes of $19,500. Accordingly, our high-income filer would pay a total of $27,670 in taxes or 5.50% of his or her $500,000 in gross reported income as compared to the taxpayer who has limited deductions and pays 24% of their taxable income in taxes. Quite a disparity, wouldn't you agree?

Now we begin to see why the tax code is so difficult to understand -- because Congress purposely makes it so in order to facilitate the shell game which, on balance, serves to victimize the middle and lower income groups (the President's and Congress's protests and promises to the contrary notwithstanding). Elected officials believe that the taxpayer who earns $500,000 is more predisposed to contribute to political campaigns and support the two-party political process than the lower-income taxpayer. And, as the elected officials know full well, turnout among high income voters is much greater than lower- income voters.

But Congress believes that it must put on a "good show" for the electorate at large by making it appear that that the wealthy bear a disproportionately larger tax burden, whereas, in actuality, the lower-income taxpayer usually pays a higher percentage of his or her income in taxes than does Mr. or Mrs. Big Bucks. Thus, in our example above, the taxman plucks one of every four dollars of hard-earned income from the low-income filer, but extracts only 1 of every 20 dollars from the high-income taxpayer, rendering the tax code regressive instead of progressive. To further compound the relatively greater burden on the average taxpayer, consider this: taxpayers with adjusted gross incomes under $20,000 pay, on average, 5.9% of this amount in compliance costs while those with adjusted gross incomes in excess of $200,000 pay, on average, .5% of their incomes for tax compliance. Nevertheless, politicians shamelessly (and shamefully) spin the hype to convey just the opposite impression by making the wealthy "whipping boys" in public, but doing so with the proverbial "wink and a nod," so wealthy can rest easy with the knowledge that the politicos will make sure the wealthy do not suffer unduly, when all is said and done, under the tax laws (apparently affirming the adage that you can indeed fool some of the people - in this case the masses - all of the time).

So then, we must ask ourselves, for whom is the Internal Revenue Code written. Certainly not for Joe or Jane Q. Public, as most taxpayers have not a clue about how to decipher the inscrutable tax code. Albert Einstein, one of the most brilliant men in history, once remarked that *"the hardest thing in the world to understand is the income tax"* and is also attributed, perhaps anecdotally, to have quipped that it was easier for him to postulate the theory of relativity and all its underpinning nuances and intricacies than to fill out a single income tax return. Even the so-called "in house experts" at the IRS have difficulty understanding the tax code-- in 2008, they were wrong 10% of the time (and on relatively simple questions at that). Since the code can only be interpreted by the "tax high priests" (CPAs, tax attorneys and other learned tax professionals), it must have been written in part then to benefit them. Consequently, the code can be characterized as a "tax specialist's relief act" or "public works program for lawyers and accountants."

Additionally, as noted above, the tax code has proven to be a rather remarkable piece of legislative legerdemain, in that Congress is able to utilize its sheer complexity to effectively conceal much of the preferential treatment afforded the wealthy. Seen in this light, there is real "method to the madness" of the tax code. By keeping the tax code largely incomprehensible to laymen, the politicians can limit discourse to the wealthy complaining about "unfair" taxes directed at them, such as capital gains or estate tax rates, which have no meaningful bearing on the bulk of the middle and lower classes.

In summary, let us just say that Congress has perfected a system whereby it can take taxpayers' money with impunity (leaving many to impecuniosities) by changing the rules in the tax code while making most taxpayers believe that a progressive tax system is fair. This is an example of what we like to call "Congressional chicanery" at its best (and worst).

There is no use complaining unless you have a solution. So, then, we must pose the question: Is there a more efficient tax system, one that is simple to understand and fair for everyone? There most certainly is -- a flat tax coming in at less than 15% of income. What are the advantages of a flat tax?

❖ **Faster economic growth**. A flat tax would serve to spur increased work, saving and investment by reducing the penalties imposed by high marginal tax rates on labor (Obama has proposed increasing the marginal tax rate to 39%), eliminating taxes on savings, and doing away with the current system of double taxation on investments. By exempting savings, at least up to a relatively high amount, from taxation, we could become a nations of savers again instead of a nation of spenders (particularly spenders of money we do not have except through borrowings), an ancillary benefit of which would be to strengthen the dollar.

❖ **Creation of wealth**. According to Harvard economist Dale Jorgensen, tax reform, which the flat tax would bring about in spades, would boost national wealth by $5 trillion. It would do this in part because all income-producing assets would rise in value, since the fair tax would increase the after-tax stream of income that they generate.

❖ **Simplicity**. As we have demonstrated, complexity is a hidden tax, in and of itself, that amounts to about $200 billion a year, not counting the billions of our tax dollars consumed by the IRS (the bloating of the tax code has quite naturally led to the bloating of the agency that has to administer it). The flat tax would streamline and simplify the process that everyone could file their returns on postcard-sized forms.

❖ **Fairness**. This is a biggie. A flat tax would treat people fairly. No longer would the tax code strive to penalize success and seek to discriminate against citizens on the basis of income. The costs of tax preparation would be equalized and would become only nominal. And the flat tax would enable us to do away with the granddaddy of unfairness, the estate (death) tax which will return with a vengeance in 2011 with a top tax rate of 55% (60% for some estates). Raymond J. Keating, Chief Economist for the Small Business and Entrepreneurship Council, had this to say about the estate tax:

"No sound economic reasons exist for a death tax. It discourages investment. It diverts resources to nonproductive tax planning and tax avoidance measures. It forces some family businesses to be sold or even closed. This destroys jobs. And after a lifetime of paying seemingly countless taxes and fees, it is grossly unfair. For good measure, once all of the costs are factored into the equation, it has been estimated by the Joint Economic Committee of Congress that the death tax generates no net revenue for the federal government. Quite simply, this tax is destructive -- it is a waste".

When Benjamin Franklin penned one of the most famous phrases in American history, *"in this world, nothing is certain but death and taxes,"* he surely did not envision that Congress would enable taxes to trump even death with the enactment of the estate tax in 1916.

❖ **Economic efficiency.** A common approximation in economics is that the economic distortion or excess burden from a tax is proportional to the square of the tax rate. Accordingly, a 20% tax rate causes four times the excess burden on taxpayers of a 10% tax, since it is twice the rate. Broadly speaking, this means that a low uniform (flat) rate on a broad tax base will always be more economically efficient than a mix of high and low rates on a smaller tax base (which the current system provides).

❖ **Increased civil liberties.** Under current law, persons charged with murder are presumed innocent and are afforded more rights than taxpayers dealing with the IRS. Because of the vague and subjective nature of much of the tax code, the criminal and certainly civil penalty provisions of the code could technically be used to imprison or seize the property of virtually everyone who signs a tax return. And the tax court is perhaps the only area of American jurisprudence where the burden of proof is upon the accused, not the government (it's no wonder then that the IRS wins 86% of all tax cases). A flat tax would eliminate almost all sources of conflict between taxpayers and the government. Moreover, IRS infringements on freedom and privacy, now relatively commonplace, would fall dramatically since the government would no longer need to know the intimate details of each taxpayer's financial assets.

Have flat tax systems worked elsewhere? Indeed. Flat tax systems have been adopted in 25 countries and more are taking a hard look at them each year. One big success story is Russia. Prior to 2001, Russia had a complicated and cumbersome progressive system of taxation, somewhat like ours. In 2001, Russia, at the behest of President Vladimir Putin, became the world's first large economy to implement a flat tax with a rate of 13%. Over the next year after the reform, while the Russian economy grew at almost 5% in real terms, revenues from the personal income tax increased by over 25% in real terms in the first full year after the new tax system was implemented, followed by a 24.6% increase in the second year, and a 15.2% increase in the third year. The tax rate was raised to 15% in 2007. Russian authorities claim that the flat tax led to a one-third increase in taxpayer compliance. Studies done each year since 2001 have indicated that the flat tax in Russia has contributed to a decline in capital flight out of the country and increased revenue.

Does the U.S. public at large support a flat tax? In almost every poll done on the issue, a majority to super majority of those surveyed support some type of flat tax. A few years ago *Parade Magazine* polled its readers about whether the current system is broken and should be scrapped and replaced with a simple flat tax rate. By a 50 to 1 margin, they said yes. One of the most intriguing findings was a report by the editors that hundreds of IRS agents had responded with a plea to abolish the current tax code.

If there are so many advantages to a flat tax, and it seems to be working well in other countries, then why do members of Congress denigrate such a system? Simple, even though a true flat tax system would appear to be inherently fairer and more efficient and cost effective than the current system, Congress would lose its ability to engineer social change and clandestinely reward the high income tax filers. Moreover, a flat tax system would minimize the need for the current army of tax professionals and tax lobbyists who make a good, albeit parasitic, living from the current system. Since they do not want to upset the applecart and they know they cannot win arguments against the flat tax on the merits, the politicians resort to their red herring grab bag and proclaim, indignantly and self-righteously, that a flat tax would benefit the "haves" to the extreme detriment of the "have-nots" and would serve to greatly exacerbate the budget crisis.

In addition, we propose the same flat tax system for corporate America. We believe that the argument for fair and equal treatment for all taxpayers must include corporate America. Corporations are asking to be treated like individuals when it comes to rights like freedom of speech and freedom of the press. They should also be required to bear their fair share of the obligations of individuals and thus should pay their fair share of taxes and no longer be favored beneficiaries of Congressional largess. It is not a fair sharing when the twenty largest U.S. corporations pay no income taxes. We advocate a flat tax for all profit and not-for-profit entities. A flat tax of not more than 4% on each and every entity's net revenues would go a long way toward correcting lawmakers' corporate tax bias. Congress will be reluctant to do this because politicians never like to bite the hand that feeds them and the business community is certainly that hand since it serves as the bank for providing politicians that highly sought after and sorely needed resource - cash!

We can make this change happen, but it will take a concerted and coordinated grass roots effort, and we will have to make tax reform an election-critical issue. At the end of the day, however, the electorate has the power to take the purse strings away from the politicians, and this must be done! We can no longer let the Washington crowd put our money where their mouth is. If we do, we can expect major tax increases to support the ever-growing government deficits -- to the point where our rendering unto Caesar all which belongs to Caesar will leave little to live on and nothing for God.

Maybe we are just dreaming, but the notion of tax reform does allow us some small solace as we turn out the light for the night -- and so we drift off to sleep with hopes for a better, dare we say *less taxing* tomorrow.

CHAPTER 8

SOCIAL SECURITY
'Never Count Your Chickens Before They Hatch'

"We can evade reality, but we cannot evade the consequences of evading reality."
- Ayn Rand, 20ᵗʰ century Russian-American novelist

"Experience should teach us to be most on our guard to protect liberty when the Government's purposes are beneficent. Men born to freedom are naturally alert to repel invasion of their liberty by evil-minded rulers. The greatest dangers to liberty lurk in the insidious encroachment by men of zeal, well meaning but without understanding."
- Justice Louis Brandeis

Today we inadvertently overheard and were struck by a passionate conversation between two 60-something fellows regarding the Social Security system. They were extremely concerned (actually agitated is a more accurate description) about the federal government being able to meet future social security obligations and the implications for their children and grandchildren. Both agreed that, unless Congress acts right away to curtail spending, balance the budget, and reduce the national debt, Social Security would not be able to pay anything to future retirees, leaving future generations with an empty nest instead of the promised nest egg.

Their comments led us to a state of contemplation, meditation and deliberation, after which we could only conclude they were right on the money (actually, the lack thereof). Simply stated,

Congress cannot continue to spend money it does not have, then print money out of "thin air" with reckless abandon to cover the shortfall. Congress cannot then stick its head in the sand and pretend no problem exists by claiming Social Security is adequately funded for at least another 25 years (the politician's horizon, you see, never extends past the next election, so 25 years is too long to have any political relevance to members of Congress).

How did the problem develop? To understand the genesis of the problem, we need a short review of the structure of Social Security. As you know, the Social Security System is funded through the Federal Insurance Contributions Act (FICA), a payroll tax paid equally by employees and their employers. Today, Social Security taxes are levied on the first $106,800 of worker income. Covered workers are eligible for retirement benefits; if a covered worker dies, his or her spouse and children may receive survivors' benefits. The program does not have individual accounts and tax receipts are not invested on behalf of workers, which in and of itself are problematic for the future health and well-being of the program, as we will see when we discuss the misuse of Social Security funds by the government.

The Social Security program works until the demographic trends begin to change, as they are today, such that the number of workers paying into the program begins to decline relative to those receiving benefits. The number of workers paying into the program was 15 per retiree in 1950, but fell to 6.1 per retiree in 1960, then was cut almost in half in 2008, to just over 3 to 1, and is projected to drop to about 2 to 1 by 2030. Further, as life expectancies continue to increase, retirees continue to be entitled to collect benefits for a longer period. The system was front-loaded so that earlier retirees have, on average, received substantially more in benefits than they paid into the system. The very first recipient of Social Security benefits was Ida May Fuller way back in 1939. Her total contribution was $24.75, yet she collected $22,888.92 in benefits (a 92,500% return on "investment" -- not too shabby).

Just how big is the problem today? It is Big (with a capital "B"), and it is BIG (all caps "BIG") when you add in Medicare obligations which are even greater. Moreover, any problem with Social Security is a major event when you consider that Social Security benefits provide more than half the income for six out of every 10 seniors and 90% of cash income for almost half of all single seniors. Social Security accounts for 40% of all income received by seniors and, for more than 20% of seniors, it is the sole source of income. Thanks to Social Security, 35% of older Americans (over 13 million) are kept out of poverty. And the magnitude of any problem with the system is surely magnified when you realize that 80 million Baby Boomers will become eligible for Social Security over the next 20 years, more than 10,000 per day, every day.

From a financial perspective, the rubber is now meeting the road for Social Security and there is a lot of nasty, smoking tread left on the pavement. The 2009 Annual Report by the Trustees of the Social Security Trust Fund refers to the financial condition of the Social Security program as "challenging" (that is government speak for extremely serious but not yet dire enough to elicit serious attention by Congress). Even the Trustees were forced to caution, however, that the pay-outs long-term (i.e., Congress can still subject Social security to its rule of "never do today what can be put off until tomorrow") "are not sustainable under current program parameters" (in other words, the light at the end of the tunnel, as we feared, is in fact that onrushing locomotive, but no worries because the tunnel is a really long one).

Well, the tunnel is not as long as the Trustees would have us believe. Not only that, but, that onrushing train is apparently on a high-speed rail line because it is actually already bearing down on us (so much so that we can hear the rumble). Read the 2009 report from the Congressional Budget Office and you will learn that, for the first time in 25 years, Social Security is taking in less in taxes in 2010 than it is spending on benefits. Therefore, instead of providing a presidential and congressional piggybank of surplus funds to help finance the rest of the federal government, as it did in the past, Social Security now needs funds from the Treasury to make its retirement benefit payments (the piggybank is empty). Not that anyone has bothered to make it official that this is the case, but if you take two numbers in the recent federal budget update, as Allan Sloan, senior editor at large for CNNMoney.com did, the "truth will out" (as the Bard wrote long ago). The first number is $120 billion, the interest that Social Security will earn on its trust fund in 2010 and the second is $92 billion, the overall Social Security surplus for 2010. This means that, without the interest income, Social Security will be $28 billion in the red this year.

Why should we disregard the interest income? Because, as people like Mr. Sloan have argued repeatedly over the years, *"the interest, which consists of (non-marketable) Treasury IOUs that the Social Security trust fund gets on its holdings of government securities, doesn't provide Social Security with any cash that it can use to pay its bills."* In other words, the interest figure is, again to quote Mr. Sloan, *"merely an accounting entry with no economic significance."*

Social Security has not been in a cash negative position since the early 1980s, when it began making plans to cease payments to retirees, which prompted the famous Greenspan Commission's urgent calls for reducing benefits and increasing payroll taxes, which Congress quickly wrote into law. And it would appear that this type of medicine (the kind that has to be taken with a spoonful of sugar, we hasten to add) is going to be administered to taxpayers again, either in the form of a hike in the FICA rates or an expansion of the wage base that pays the tax beyond the current $106,800 annual limit or both. Indeed, even the Trustees' Report admits that the Social Security System will begin bleeding profusely in 2016, a year earlier than the Trustees estimated just one year ago. Small wonder then that benefits, for the first time in 35 years, received no cost of living increase this year and will not for at least the next two years.

A truly astounding (we say terrifying) statistic is that, overall, the Social Security system's total unfunded liabilities -- the amount it has promised in excess of what it can actually pay -- is already $18 trillion, $2 trillion worse than last year (and this is according to Social Security's own actuaries). This means the program would need that much money today in a real trust fund outside the government earning a true return to pay for all of the benefits that have been promised over and above future Social Security taxes. Folks that would require an immediate 4% increase in FICA or a 13% increase in the income tax rate. And here is a (not so) tasty tidbit you never hear about that makes matters much worse -- the unfunded obligations for the United States military and federal civil service retirement programs is about the same as Social Security.

The Report of the Trustees seeks to allay some of the fear by noting that the deficits will *be "made up by redeeming trust fund assets until reserves are exhausted in 2037, at which point payroll tax receipts will be sufficient to pay only "three-fourths of scheduled benefits through 2083."* Moreover, many experts find this prediction far too optimistic since it is conditioned on the economy improving, unemployment declining, and GDP growing consistently during the next fifteen years. What are the chances of those coming to pass?

Moreover, the estimates are misleading because the Trust Fund contains no actual assets. Instead, as noted above, it contains only non-marketable government bonds, IOUs, a measure of how much money the government owes the Social Security system. Think about that for a second. The system has been generating surpluses (as receipts exceeded payouts) for the past 26 years. Now, you might have thought that these surpluses were being set aside in a separate account and not made available for any other purpose than the payment of retirement benefits -- we mean, isn't that what a trust fund is supposed to be, a segregated account which can only be used for the specific purpose for which it was established? Unfortunately, for all of us, this is not the case. Instead, all of those surpluses have been diverted straight to Treasury and into the general budget, with the Trust Funds getting those non-marketable IOUs in return. This is the way the Clinton Administration was able to "balance" the budget, an achievement that Martin Gross, author of *The End of Sanity* and *The Government Racket* called *"the single biggest lie by the U.S. government in its history."* The federal government treated the trust monies taken from Social Security as revenues, which enabled Clinton to claim he had balanced the budget. Never mind that it was all a charade, what we call a "debt defying, high liar act." Of course, if anyone in private industry looted their employees' pension plans each year and treated the money as operating revenues, they would be criminally prosecuted for fraud and embezzlement. Not so for the government, as Steve Forbes noted -- "for the federal government, the moral equivalent (of theft) is perfectly legal." In crying foul, Mr. Gross said that the *"dirty little secret of Washington's cooked books has been maintained through a conspiracy of silence by the leadership of both major political parties."*

So, are those of us approaching retirement age and those of us receiving Social Security benefits (the Baby Boomers) going to be left high and dry? Possibly, if we do not make something happen and address the situation forcibly. Now, if Congress and the administration truly desire to rehabilitate Social Security, they must first eliminate the cap on Social Security taxable wages and enact "lock box" legislation strictly prohibiting FICA receipts from use for general budgetary purposes. They may also have to push back the retirement age a few years. In addition, Social Security benefits should be restricted to recipients who cannot afford and do not have a private retirement plan or a private insurance plan. Some brave souls (politically speaking), like Ron Paul, have proposed abolishing Social Security for the younger generations and letting them provide for their own retirements through individual tax advantaged retirement plans. This would require a phase-in period and would maintain Social Security for the Baby Boomers.

At the end of the day, if we truly believe capitalism (real capitalism, not the distortion -- some might say perversion -- of socialized or managed capitalism) is superior to any other economic system, then we need to rein in excessive government spending at all levels, in furtherance of future financial self-preservation. If the Social Security fiasco teaches us anything, it is this -- government is more often the problem (or at least the cause of the problem) than the solution to the problem.

The real problem is the lack of honesty on the part of lawmakers with the electorate. The truth is the government is broke and cannot afford to pay what it obligated itself to do. Only because the Fed is allowed to print money does the system continue. No one could operate their own finances as the government does theirs, simply because they operate their own ATM, we do not. What the Fed is printing is worthless. There is no collateral, metal standard, warehouses full of whatever to back up the trillions of dollars now in circulation. And always remember that money is simply debt.

The following steps are very simple and would help to resolve some of the immediate problems of Social Security and other entitlement programs: (i) lawmakers must tell the electorate the truth that we are broke as a nation and cannot afford to pay out on entitlement programs as in the past; (ii) an immediate freeze in entitlement spending; (iii) an immediate reduction in the number of Social Security recipients based on reportable taxable income whereby any recipient reporting $250,000 in taxable income is immediately barred from the Social Security program and shall have returned any excess employee paid contributions; (iv) immediately increase the minimum age eligible to receive benefits from 62 to 65; (v) the federal government must reduce spending across the board by at least twenty percent for the next 10 years and take immediate steps to repay the national debt; and (vi) lawmakers must stop making economic promises that they cannot deliver -- no money, no promise!

Although the aforementioned steps do not address all of the issues, they provide a firm foundation to staunch the hemorrhaging. We must begin to make changes now and not wait another ten years, all the while blaming others for the problems. Fellow Americans, we hate to break it you, but this country is broke (but you already knew that), broke. And we must take a stand and demand the federal government stop spending and, conversely, stop expecting government to be our financial fairy godmother. And speaking of fairy godmothers, we would do well to remember how the story went. If you recall, even the fairy Godmother's spell of enchantment lasted only one evening and then it was up to Cinderella to return to harsh reality and either make it or break it with the Prince -- likewise, our evening at the Ball enjoying the transitory riches paid for by government largesse is over and done with and it is now our time to make it or break it.

CHAPTER 9

THE SIZE OF THE FEDERAL GOVERNMENT
'Bigger is not Better'

"A government big enough to give you all you want is a government big enough to take from you everything you have"
- Gerald Ford

"The Constitution is not an instrument for the government to restrain the people; it is an instrument for the people to restrain the government- lest it come to dominate our lives and interests."
- Patrick Henry

If you thought last year's federal deficit of $1.4 trillion was bad (and it was), this year's will be even worse. The 2010 budget sent to Congress by President Obama, a record $3.8 trillion, also calls for a record deficit of $1.6 trillion, about 11% of GDP (and current numbers indicate that it could hit $2 trillion, which would equal almost 14% of GDP). Most economists agree that a budget deficit in excess of 3% of GDP is not sustainable long-term. Certainly, a deficit more than three times that is tantamount to sailing the Ship of State onto economic shoals. And the Obama Administration is projecting that the deficit will increase by over $8.5 trillion over the next decade (remaining well above that 3% danger threshold), an estimate itself based on very (probably overly) optimistic projections of relatively robust economic growth during the period. The past does not offer us much hope -- even under President Reagan who regularly spoke out against government spending and government growth, the national debt almost tripled to $2.8 trillion.

However, the post-Reagan era has proven exceedingly worse for opponents of big government and big spending. Since the Reagan years, the total national debt has increased a whopping 450%, to more than $12.5 trillion, which represents a dangerously high 83% of GDP. And it will exceed $14.3 trillion in less than a year, which will take it to almost 100% of GDP. Now, as you will recall from an earlier chapter, it took every President from George Washington to Jimmy Carter to create a paltry $1 trillion of national debt. To say federal spending (and, worse, deficit spending) is out of control is to state (or understate) the obvious.

This year's proposed U.S. budget amounts to an expenditure (in just one year, mind you) of more than $12,000 for every man, woman and child in the country. Compare that with China, where the central government is supposed to play a much greater managerial role in the lives of its citizens -- it spends only $550 per citizen. Japan is the closest "free-wheeling spender" to the United States. It spends about $8000 per citizen (50% less than America) and its annual deficit this year will run over 8% of its GDP, compared to about 11% for the United States. However, our similarity to Japan should provide no comfort. Quite to the contrary, it should be viewed with serious trepidation. Japan has been trying to spend its way out of its economic malaise for the past 20 years, to no avail. Like us, Japan has seen its deficits increase dramatically over that period and many now believe that Japan, whose national debt has soared to over 200% of its GDP and heading higher, is poised to suffer an economic Armageddon if it does not get its spending house in order (and in short order, to boot). Over the last two decades, Japan has fallen (and fallen hard) from the ranks of the world's economic superpowers to a second-tier economy. And Japan has conned its citizens into buying up its debt, but guess what? Their savings have been exhausted so the government can no longer dip into that well. The new Prime Minister of Japan, Naoto Kan, recently warned that Japan is risking defaulting on its borrowing if drastic measures are not taken to rein in its massive public debt.

Since spending begets size, the size of our federal government, as you might expect, is immense. Not counting the Postal Service or the military, over 2 million people are employed by the federal government. When you add in the Postal Service and the military, that number more than doubles to over 4,000,000 government workers. Moreover, to exacerbate the situation, the average federal worker now makes over $75,000 per year, twice the average pay of workers in private industry. We believe that is unconscionable and unsustainable.

The federal government has over 400 departments, agencies, commissions, and bureaus. Under many of these are sub-departments, agencies, commissions, and bureaus. For example, there are at least 37 separate offices, councils and boards under the Executive Office of the Presidency, and there are more than 30 subsidiary institutes and agencies under the National Institute of Health. On average, 2010 budgets for the federal departments and agencies have been increased 10% from 2009 levels (never mind that almost everyone on Main Street has had to slash spending, many just to survive).

The growth in government might be best compared to a virus -- science tells us that all a virus is programmed to do is create more viruses -- which just keeps growing and growing by feeding on the once healthy "cells" of the economy. By way of example, Congress is on track to launch a Consumer Financial Protection Agency supposedly to protect consumers from the rapacious acts of our financial institutions. Right, just like the Securities and Exchange Commission did such a sterling job in protecting hapless investors from the Bernie Madoff Ponzi scheme, or ferreting out the frauds of the Enrons and WorldComs, and monitoring and checking the speculative, high-risk behavior of the big investment banks, like Bear Sterns and Lehman Brothers. What we the taxpayers will receive from this new agency is nothing more than a huge invoice for the support of more great intentions (which, as you might expect, can be used as more paving material for the road to you know where).

As we evaluate the various federal departments and agencies, which comprise our big and bloated bureaucracy, we are confused as to why we allow such duplication of services between state governments and their federal counterparts. For example, why do we need a federal department of education when we already have fifty state departments of education? Further, why is there so much duplication and redundancy of function within the federal government itself? What is the purpose of having a Department of Energy when we have a Department of Interior and, besides collecting data for other agencies and departments and conducting the census, what is the purpose of the Department of Commerce?

It seems that the response of the government to every crisis is to create more bureaucracy, as if that ever helps solve the problem. A good example is the plethora of new bureaus and agencies included in the health care reform and financial reform legislation and the legions of new bureaucrats who will be hired to staff them. Similarly, we count at least five new agencies to be formed under the new financial reform legislation and the throngs of new bureaucrats who will fill their ranks. And what of the enormous cost to office and equip these thousands of new bureaucrats (we guess today they should be called "keyboard pushers" rather than the "pencil pushers" -- unfortunately, the cost of a computer for each of these new governmental minions will be a lot more than a pencil). The projected administrative and associated cost to implement the financial reform legislation is a whopping $19 billion over the next ten years (and it will be a lot more than that).

Another example of throwing more government personnel and more governmental red tape at problems can be found in the President's proposal to better address the oil spill crisis by breaking the Mineral Management Service agency ("MMS") into three new agencies. Please! That is just more window dressing and everybody knows it. One reason cited for the change is that it will help diffuse the influence of lobbyists which has so permeated the MMS. In truth, this change will simply give the lobbyists three bites at the regulatory apple instead of one.

In addition, what about all of those agencies that do little of anything? A prime example is the Small Business Administration (SBA) -- what in the world is it doing these days, obviously not issuing loan guarantees to help small businesses. And are we, as Americans, getting our tax money's worth from the federal government? Does anyone believe for one second that the people of this country are getting $3.8 trillion worth of services? Of course not! And how helpful are the agencies, really, to John and Jane Q. Public? Ronald Reagan was right when he said, *"The nine most terrifying words in the English language are, 'I'm from the government and I'm here to help.'"* He was also right on point when he said, *"No government ever voluntarily reduces itself in size. Government programs, once launched, never disappear. Actually, a government bureau is the nearest thing to eternal life we'll ever see on this earth!"*

We, as a nation, are about to be saddled with more than $14 trillion dollars in sovereign debt, not to speak of the unfunded entitlement programs portion, which will eventually add another add another $42 trillion or so to the debt, and yet the politicians are busy redecorating their offices in Washington and working out seating arrangements on the House and Senate floors, claiming we are out of the recession and onto recovery. But you know what they say about recovery and addiction -- an addict can never quit, never recover, unless he or she freely and openly admits that there is a problem and commits today and recommits every day thereafter to stop using and abusing. And no addict can do it alone. He or she has to have support from others. The result of unchecked addiction is one we know all too well -- destruction and death. This nature of the recovery process applies with equal force to the federal addiction to debt. It has to be checked before it is too late and all of us have to support the weaning of the country from its dependence on debt. If we do not, then we are the enablers.

We need an "intervention" and we need it now. If we don't stop the bleeding (of red ink), there will come a time when no one will buy our bonds and interest will go through the roof and our debt service alone will consume the lion's share of our nation's productivity and resources -- and then we will be subjected to the vagaries of a debased dollar and horrific hyperinflation (ala Weimar Germany in the 1920s which sowed the seeds of discontent for the rise to power of Adolph Hitler). Some will say we are being overly melodramatic, but we doubt those folks would have said that just a short while ago when it appeared the whole financial system was about to crater.

It is just like the junkie who says to his friends and family that he will go into a rehab program tomorrow, next week for sure, just let him or her have one last "fix" or one last drink to get through today, when Congress and the White House promise the taxpayers they will reduce expenditures next year, but have to take just one more "hit" on the debt pipe this year. But, hey, you know they will go "straight" tomorrow, you can count on it. And so we do, count on it that is, but why, we don't know (as the old saying goes, *"fool me once, shame on you, fool me twice, shame on me"* -- but to what degree of shame (and blame) must we then lay claim for allowing ourselves to be fooled for the "umpteenth" time).

We now must stop writing and find an aspirin (or maybe three) to relieve the raging headache brought on by thinking that we, the taxpayers, are cruising merrily along on the ***RMS Titanic*** minutes before Captain Edward John Smith receives a communiqué warning of an impending collision with a massive iceberg. Moreover, our headaches are compounded by a fear that our politicians believe, like Captain Smith, that the Ship of State is unsinkable. As we open the medicine cabinet and reach for the aspirin bottle, we repeat to ourselves a very simple maxim practiced by most people today (by necessity) in mainstream America -- if you cannot pay cash, do not buy it! Too bad our lawmakers do not understand what the people who have to stay within their means have long known and had to live by!

Strangely, Democrats contend that they only want to help the electorate in providing new government agencies, funding new entitlement programs and supplying something for everyone whereas the Republicans want to minimize taxes for their constituents, find wars to wage, and protect Wall Street from governmental regulators. Just crazy stuff as lawmakers have become so self-absorbed with protecting their own special interests that they forget that they were elected to serve the interests of all of the electorate. It seems that Democrats cannot find a project too small not to fund and Republicans are always protecting their largest contributors. In the meantime, the size of the federal government grows larger daily and we, the taxpayer, allow this craziness to continue.

While millions of Americans are without jobs, homes, health insurance, retirement or savings accounts we allow lawmakers and the Administration to create a bureaucracy larger than ever in our history. We need jobs, real jobs, not "make believe," "make work" government jobs where the job descriptions and the jobs are just like government's pledge to rein in excessive spending -- bogus, bogus, bogus, just plain bogus!

We demand the end to bloated government bureaucracies and a radical reduction in the size of the federal government -- by at least 40% over the next five years!

CHAPTER 10

THE FED AND MONETARY POLICY
'Who Died and Made You King?'

"It is well that the people of the nation do not understand the banking and monetary system, for if they did, I believe there would be a revolution before tomorrow morning."
- Henry Ford

"Whoever controls the volume of money in any country is absolute master of all industry and commerce."
- James A. Garfield

Today is a new day, but the news is not new -- politicians doing more "speechifying," trying to convince anyone who will listen that their point of view is better for America. We have been listening to a discussion between a senator and a congressional representative regarding monetary policy. The Senator is trumpeting the Senate's having passed a Fed audit measure which he says will lift the veil of secrecy on one of the most important and powerful institutions in the world. The Representative responds that the Senate sold the American people out by watering down the bill that had passed in the House of Representatives. He points out that the legislation passed in the Senate is only a one-time audit by the Government Accountability Office (GAO) of the Fed's emergency actions during the economic crisis and a requirement to post on its Web site the names of institutions to whom it lent money during the crisis. He contends that the Senate measure, for all practical purposes, gutted the House bill (the Federal Reserve Transparency Act) which would have required the GAO to regularly audit the operations of the Federal Reserve.

The Representative further notes that the fact the Fed lobbied aggressively against the House measure and yet said not a word against the Senate version tells us everything we need to know -- meaning, he says, that the Senate measure will continue to let the Fed operate in an unmonitored world shrouded in secrecy that "Bernanke and Company" claim is necessary to preserve the Fed's "independence." The Senator responds that Congress has no business intruding into monetary policy -- that function, he says, is the exclusive province of the Fed. The Congressman responds that the Fed's control of and influence over trillions of Americans' dollars absolutely obligates Congress to know what the Fed is doing with those dollars and contends that knowledge can only come from systematic, detailed audits of the Fed.

The Senator tries once more to defend the Senate's rejection of the House measure by arguing that the House bill would compromise the Fed's political independence and calls the vote in the House in favor of H.R. 1207 "pandering to the populist movement." The Representative responds, rather heatedly, that anyone who thinks the Fed is truly "politically independent" is "naïve" at best and "just plain ignorant" at worst and that the citizens want and deserve "real transparency" in the actions of an institution whose decisions can "make or break them, financially speaking"-- transparency which can only occur by auditing all of the Fed's operations. He notes, as one example, no one outside the shadowy inner sanctum of the Fed has any idea what the Fed is doing with our money to aid Greece and other ailing sovereignties in the European Union, but we do know they are buying Euro bonds (which may be prohibited under its charter) and providing other financial assistance to European Central Banks, which should be *verboten*. The Senator has no answer to this charge.

In our opinion, the Representative's points rather handily triumph over the Senator's in the mini debate. Although the Senator hails from the "senior" chamber of our bicameral legislature, the senior parts of his defense of the Senate bill and denigration of the House bill are several "senior moments" when he was at a loss for valid commentary.

Our initial reaction to this give and take (in this case, the Senator "giving" ground and the Representative "taking" it) is this -- maintaining the status quo and allowing the Fed to continue to operate with no genuine accountability means there is a high likelihood we will continue to experience catastrophic monetary interruptions such as the housing bubble and the credit debacle and the near economic collapse (if you believe the political leaders and economic "experts") of the world's financial systems. As you might well expect, however, the current Fed Chairman, Ben Shalom Bernanke, has categorically denied that the Fed had any responsibility for fueling the housing bubble and that the Fed had sufficient regulatory power to prevent the credit and banking debacle. It is difficult to believe that Dr. Bernanke could make these assertions with a straight face, and, worse, that the vast majority of politicians were willing to take him at his word.

Let's examine first the housing bubble. It was the low interest rate policy implemented by Bernanke's predecessor, the legendary (mostly in his own mind, as it turns out) Alan Greenspan (a/k/a the "Maestro" and the "Oracle"), and extended down to zero by Big Ben, that directly contributed to the rapid inflation of housing prices which resulted from the low monthly mortgage payments made possible by the artificially low interest rates. And lest we forget, the Fed, through Chairman Greenspan, backed the sub-prime mortgage market "whole hog" by urging homebuyers and homeowners to swap fixed rate mortgages for variable rate ones (ARMs), which left many mortgage holders unable to pay when the initial ridiculously low teaser rates gave away upon "reset" to unaffordable high rates.

An even greater contributing factor was the continued flooding of money into the banking system, both directly by the Fed ramping up the money supply and indirectly by the Fed relaxing the capital standards. These moves allowed even encouraged, banks to aggressively lend many more dollars against their balance sheets and assume greater lending risk through larger mortgages and substantially higher debt to equity ratios.

So the Fed helped usher in a world of high finance in the housing industry, the likes of which had never before been seen. And surely, you say, the Fed is not doing anything now that might be perceived as re-inflating the housing bubble and maintaining ludicrously cheap money for Wall Street to use and abuse. Wish that were so, but the head of the Fed apparently plans to keep the cost of Fed funds at zero to .25% well into the foreseeable (even unforeseeable) future and the Fed has loaded up its balance sheet with another $1.25 trillion of mortgage-backed securities (MBS) and another $175 billion of housing agency debt to "lubricate" (the Fed's word) the housing market. All of this "lubrication" and buying of the federal government's debt has increased the Fed's balance sheet from $800 billion in 2008 to $2.4 trillion, a 300% increase in less than two years. Bernanke, under questioning by Representative Ron Paul (R-TX), in a recent congressional hearing, a lifetime advocate for a less intrusive federal government and abolition of the Federal Reserve, indicated that, to be on the safe side, the Fed should get its balance sheet under $1 trillion. That's a tall order given that his predilection seems to be just the opposite. In fact, news broke in late June that the Federal Reserve, in "closed-door" "back room" meetings (we would expect nothing else), was considering buying another $2.6 trillion in toxic assets which would bring its balance sheet to an almost inconceivable (well, not with Bernanke at the helm) $5.0 trillion. Why not? It's only money!

And will it stop there? Probably not, as there have been strong hints of further Fed stimulus monies being made available down the road, despite Bernanke's carefully worded statements to the contrary, sometimes in prepared testimony to the Senate Finance Committee -- where he stated earlier this year the Fed would begin withdrawing its easy money policies at some future date, but hastily added that the shift would not be imminent (in other words, no time soon). In recent testimony before the House Committee on Financial Services, Bernanke indicated the Fed's near zero interest rate policy would continue for an extended period because, "although showing signs of recovery, the economy is not out of the woods yet." In fact, in July he reiterated (for the ninth time this year) the need for continuing the Fed's easy money policy long into the future. In testimony before the Joint Economic Committee of Congress, Bernanke had this to say: *"The Federal Open Market Committee has stated clearly that they currently anticipate that very low, extremely low rates will be needed for an extended period."* Our guess is engaging in a game of "one upsmanship" vis-à-vis Greenspan in a contest of who can keep rates the lowest for longest. The winners of this game will, as always, be the financial institutions that can borrow low and sell high (interest rate arbitrage) and the losers will be, as always, the masses.

It should also be noted that the deluge of capital orchestrated by the Fed fueled the Wall Street securitization machine, which allowed lending and investment institutions to raise trillions of dollars in high-risk capital and the toxic off-balance-sheet derivatives (Wall Street bankers sold over $60 trillion in credit default swaps alone). Greenspan staunchly defended the risk-fraught credit derivatives business by actively campaigning against government regulation of the instruments and the burgeoning derivatives market -- on his watch, credit derivatives grew from less than $2 trillion in 1989 to $8 trillion in 1994, then $100 trillion in 2002, reaching $300 trillion or so before he was replaced by Ben Bernanke, who, not to be outdone by his predecessor, witnessed the skyrocketing of the global derivatives market to (we hope you are sitting down for this, or better yet, lying down) **1 quadrillion dollars** (that's $1,000,000,000,000,000, 15 times the size of the entire world's economy), according to the Bank of International Settlements, the leading authority on the subject.

By the way, more than a quarter of this staggering amount ($281 trillion to be exact) is held by the usual suspects, JP Morgan Chase, Bank of America, Goldman Sachs, Morgan Stanley, and Citigroup. Even Warren Buffet who called them "weapons of mass destruction," owns $63 billion of them, which has prompted him to ask that existing derivatives be exempted from the proposed financial regulation bill before Congress which would force all derivatives to trade on an exchange. So, then, even Buffet talks out of both sides of his mouth when need be to serve his personal financial interests. Well, we never really thought the "Oracle of Omaha" became the second richest man in the world by being philanthropic all or even most of the time, did we really?

To give you some perspective on the immensity of a quadrillion, consider these facts: a quadrillion seconds would last more than 30,000,000 years; if you built a cube out of a quadrillion pennies, the cube would be more than a half mile wide, thick and high and would weigh over 3 billion tons; if you stacked a quadrillion pennies one on top of another, the stack would stretch from the Sun past Saturn. Now this is not to say there is a risk of total loss of this magnitude. This is nominal or face (notational) value which does not mean the value always changes hands and in fact the majority of the instruments cancel each other out (we hope). Although, then, the actual risk of loss hanging out here may be unquantifiable, one thing we do know -- it is substantial.

Well then, what about Chairman Bernanke's complaints that the Fed needed more regulatory power to ward off the banking crisis? The regulations that did come came too late to stave off the crisis. Again we must take exception to Big Ben's claims. There were numerous regulatory checks and balances in place, held by numerous agencies and instrumentalities, including the Fed itself, the Securities and Exchange Commission (SEC), the Commodities Futures Trading Commission (CFTC), the Treasury Department, Financial Industry Regulatory Authority (FINRA), and the Federal Deposit Insurance Corporation (FDIC), among others, but there was a lack of enforcement of existing regulations that enabled the massive ratings fraud perpetrated by the ratings agency and the "house of cards" leverage which fostered the deterioration of the mortgage underwriting standards that in turn fueled the subprime boom and the ensuing housing bubble. Bernanke should have known this, but he either missed it (which would question his competence) or chose to ignore it (which would question his integrity). Early in his tenure with the Fed, when asked about the dangers associated with escalating the subprime mortgage market, he replied, somewhat cavalierly, "The impact of the problems in the subprime market seems likely to be contained." Wrong!

Another oft-cited reason for the failure of the enforcement mechanisms in place at the time of the financial meltdown was the highly incestuous relationship between the banking community and the regulators. Interestingly, the esteemed Nobel Laureate in Economics, Paul Krugman, questioned Bernanke's independence when he claimed earlier this year that, *"to a greater degree than I had hoped, Bernanke has been assimilated by the banking Borg"* (you will recall the Borg from ***Star Trek*** as the race of aliens who absorbed all cultures with whom they came into contact with the catch phrase *"resistance is futile"* and made them part of the greater collective).

Simply stated, then, under both Greenspan and Bernanke, the Fed did virtually nothing to rein in (or, as they now wont to say, "fence in" or "ring fence") the excesses of mortgage finance and synthetic credit market run amok. To the contrary, it provided great gobs of operating fuel for the Wall Street machinery to run at a 24/7 clip.

We are not saying that the Fed was solely to blame for the financial crisis, far from it, but it was most definitely, contrary to the Fed Chairman, derelict in its duties. Ron Paul, Congressman from Texas and a long-time, well-known champion of individual rights and personal liberty, claims that:

> *"Every economic downturn suffered by this country over the last 80+ years, from the Great Depression to the*

stagflation of the seventies, to the bust of the dotcom bubble, to the current Great Recession can be traced to Federal Reserve Policy." Congressman Paul observed that *"middle and working class Americans have been victimized by a boom-and-bust monetary policy since the creation of the Federal Reserve"* and *"have suffered a steadily eroding purchasing power because of the Federal Reserve's inflationary policies."*

Paul's New York Times best-selling book, **End the Fed**, published last year, persuasively advocates for abolition of the Federal Reserve Bank. We find many of his arguments compelling, but we do not see such a result being in the "political cards" as it were and we worry that, even if such a radical move were somehow to be taken, Congress would replace the Fed with an even more suspect organization. Or, in taking on the monetary powers itself, Congress would exercise them in just as short-sighted, or, worse "no-sighted" manner and we might end up out of the proverbial frying pan and into a fire (sometimes the devil you know is better than the devil you don't). Nonetheless, we firmly believe that the Fed's policies, on balance, have done more harm than good, at least for mainstream America, and that it should be audited and retooled and its powers curtailed, not expanded. So we disagree vehemently with Senator Dodd's 1,336-page proposed legislation to grant the Fed a greatly expanded role in banking regulation.

What is it exactly the Fed is supposed to do? According to the Fed's official documentation, these are its primary functions:

❖ Conducting the nation's monetary policy by influencing monetary and credit conditions in the economy in pursuit of maximum employment, stable prices, and moderate long-term interest rates.

❖ Supervising and regulating banking institutions to ensure the safety and soundness of the nation's banking and financial system, and protect the credit rights of consumers.

❖ Maintaining stability of the financial system and containing systemic risk that may arise in financial markets.

❖ Providing financial services to depository institutions, the U.S. government, and foreign official institutions, including playing a major role in operating the nation's payments system.

However, one thing the Fed is not supposed to do is engage in setting or implementing fiscal policy, which is the use of government spending and revenue collection to influence the economy. Fiscal policy is supposed to be a purely political province, the bailiwick of Congress and the White House. But if the Fed engages in actions which serve to increase the federal debt, isn't that crossing the line into influencing fiscal policy? You betcha! One of the worst kept secrets in Washington is the Fed's role in monetizing the federal debt, a charge Dr. Bernanke has repeatedly denied. For example, consider this colloquy during Bernanke's testimony before the House Budget Committee in June 2009: Representative Paul Ryan of Wisconsin, the ranking Republican member, observed: "The Treasury is issuing debt and the central bank is buying it. It gives the alarming impression that the U.S. one day might begin to meet its financial obligations by simply printing money."

Bernanke adamantly denied that would ever happen: "The Federal Reserve will not monetize the debt," he said. "Either cuts in spending or increases in taxes will be necessary to stabilize the fiscal situation."

Unfortunately for Bernanke (and even more so for us), actions speak louder than words, so let's take a peek at the Fed's actions under the tenure of Big Ben (well-named, we might add, since his pronouncements on keeping a loose monetary policy are as regular as "clockwork") to see if he just might have committed perjury during the referenced Congressional testimony. What exactly does it mean to "monetize" debt? Bill Bonner, well-known writer on economics and finance and author of the wisely read financial column, **The Daily Reckoning**, calls it *"larceny on the grandest* *scale."* San Jose State economics professor Jeffrey Rogers Hummel, says it is essentially the Fed's *"giant, legalized counterfeiting operation."* The Fed calls it *"quantitative easing,"* an innocuous sounding phrase, but one which, in practice, is quite serious and frequently insidious. Quantitative easing is actually an extreme form of monetary policy used to stimulate an economy when the interbank rate, which in the US is called the federal funds rate, is either at, or close to, zero. In practical terms, the central bank, the Fed, purchases financial assets (mostly short-term assets), including government paper and corporate bonds using money it has created *ex nihilo* (out of nothing). I can almost hear the Fed now, parodying some lyrics from the 1980s British rock group Dire Straits, and singing, with gusto and glee, *"hey, that's the way we do it, money from nothin' and our checks for free."* Japan has tried it for two decades and it has not helped that country get out of its economic doldrums. But non-supporters' obvious reply to such criticism is that the U.S. is not Japan. Maybe not, yet!

Normally, a central bank like the Fed stimulates the economy indirectly by lowering the discount rate or reserve requirements, but when it cannot lower them any further, as is the case today, it may attempt to flood the financial system with new money through a quantitative easing, one result of which is the monetization of government debt. Now, Treasury and the Administration, needing to sell huge amounts of government debt, would say this is a benefit, while the American people, whose purchasing power is being constantly eroded over time by such activities, would beg to differ and say it is a "detriment." Bernanke and his Fed cohorts have sided with the government, not the people, as they implemented an aggressive policy of quantitative easing in March 2009 and are keeping it in full swing even today. But even the Fed knows that the party has to end sometime, presumably before the inflation that will eventually and inevitably ensue from the easy money policies (a/k/a quantitative easing) gets legs and starts running off with our purchasing power. Yes, the Fed knows that the aftermath of the big party is likely to be one raging hangover, but does this mean the Fed is likely to take its foot off the debt monetization accelerator any time soon? We don't believe so, not when fiscal 2010 gross coupon issuances of U.S. Treasury bonds is expected to exceed $2.5 trillion, a $700 billion increase from 2009, which represented a $1.1 trillion increase (almost 40%) from 2008. Moreover, when we examine estimates from Morgan Stanley for 2010 Treasury supply and demand, we are led to the conclusion that there is likely to be a shortfall of "private" demand for the issuances of at least $700 billion. You can be sure that the federal government will be looking to the Fed to cover this shortfall. After all, the Fed bought 80% of all U.S. Treasuries in 2009 and they are not about to stop now.

Why has it not yet proven to be inflationary? Well, the Fed can infuse all the money it wants into the banking system, but it cannot force institutions to lend. And it is abundantly clear to everyone that the banks are not lending. Instead, they are hoarding cash. Take for example the growth in "excess reserves," the amount of reserves banks hold in excess of the amount the Fed requires them to hold. Until September 2008, excess reserves hovered at or below $2 billion. Today they have ballooned to over $1 trillion. Why? One reason is that they now earn interest (due to the Economic Stabilization Act of 2008 which went into law in October 2008) for the first time in history. With banks now being able to derive earnings from capital completely risk-free, how much incentive is there for them to put their money to work as risk capital in the form of loans to businesses and households? To date, very little.

The Fed's easy money programs have, for the most part, substituted for, rather than elicited, private sector lending activity. For example, when the Fed offered commercial paper to GE at the height of the credit crisis, not one private sector participant stepped in to effectively compete. And there is another reason that banks are keeping large reserves to the detriment of commercial lending - keeping a healthy balance sheet puts banks in a better position to be given the loans and deposits of failed banks (and bank failures are still running apace) by the FDIC. So sound banks who are in competition with their peers to take over fallen institutions need to maintain a strong balance sheet to make the "short list" of viable takeover candidates and one way to do this is to keep reserves on deposit with the Fed.

So we should ask how much debt the Fed has acquired. The short answer is "a heck of a lot." In 2009, as noted above, the Fed bought 80% of the federal debt issued in the form of U.S. Treasuries. This is, to say the least, unprecedented. In the current economic morass, where numbers are bandied about with reckless, sometimes feckless, abandon, it is easy to get lost in a statistical thicket and lose sight of the forest for the trees. In calendar year 2009, the national deficit grew by $1.4 trillion. During that time, the Fed grew its securities holdings from about $500 billion to $1.85 trillion, a $1.34 trillion increase. In its simplest terms, then, 91% of the budget deficit increase was effectively funded by or through the Federal Reserve. If that is not monetizing the debt, I do not know what is.

Some might even say the Fed has gone beyond monetizing to *ponzitizing* the debt (as in a Maddoff style Ponzi scheme). Others refer to it as legalized check kiting. How is this possible? The Treasury issues debt which it has neither the intention nor the means ever to repay. This debt is used as backing for the issuance of Federal Reserve notes and deposits, which the Fed has neither the intention of redeeming nor the means to redeem. When the Treasury debt matures, it is paid in Federal Reserve credit issued on the collateral security of new Treasury debt. When Federal Reserve credit is presented for redemption, the Fed offers interest-bearing Treasury debt in exchange. This then is a shell game and would be illegal check kiting if done by you or me. Neither the Treasury debt nor the Federal Reserve credit is issued in good faith. Neither is redeemable any more than Charles Ponzi's illicit coupons were. The Federal Reserve has the luxury of being able to continue this charade because it can continue to create money out of nothing, loan it to the U.S. government, collect interest on the loan and then rebate the interest earned to the Government. Bernie Madoff, eat your heart out!

Not only this, but the Fed's intervention is keeping the interest rates on Treasury bonds artificially low. Think about it. In a true "free market," interest rates on U.S. Treasuries would rise to reflect the declining economic situation such as what Greece's debt is now doing. With the massive increase in the size of the federal debt, the very weak U.S. economy and the rapidly diminishing appetite by foreign governments and private parties for the debt, interest rates on Treasuries should have gone through the roof by now. After all, rational investors would normally demand an increased return for the increased investment risk represented by Treasuries today. But that is not happening because, when there are no buyers at the current low interest rates, the Fed just steps in and buys up the excess bonds that need to be purchased. If this were to stop, the consequences could quickly turn disastrous because the free market would push rates up and, in turn, the federal budget deficit would skyrocket (even more than it has). The ripple effect would trigger a cascade of higher interest rates throughout the economy which would bring the housing and credit markets back to their knees (if not flat on their backs) and leave the economy in tatters. At some point, this flood of cheap money and escalating monetization of debt will take a serious toll on the dollar and the value of the savings and earnings of the American public will take a huge hit.

If the Fed should decide it can no longer continue playing the shell game with the government vis-à-vis the federal debt, then the "powers that be" might have to go to work to purposely "tank" the stock market. If the DOW and the S&P were to take precipitous drops and break through to new lows, the domino effect on global markets and consequential worldwide investment anxiety that would be engendered would trigger a flight to safety to Treasuries. This sudden increase in the world's appetite for Treasuries might forestall the Fed's having to raise interest rates, at least for a while, but only for a while -- after all, the federal government is like an alligator -- both have to be fed (an alligator with meat and the government with debt), and both have to be fed plenty and often. Plus, the bigger both become, the more they have to be fed (no pun intended).

One final point regarding the Fed's excursions (more aptly incursions) into the realm of fiscal policy; the Fed has now purchased $1.25 trillion of mortgage-backed securities. This action by the Fed is designed to keep mortgage rates low and in turn artificially stabilize housing prices. Hmmm. Bernanke wants folks not to worry and stay nestled all snug in their beds, but what about those disturbing visions of housing bubbles dancing in their heads? And providing money to one specific sector of the economy is plainly fiscal, not monetary policy, and is encroachment on the power reserved to Congress and an erosion of the Fed's credibility (what precious little is left) as being apolitical.

By the way, it is also worth noting that open-market operations (in effect, net purchases of T-bills) by the Fed (the tool which the Fed uses to increase the money supply through monetizing government debt as needed) were illegal when the Fed was created in 1913. The original legislation establishing the Federal Reserve System looked at monetization of government debts as anathema. Illegal open-market operations started in the early 1920s and were legalized ex post facto in 1935 by an amendment to the original act, after the gold standard was destroyed by a proclamation of President Roosevelt in 1933.

As long as we are talking about history, how could we have a chapter on the Fed without a brief look at its origin and how the Fed came to be one of the most dominant players in our economic and financial lives and well-being (well, at least "being")? And, no, we are not conspiracy theory advocates, out to prove the Fed is and always has been controlled by the Illuminati or the New World Order or that the Fed members meet only at night wearing black hooded cloaks and sit in high-backed wooden chairs with ornate carvings of demons and such passed down for generations from the House of Rothschild, or that the Fed members take blood oaths of brotherhood and secrecy (well, now, this one we are not too quick to cast aside) or that each member is given a special 24/7 telephone number, the only number in this country with a "666" area code (the infamous "Mark of the Beast"). We do believe the Fed was formed in a shroud of secrecy and that its workings are still far too opaque (not nearly enough transparency) and that it wields far too much power, but we do not subscribe to talk about Ben Bernanke or one of his future successors proving to be the anti-Christ (now, as for Timothy Geithner, who knows). Nevertheless, the history is nothing if not interesting.

Alexander Hamilton lobbied for the first private Federal Bank and in 1789 Congress chartered the bank. Thomas Jefferson was adamantly opposed to the idea of a privately owned federal bank and cautioned, *"I sincerely believe the banking institutions having the issuing power of money are more dangerous to liberty than standing armies."*

In 1811, under President James Madison, Vice President George Clinton broke a tie vote in Congress to cast the bankers out, refusing to renew the charter for the bankers. But it was President Madison who proposed a second United States privately owned central bank and it came into existence in 1816.

However, in 1836, President Andrew Jackson (known as the "Bank Buster"), overriding Congress, closed the central bank, stating, *"The bold effort the present bank had made to control the government are but premonitions of this institution or the establishment of another like it."* He also charged, when speaking to the bankers, *"You are a den of vipers and thieves. I intend to rout you out, and the eternal God I will rout you out."* In a letter to his closest friend, Martin Van Buren, Jackson claimed, *"The bank is trying to kill me, but I will kill it!"* (and so he did). But, like the undead, it did not stay dead.

During the Civil War, President Lincoln needed money to finance the North's operations. The bankers got together and were going to charge him 24% to 36% interest. Lincoln was aghast and distressed to the extreme, recognizing that such usurious rates would plunge his beloved country into a debt that would keep the nation and its citizens in debt forever. So Lincoln advised Congress to pass a new law authorizing the printing of full legal tender Treasury notes to pay for the War effort. Lincoln recognized this as a great public benefit. At one point he wrote, *"We gave the people of the Republic the greatest blessing they have ever had -- their own paper money to pay their own debts."* The Treasury notes were printed with green ink on the back, so the people called them "Greenbacks." Lincoln printed over $400 million worth of Greenbacks, money that he created debt-free and interest-free to finance the War. He used it to pay the soldiers and the civil service employees and for supplies. Lincoln was of course assassinated shortly after the War and Congress proceeded to revoke the Greenback Law and enacted in its place a new National Banking Act pursuant to which national banks were to be privately owned and the national bank notes they issued were to be interest-bearing. The Act also provided that the Greenbacks were to be retired from circulation as soon as they came back to the Treasury in payment of taxes.

The plan for the Federal Reserve System as we know it today originated at the famous "Jekyll Island Meeting" 100 years ago. At that time, Jekyll Island, a small island off the coast of Georgia, was privately owned by a small group of New York millionaires and banking magnates, perhaps most notably J.P. Morgan and William Rockefeller. These titans of industry, commerce and banking wintered there with their families. They had erected a magnificent clubhouse which served as the birthplace of the Fed.

It all began with Senator Nelson Aldrich, the Republican Whip in the Senate and Chairman of the National Monetary Commission, a special committee of Congress established to make recommendations to Congress for proposed legislation to reform the banking industry. He was also the business associate of J.P. Morgan and the father-in-law of John D. Rockefeller, Jr. In November of 1910, Senator Aldrich sent his private railroad car to the railroad station in New Jersey and there it was in readiness for his arrival and that of six other men who were told to come under conditions of great secrecy. For example, they were told to arrive one at a time and not to dine with each other on the night of their departure. They were told that should they arrive at the station at the same time they should pretend that they did not even know each other. They were instructed to avoid newspaper reporters at all costs because they were well-known people and, had they been seen by a reporter, they would almost certainly have been asked questions. Especially if two or three of them had been spotted together, this would raise eyebrows and they would likely be asked a lot of questions. One of the men carried a shotgun in a big black case so that, if he had been stopped and asked where he was going, he was prepared to say that he was going on a duck hunting trip. Of some interest, however, is that this man never fired a gun in his life, and, in fact, he borrowed that shotgun just to carry with him on this trip to promote the deception.

Once they boarded the private railroad car, this clandestine pattern continued. They were told to use first names only, never to use their last names. A couple of the men even adopted a code name. The reason for this subterfuge -- so that the servants on board the train would not know who these people were. They were afraid that word would leak out and it might get into the press if the servants knew who they were. They traveled for two nights and a day onboard this car and they arrived after a 1,000 mile journey at Brunswick, Georgia. From there they took a ferry across the inland straits and ended up on Jekyll Island in the clubhouse, where, for the next nine days, they sat around a big table and hammered out all the important details of the central bank that eventually became the Federal Reserve System. When they were done, they went back to New York, again taking great care to conceal their true identities.

For quite a few years thereafter these men steadfastly denied that any such meeting took place. It was not until after the Federal Reserve System was firmly established that they then began to talk about their journey and what they accomplished. A few of them wrote books on the topic, one wrote a magazine article, and several gave interviews to newspaper reporters.

Who were these seven men? The leader and organizer was of course Senator Nelson Aldrich. The second important person there was Abraham Andrew, Assistant Secretary of the Treasury who later became a Congressman and a very important person in banking circles.

Frank Vanderlip was also present. He was the President of the National City Bank of New York which was the largest of all of the banks in America representing the financial interests of William Rockefeller and the international investment firm of Kuhn, Loeb & Company.

Henry Davison, the senior partner of the J. P. Morgan Company, was also a participant, as was Charles Norton, the President of the First National Bank of New York, another of the banking giants of the day. Benjamin Strong also attended. He was the head of J. P. Morgan's Banker's Trust Company and three years later would become the first head of the Federal Reserve System.

Finally, there was Paul Warburg who is now considered to have been the most influential person at the meeting due to his knowledge of banking as it was then being practiced in Europe. Paul Warburg was born in Germany and eventually became a naturalized American citizen. He was a partner in Kuhn, Loeb & Company and was a representative of the vast House of Rothschild banking dynasty in England and France, and with whom he maintained a very close working relationship throughout his career, together with his brother, Max Warburg, the head of the powerful Warburg banking consortium in Germany and the Netherlands. In 1910, Paul Warburg was reputed to be one of the wealthiest men in the world. As an aside, those of you who are familiar with Little Orphan Annie may remember Daddy Warbucks. Daddy Warbucks was a caricature of Paul Warburg and the public at the time was well aware of that fact.

So, then, these were the seven men aboard that railroad car who were at the famous Jekyll Island meeting (in banking circles they would have been known as "the Magnificent Seven"). As amazing as it may seem, they represented approximately 25% of the wealth of the entire world. They gave us the Federal Reserve pretty much as we now know it today. Strangely enough, the purpose of the meeting and their mandate was to fashion laws to break the money trust, but the people picked for this important task were card-carrying members of the money trust. Consider the composition of this group. Here we had the Morgans, the Rockefellers, Kuhn, Loeb & Company, the Rothschilds and the Warburgs, the top investment and commercial bankers in the world, without question. However, at this time they also were the major competitors in the investment and banking world and, prior to this point in time, they could often be found going toe to toe, fighting for dominance in the financial markets. But here they were on Jekyll Island given a rare, almost unfathomable, opportunity to stop their costly competition and form a cartel which in turn would be legalized by Congress. It could not have been scripted any better -- oh, almost forgot, it was scripted -- by the Jekyll Island Seven. It is almost tantamount to hiring a group of clever foxes to design and build chicken coops. And, as they say, the rest is history -- but history we are still living.

Back to the story. In December 1913, three years after the master plan was conceived at the Jekyll Island Club, and a year after Woodrow Wilson was elected President, while many members of Congress were home for Christmas, the Federal Reserve Act was pushed through Congress. It was later signed into law by Wilson (his having reluctantly agreed during his run for the presidency, in return for then desperately needed campaign contributions from the banking and investment community, to sign the Federal Reserve Act, if elected). At a later date, however, Wilson lamented when referring to the Fed,

> *"I have unwittingly ruined my country. A great industrial nation is controlled by its system of credit. Our system of credit is concentrated. The growth of the nation, therefore, and all our activities are in the hands of a few*

men. We have come to be one of the worst ruled, one of the most completely controlled and dominated Governments in the civilized world no longer a Government by free opinion, no longer a Government by conviction and the vote of the majority, but a Government by the opinion and duress of a small group of dominant men."

On June 4, 1963, President John F. Kennedy signed a Presidential Decree, Executive Order 11110 which virtually stripped the Federal Reserve Bank of its power to loan money to the United States Government with interest. President Kennedy declared the privately owned Federal Reserve Bank would soon be out of business. This order gave the Treasury Department the authority to issue silver certificates against any silver in the treasury. This executive order still stands today. In less than five months after signing that order, President Kennedy was assassinated. Unlike the conspiracy theorists, we do not draw a causal link between the two events, but it is interesting that the United States notes (silver certificates) he has issued were immediately taken out of circulation by his successor, Lyndon Johnson, and Federal Reserve Notes became the sole legal currency of this nation.

And from that time on, the Fed never looked back and its powers began to grow, enabling it to become today's financial and economic potentate. When the Fed speaks today, almost everyone in the world stops what they are doing and listens with baited breath. It all reminds us of Pharaoh Ramses II (played by the inestimable Yul Brenner) in the movie ***The Ten Commandments*** when he would make his major pronouncements to a rapt audience, *"So let it be written, SO LET IT BE DONE!"*

One revelatory footnote is closing. Did you ever wonder why so many economists seem to sing out of the Fed hymnal? Or why the Fed, even though it failed miserably to foresee the greatest economic collapse since the Great Depression has largely escaped the slightest criticism from academic economists who are supposed to be what we like to call "objectively astute"? Well, we did, and so we did a little digging, and, as is usually the case with digging, we uncovered some dirt.

We found out that the Federal Reserve pretty much dominates the community of economists, so much so that criticism of the Fed can be hazardous to the health (career-wise) of the profession. According to Joshua Rosner, a Wall Street analyst who predicted the meltdown, *"the Fed has a lock on the economics world."* He claimed that the Fed's control over economics academia hampered his efforts to warn colleagues of the impending crash.

One way the central bank keeps control is by "buying" it. One example is the Journal of Monetary Economics, a sort of "publish or perish" periodical for up and coming economists. More than half of its editorial board is on the Fed payroll and the rest were at one time.

And the control is nothing new. The first seeds of Fed domination were sowed almost 30 years ago and they really started to bear fruit by 1993, when then Chairman Greenspan reported that 189 economists worked for the Federal Reserve Board itself and another 171 for the various regional federal banks. When you added statisticians, support staff and officers (mostly economists) the number totaled 730. On top of that were the consulting contracts. Over the three-year period ending in October 1994, the central bank gave out over 300 contracts to over 200 economics professors worth in excess of $3 million.

How about today? The Federal Reserve Board of Governors employs 220 economists with doctorate degrees and many more economic researchers and support staff. The twelve regional banks employ hundreds more. Plus the Fed pays out many millions of dollars to economists for consulting contracts, research projects and papers, presentations, workshops, and for serving in the "visiting scholar program" (a rather impressive sounding post, but really a vacuous mechanism for the Fed to funnel money to economists for spending some time "glad-handing" with staff economists at the various Fed offices) or the "resident scholar program" (more time and more money for, to use the words of the New York Fed, *"pursuing their own research while providing intellectual leadership by advising and collaborating with our staff of more than fifty economists"* -- wow, is that not a "gussied up" way for the Fed to say "we want you to be our friend and we don't expect you to do it for nothing"). The Federal Reserve spent over $430 million last year on analysis, research, data collection and studies on market structure. That's a lot of money for a relatively small number of economists, maybe a thousand.

And the Fed keeps many influential editors of top academic publications on its payroll. It is disturbingly common for an editor to review submissions dealing with Fed policy even while receiving money from the central bank. Has the Fed ever heard the term "conflict of interest"? Guess not.

Furthermore, an affiliation with the Fed may be critical to career advancement. Jane D'Arista, a Fed critic and an economist with the Political Economy Research Institute at the University of Massachusetts, commented:

"It's very important, if you are tenure track and don't have tenure, to show that you are valued by the Federal Reserve."

And the Fed does not cotton to criticism or dissent. Ask esteemed economist Paul Krugman. He claimed to have been blackballed by the Fed for years after criticizing Alan Greenspan. And even when his criticisms were shown to have been well-founded, he was not invited back into the club (kinda gives the term "Club Fed" a whole new meaning, or does it).

At any rate, it is small wonder that so many economists kneel before the altar of the Federal Reserve. Perhaps in their acclaimed closed door meetings, worthy economists are allowed to kiss the Chairman's ring as they are ordained into the Fed "brotherhood" of economists.

As the day winds down and comes to a close, and, as we withdraw from the keyboard, we are once again reminded about the essential goodness of the people who make up this great country of ours and we wonder when the "sleeping giant" will awake and decide enough is enough and stop kowtowing to the power-mongers who want to control us and our destiny. And we hearken back to our time in the sixties and seventies when we clamored for "Power to the People" and really meant it, well, sort of, maybe, at least we thought so at the time. This time around there can be no half-hearted, "flash in the pan" efforts. This time it's for all the marbles (and let's not forget they're our marbles, after all)!

CHAPTER 11

THE ALMIGHTY DOLLAR
'When the Dollar Fails to Make *Sense*'

"The almighty dollar, that great object of universal devotion throughout our land, seems to have no genuine devotees in these peculiar villages; and unless some of its missionaries penetrate there, and erect banking houses and other pious shrines, there is no knowing how long the inhabitants may remain in their present state of contented poverty."
- **Washington Irving, early 19th century American novelist and historian**

"A strong dollar policy is the yeti of economics. Despite occasional sightings ... scientific evidence indicates that no such species exists."
- **Dr. Ben Craig and Dr. Owen Humpage, economists and financial and banking experts**

"The reality is that America's 'weak dollar' policy – its long-standing practice of allowing its currency to depreciate in order to lower the value of its foreign debts – amounts to the biggest currency manipulation in human history."
- **Dr. Mark Perry, Chairman of the Department of Economics at the University of Michigan**

Again restive (little wonder with the rampant negativity and pervasive pessimism in current events) we are up early, taking a quick look at a newspaper (and yes, believe it or not, we still get some of our news from the traditional hard copy sources that you can hold in your hands and get them blackened with newsprint) and find sprawled across the front page articles on the United States dollar policy (or lack thereof). One story advocates a weak dollar policy and another gives the countervailing view for a strong dollar policy. We reflect for a few minutes, wondering which of the two would better serve the best interests of this generation and future generations. So, we contemplate the respective pros and cons of each, but before we can answer the question, we first must compare the dollar policies of prior administrations with today's.

Over the years, presidents from both parties, in concert with the Federal Reserve, have regularly sought to use the dollar as a tool to manipulate interest rates. Today, for example, the flood of dollars from the Fed has helped keep interest rates artificially low. By keeping interest rates artificially low, the value of the dollar is likewise kept artificially low.

Let's take a look at 1971 for a story of dollar manipulation in all its glory. In an attempt to curb runaway inflation and reduce the supply of money in the system, which resulted largely from the refusal of Congress to pay the debts incurred to fund the Vietnam War, Richard Nixon attempted to defuse the excessive spending by, among other things: (i) decreasing the money supply; ii) implementing price controls; (iii) imposing a 10% surcharge on imports, and (iv) most notably, closing the gold window, thereby cancelling the convertibility of dollars into gold, which in turn allowed the dollar to float against other currencies.

The result was the 1973-75 recession, which President Carter sought to address by flooding the system with excessive liquidity, so that, by the late 1970s, the nation was again reeling from runaway inflation, with interest rates topping a whopping 20%, and the value of the dollar dropping to a post-depression low. Then, in an effort to control the rampant inflation, the Fed drained much of the excess liquidity from the system, leading to the 1981-1983 recession, which was deliberately triggered by Paul Volcker, who had been appointed by Carter, to bring inflation to a grinding halt (the recession actually took a turn for the worse, causing substantially more pain and suffering than Volcker and his Fed buddies had expected, demonstrating once again that the free market frequently defies "soft landings" orchestrated by Fed and/or government intervention).

With the "misery index" (inflation plus unemployment) reaching a post-World War II high under Carter and Carter being blamed by the electorate for the economy's woes, in particular stagflation (inflation coupled with stagnation), Carter's bid for reelection soon became a long shot, particularly when the Republicans tapped the formidable Ronald Reagan as their presidential contender. The rest is history as they say and Reagan swept into office on a strong anti-status quo sentiment. He soon caught the wave of the business cycle upturn and rode it for most of his presidential tenure.

Under Chairman Volcker's firm hand (which, at the outset, was unpopular because he had to administer a bitter pill to tame inflation), the country enjoyed seven years of economic expansion, as the money supply was re-inflated, inflation was reduced from 13.5% to 3.2%, interest rates stabilized and the dollar gained in value relative to other world currencies. The Reagan Administration was quick to let Volcker be the public "whipping boy" or "fall guy" at the outset when he implemented the harsh measures to rein in inflation, but even quicker to take the credit when prosperity returned. Notwithstanding the "Seven Fat Years" (as the conservatives dubbed the Reagan years of prosperity), as if to prove that all good things must come to an end (especially when the government is involved) and what goes up must come down (particularly when the money supply is too free and easy), in October 1987, the economic cycle began again with the stock market implosion, followed by inflation and rising interest rates and then the S&L crisis, and eventually another (although relatively brief) recessionary period in 1990 and 1991.

And each subsequent administration (more often than not in close collaboration with the "politically independent" Fed) has attempted to manipulate interest rates, the money supply and the dollar in order to promote that administration's monetary and fiscal objectives.

The problem we have today with a low dollar, and one perceived at times to be under siege, reflects the Greenspan-Bernanke policy of excess liquidity which we discussed briefly in the previous chapter. Last fall, famed financier Warren Buffet wrote in a New York Times commentary that the dollar is under threat from the "monetary medicine" that has been pumped into the financial system. Buffet noted that the cure could end up being worse than the disease and that, probably sooner rather than later, we will have to deal with the deleterious side effects of "greenback emissions." Paul Volcker has also returned to the economic and financial center stage and recently warned of the high costs and risks associated with a weak dollar, noting that *history is littered with examples of countries that tried and failed to solve their economic woes through a devalued currency.* Volcker even went so far as to say we are already in the midst of a *"dollar crisis"* but nobody seems willing to acknowledge it, much less willing to tackle it.

Currently, the world financial markets are awash with liquidity in line with the Keynesian economic theory that hard assets must be re-inflated in times of recession in order to jump-start the world's financial markets. Now, most of the financial markets have recovered from the March 2009 lows due in part to the unprecedented collaborative effort by the world's central bankers to inundate the capital markets with liquidity. We are by no means out of the woods, however, as even Bernanke said recently. Furthermore, once a government's central bank decides to print itself out of recession (by printing more dollars) it then must deal with the consequences, intended and unintended, of its actions.

Since Nixon's employment of this methodology to tame inflation met with initial success, this approach has apparently become the prototype for subsequent administration's handling of their monetary and dollar dilemmas. One problem, however, lies in the fact that the fix is transitory and usually leaves the following administration with immediate and often severe financial issues to resolve -- a prime example being the monetary and dollar imbalances the Bush Administration left for the Obama Administration to deal with. Under George W. Bush's eight years in office, the dollar lost about 40% of its value against the Euro and more than 15% against the Yen. The Bush White House felt a weaker currency was critical to its desires to rebalance the global economy plagued by a U.S. trade deficit and huge Chinese surplus. The Bush Administration repeatedly claimed it believed in a strong dollar and would do all it could to keep the dollar the most robust currency in the world (words it had no choice but to utter in order to continually calm foreign governments and keep them buying our debt). When the actions failed to live up to the words, the world at large began to see the Bush Administration claim as empty rhetoric and thus began to lose faith in the dollar.

From the outset, the Obama Administration voiced rock solid support for a strong dollar policy (so what else is new) and took pains to convey publicly that, unlike Bush, they "really meant it. " Less than 48 hours after Barack Obama took office, his selection for Treasury Secretary, Timothy Geithner, committed his office to a strong dollar policy, observing that such a policy is in the national interest. In February of this year, Geithner reaffirmed his support of the policy and he went so far as to take credit for the strong dollar policy which he claimed actually originated in his office at Treasury in 1995 when he worked under Robert Rubin in the Clinton Administration.

But, as is so often said, "Talk is cheap" and so has the dollar been (cheap that is) for most of Obama's term in office. For all the strong dollar talk, the dollar continued its 10-year slide throughout much of 2009, and, although it has gained ground recently, the global consensus is that the dollar will continue to lose value over the longer term. In the case of China, the Obama Administration, behind the scene, may actually favor a weaker dollar due to the large U.S. trade gap with China (around $250 billion) and the large amount of our debt held by China (about $760 billion). A weaker dollar would serve to encourage U.S. exports and discourage imports which in turn could work to reduce the balance of trade imbalance that we currently have with China. And a weak dollar would mean that we could pay off the debt to China (not to mention Japan, Brazil, and other countries) with cheaper dollars, resulting in a bonanza of sorts for the U.S. But China at least is wise to our game and has begun to reduce the U.S. debt it is holding, a reduction which is likely to gain momentum over the next few years. And where will that leave us? Whipsawed by having to support the dollar by raising the interest rate on our debt to entice enough buyers which in turn will increase the cost of our debt putting more pressure on our ability to sell new debt or refinance (roll over) old debt, starting the deadly cycle all over again.

See, here's the dilemma the Treasury and the Fed now find themselves facing regarding dollar policy. A weak dollar policy will inflate the value of hard assets and improve American export pricing over a period of time, but the financial community's perception of a dollar in decline reduces demand for the purchase of dollars and U.S. debt (and the U.S. has a load of debt to sell this year and for the foreseeable future).

Is the Obama Administration talking out of both sides of its mouth? Of course it is and it isn't the first time and it won't be the last time. It's what politicians do, for crying out loud. In this case, Obama and company are trying to play a deft (which might prove daft) balancing act. While proclaiming publicly that it is working fervently to keep the dollar strong, in reality, the Obama Administration has taken steps to ensure continued dollar depreciation in the hope that the value of hard assets will re-inflate, even while the Fed floods the financial markets with debt in order to finance the huge deficits that are being used to re-liquidify the world's credit markets. This "Goldilocks" approach to manipulating the dollar, money supply, interest rates and government debt in an effort to make the amount and pace of economic growth "just right" (not too hot and not too cold) will not work over the long haul. Understand the current policy is a short-gap plan whereby our government hopes that world economies substantially improve within the next twelve months in order for it to reduce the amount of debt it now must sell in order to pay its bills. But, if world economies fail to comply including ours, we will dip back into a double-dip recession and the dollar will tend to increase in value due to risk aversion by investors towards other currencies. Then, the real winner will be gold as investors will seek to buy the only currency not backed by paper.

Interestingly, the Asian markets, except Japan, along with Brazil, Russia, India, and China (the so-called "BRIC" countries) and Australia and Canada, among others, have not been affected by the credit meltdown in equal measure compared to the United States and European financial markets, not nearly so. This is the result of their not having purchased the trillions of dollars of securitized sub-prime instruments (mortgage backed securities), credit derivatives like the default swaps, and other more esoteric Wall Street-engineered debt securities bought and sold throughout the U.S. and Europe. Moreover, many of the non-affected countries are the hard-asset based economies whose currencies tend to appreciate when the dollar depreciates. Additionally, countries such as China continue to purchase our debt in order to maintain stability in their own currency which they seek to artificially undervalue versus the dollar -- meaning, they buy our debt in order to buffer the depreciation in the American dollar. This policy works as long as the dollar continues to decline in value, but, once the dollar starts to appreciate, debt buyers will demand higher payouts in the form of increased interest payments in order to protect the value of their own currencies vis-à-vis the dollar. And, as the dollar climbs, China and Japan will most likely sell our debt, driving interest rates higher. China's strategy seems to be to maintain equilibrium in their currency and to use our currency as a buffer against any head winds in doing so. And remember, as long as the dollar declines in value, materials such as copper, oil, and gold will escalate in value, as if they operate on a fulcrum. Disruptions occur when the dollar heads up and materials head down, resulting in the decline of foreign currencies.

It stands to reason that buyers of our debt eventually will reach a point at which they will demand a greater premium (rate of interest) for the purchase of dollars if they believe the currency is risk intolerant. When this occurs, the Fed will then reduce the amount of liquidity in the system in the hope that it can reduce not only the flow of liquidity but also the speed or velocity of money moving through the monetary system before inflation rears its ugly head and pushes up the price of food and raw materials and in turn finished goods -- the question is not if this will happen, but when. And the two "feds" (the Federal Reserve and the Federal Government) are trying to ease us into and maintain a modicum of control over the inflation pump without falling back into deflation. It is one of the ultimate timing games, economically speaking, and slight miscues can have disproportionably negative results. The bane of low interest rates is high employment. But do not believe that the Fed does not wish for inflation, for it does. The Administration just cannot tell the electorate because inflation is a good friend to debt-ridden central governments. Inflation allows governments to pay back its debts with cheaper dollars.

As interest rates start their inevitable trek higher, employers will have to increase wages in order for employees to stay up with expanding prices for goods and services. As this happens, the Fed will act as if it is oh so worried, but in reality the central banks covet controlled levels of inflation because it allows them to repurchase their debt with cheaper dollars as prices escalate and the dollar loses purchasing power. In addition, the cost of money begins to escalate, ordinarily to the benefit of the banks. Plus, as inflation starts its march higher, the forces of capitalism may work to play a cruel trick in the form of a "hidden tax" upon the public, particularly the poor and middle classes, who are robbed of purchasing power without any legislative action by lawmakers (a form of taxation without representation, to be sure). And, if prices and wages go higher, tax receipts also become larger so the government wins, while the people lose. It is worth noting that, even though inflation has been modest over much of the last decade, the dollar has still lost almost 25% of its purchasing power over that span.

It's interesting to watch the U.S. accuse China of manipulating its currency to unfairly benefit its economy at the expense of others, ourselves included (talk about the proverbial pot calling the kettle black). If it takes one (currency manipulator) to know one, then we certainly should know of what we speak. Listen to the words of economics researcher, historian and author Frederick William Engdahl:

> *"The Dollar System is the real source of global inflation which we have witnessed in Europe and worldwide since 1971. In the years between 1945 and 1965, total supply of dollars grew a total of only some 55%. Those were the golden years of low inflation and stable growth. After Nixon's break with gold, dollars expanded by more than 2,000% between 1970 and 2001!*

> *The dollar is still the only global reserve currency. This means other central banks must hold dollars as reserve to guarantee against currency crises, to back their export trade, to finance oil imports and such.*

> *What is little understood is how the role of US trade deficits and the Dollar System are connected. The United States has followed a deliberate policy of trade deficits and budget deficits for most of the past two decades, so-called benign neglect, in effect, to lock the rest of the world into dependence on a US money system. So long as the world accepts US dollars as money value, the US enjoys unique advantage as the sole printer of those dollars.*

> *What has evolved is a mechanism more effective than any the British Empire had with India and its colonies under the*

Gold Standard. So long as the US is the sole military superpower, the world will continue to accept inflated US dollars as payment for its goods. Developing countries like Argentina or Congo or Zambia are forced to get dollars to get the IMF seal of approval. Industrial trading nations are forced to earn dollars to defend their own currencies. The total effect of US financial and political and trade policy has been to maintain the unique role of the dollar in the world economy. It is no accident that the greatest financial center in the world is New York. It's the core of the global Dollar System.

Today, most foreign central banks hold US Treasury bonds or similar US government assets as their "currency reserves." They in fact hold [trillions of dollars] of US Government debt. Here is the devil of the system. In effect, the US economy is addicted to foreign borrowing, like a drug addict. It is able to enjoy a far higher living standard than were it to have to use its own savings to finance its consumption. America lives off the borrowed money of the rest of the world in the Dollar System.

Because the world payments system, and most importantly, the world capital markets -- stocks, bonds, derivatives -- are dollar markets, the dollar overwhelms all others. The European Central Bank could offer an alternative. So far it does not. It only reacts to a dollar world."

Next, it is important to examine the consequences of governments and central banks printing money which is not backed by any collateral (gold, silver, something of value other than the near worthless paper it's printed on) in order to spend themselves out of a recession. Understand that new dollars are issued when the Federal Reserve elects to fund the purchase of debt, primarily U.S. Treasury Bonds, by creating new reserves rather than financing the purchase with existing reserves. When the bond issuer spends the money, new dollars enter circulation in theory; Federal Reserve Notes are like checks: liabilities drawn on the Federal Reserve Bank. The Fed offsets these liabilities by holding U.S. Treasury Bonds as assets, which are backed by the full faith and credit of the U.S. Government's through its ability to levy taxes and repay. As compared with hard money backed by gold or silver, this debt-based approach has the advantage of making the currency elastic, giving the government a means of rapidly expanding or contracting the money supply in response to changing economic conditions. The disadvantage of this approach is, however, inflation. The money supply must be continually expanded in order to finance interest payments on the debt by which it is issued. This devalues the currency, causing inflation. Remember, money is debt. The more money in circulation the more likelihood of inflation, especially if governments can reduce the slack in their economy by creating demand. And demand is created by employment!

Now the Fed could literally print money, with the help of the Bureau of Printing and Engraving. After all, take a look at the dollar bills in your wallet or purse and you will notice the central bank's name sits atop them. But the Fed doesn't use this power to flood the system with cash. It doesn't need to. Instead, as noted above, when the Fed wants to print money, it simply purchases securities or other assets (Treasury Bonds and now Mortgage Backed Securities and other agency bonds) from securities dealers. In return, it gives them electronic credits that amount to cash which is kept on deposit with banks to lend out. The Fed can create as many of these electronic credits as it wants, giving it virtually unlimited power to mint cash. These cash credits -- known as bank reserves -- have grown in less than 18 months from less than $3 billion in August 2008 to more than $1.1 trillion in February of this year.

We all witnessed the results of the Fed flooding the monetary system with an abundance of liquidity beginning in 2001 -- the housing bubble and credit bubble within six years thereafter which, when they burst, wreaked havoc on the whole system. Debt was chasing debt -- debt was everywhere and much of it worthless!

Now, one might expect, given that the near collapse of our system, thanks in part to the easy money actions of the Fed, that the Fed would stop printing excessive amounts of money. Uh no, sorry. In fact, just the opposite has occurred. Irrespective of the TARP funds, the Fed has printed trillions of dollars of new debt in order to pay for the excesses that it helped to create. "Impossible" you say! Hardly. Remember now, when you deal with Dr. Bernanke, you are dealing with one of the consummate Ivory Tower mentalities, who also suffers from a classic case of short-term memory loss or voluntary denial. By the way, in case you ever wondered how he came by the nickname "helicopter Ben," it was due to the Fed printing money and increasing the money supply on such a high scale it was as if it was dropping money from a helicopter (and the helicopter he is currently operating must be bigger than a Columbia Chinook, the largest helicopter in service in this country today, with a rotor span covering an astounding 5,000 square feet).

Also, have you ever wondered what happened to the so-called toxic assets which were being held on the books of the institutions referred to as *"too big to fail"* (AIG, Citibank, Goldman Sachs, JP Morgan Chase, Wells Fargo, Bank of America, etc.). The Fed purchased the assets in order to remove the non-performing debt from the banks' books to shore up their capital ratios in order to make the failed institutions appear solvent. Simply stated, if a dollar of assets that a bank was holding was suddenly worth only 50 cents, the bank would have to raise the other 50 cents to avoid being classified as insolvent, which would mean its forced liquidation. But thanks to the Fed (the organization whose primary objective is to protect the viability of the major banks), backed by the taxpayers and paid for in large measure by foreign governments, the needed 50 cents in capital for the banks was arranged through the sale of government debt (bills, notes, and bonds). In effect, the, Fed bought the toxic assets from the too big to fail banks and re-capitalized their balance sheets to regain solvency.

But guess what? In one of the greatest hoaxes ever perpetrated on the American taxpayer, we have been saddled with paying the interest on the debt that the Fed sold to in order for the Fed to save its constituency, the *"too big to fail"* banks. All the while, like children fighting over pieces of candy, those "too big to fail" institutions demanded extortion payments, by the way of bonuses, for their efforts in helping to bring our financial system to its knees -- while the Fed looked the other way. Those institutions woke up on Christmas to stockings chock full of goodies when they should have had stockings overflowing with lumps of coal (their having been oh so naughty, not nice).

Now back to the inflation story and the dollar. The law of supply and demand will ultimately determine the fate of the dollar -- meaning that the more dollars are printed and the more debt grows, the more the value of the dollar should decline. Consequently, until the Fed decides to grow a backbone and defend the value of the dollar by withdrawing the excess liquidity now by raising interest rates and /or selling some of its assets and drastically reducing its purchase of debt instruments, the dollar will continue to slide. This is not to say that there will not be dollar rallies and sharp ones at that. Witness the recent rally against the Euro as the sovereign debt crisis in Europe went from a trot to a full-blown gallop.

But, make no mistake, the rallies will be traps for the unwary and the dollar will ultimately resume its long-term decline. Why? Because, the Fed is bent on continuing, far into the future, its (too) easy money policy because the housing market remains extremely weak, the pace of bank failures is running high (the most since the Great S&L crisis of the 1980s), and prices for commodities are still not showing signs of the much anticipated price creep -- i.e., in a nutshell, inflation still seems quite tame. Even gold, although having enjoyed an incredible run, still has not reached its inflation-adjusted high reached in the 1970s. In all likelihood, by the time the Fed change course and decides to withdraw the excess liquidity, its corrective course of action will come too late and be too little and hence we will find ourselves in the throes of painful inflation. Meanwhile, the stock market will continue rising, buoyed by an artificial high of excess liquidity orchestrated by the Fed to instill consumer confidence.

We would be remiss if we failed to mention one other consequence of a falling dollar -- a rise in oil prices. Under an OPEC ("Organization of Petroleum Exporting Countries") agreement, all oil has been traded in dollars since 1971(after the elimination of the gold standard). Thus, as the dollar declines in value, there should be a corresponding (inverse) upward pressure on the price of oil and calls to replace the dollar as the petroleum reserve currency will grow in both volume and number. And, as those demands grow, there will be added upward pressure on oil prices. The only reason we are not seeing greater price escalation in oil today is the general weakness of demand for oil in the United States and Europe and the brief stability of the dollar versus the Euro.

Of course, it is still highly unlikely that the dollar will be replaced any time soon as the world's benchmark reserve currency. Statistically speaking, the share of global transactions using the dollar, according to the Bank for International Settlements which serves as a bank for central banks, is still around 8% (down from 91% in 2001) and dollar assets still account for almost two-thirds of the total reserve assets of industrialized and developing countries. The dollar's retention of its status as the world's preeminent currency is further exemplified by its share of all outstanding debt securities, issued anywhere in the world. According to this measure, the dollar's share stands at just under 40%, down only slightly from a high of 42% in 1999.

Consequently, while it would be wrong to write off the U.S. dollar as the top global reserve currency, it is also fair to say that its roughly 90-year iron grip on that position is loosening. Many experts agree that the use of the dollar as the preeminent international reserve currency is in a state of decline, a decline which must accelerate over the next decade if we do not get our sovereign debt under control (and that's a very big "if" indeed). All in all, though, we should not have to be exposed to the vagaries of either inflation or deflation, provided we have the courage to follow a strong dollar policy, whereby the dollar is backed by tangible assets. It could be gold, silver, natural gas, whatever, something real that we have plenty of (other than thin air) and that is fungible. Opponents will roundly criticize basing the dollar on some hard asset and will argue that economic growth will be limited by the amount of the hard asset on hand -- i.e., the Fed's monetary powers will be limited because it will not be able to print more dollars than the aggregate value of the hard asset standing behind it. And this is bad? We don't believe so.

The goal should be to drastically reduce, then eliminate, our national debt while implementing an economic growth policy based on manufacturing, technology, energy, and transportation. We need to become a nation of makers again and shun being a nation of takers. We need to return to the status of a creditor country and stop being the largest debtor nation in the world. If our creed is to lead and if the most effective way to lead is by example, we have to alter our wayward ways because our leadership is being compromised daily by the bad example we are setting for the rest of the world. By way of example, consider the economies of Australia, Brazil, and Canada. All three are natural resource-based, mining-based, and manufacturing-based economies, and all have weathered the financial crisis far better than we have -- and their strong currencies and relatively high standards of living, especially with regard to their middle classes, reflect the positive results of their economic policies.

And so another day comes to a close and we have discovered that, as long as we do not either listen to or watch the talking heads on the cable babble stations, we can get through the day without too much anger or angst - and that is a good thing. However, we know we must also address the babble guys and gals if we truly desire to understand and hope to improve the lot of our fellow citizens, as it appears the talking heads, with their scripted political agendas, being paid big money to rail against the other political party's view points, are an integral part of the problem -- we like to call them the diabolical dealers of drivel. Surprisingly, many of those who watch them are absolutely avid, frequently addicted, viewers, and most believe they have been endowed with inalienable political insight and that the message they deliver is nothing short of prescient political journalism. Sadly, this perception could not be more distant from the truth, for these commentators are, journalistically speaking, mere mountebanks, entertainers posing as newsmen, paid to read whatever verbiage is printed before them on their Teleprompters. They are broadcasters who "say for pay" (whatever it is their editors and sponsors dictate).

At any rate, we are now growing a bit weary of this topic and so it is time to close this chapter -- but, not to worry, more, much more later on one of our favorite subjects, the "talking heads."

A final thought occurs to us before we close. Why not adopt our Canadian brothers' unit of currency, the *Loonie*, in place of the dollar -- that way we can really keep the rest of the world off balance and confused because no one will know when our politicians are talking about the actual currency itself or the policies behind it. It's at times like these you have to laugh to keep from crying! Maybe that's why Ben Franklin on the $100 bill has such a grim countenance. Or is that a smirk?

CHAPTER 12

ENERGY POLICY
'Running on Empty'

"Ours is the most wasteful nation on Earth. We waste more energy than we import. With about the same standard of living, we use twice as much energy per person as do other countries like Germany, Japan, and Sweden. Energy will be the immediate test of our ability to unite this Nation, and it can also be the standard around which we rally. On the battlefield of energy we can win for our Nation a new confidence, and we can seize control again of our common destiny."
- **Jimmy Carter**

"Right now we are not at the forefront of the global race in clean energy and the reason we are not leafing that - and China, India and Germany are moving ahead of us- is because we haven't put in place the right domestic policy. In order for companies to make investments here in the United States in clean energy technologies, they need to know there's going to be an opportunity for them to sell their technologies here. The best way to give them that predictability and certainty is with a comprehensive energy policy."
- **Carol Browner, Director of White House Energy and Climate Change Policy**

Another day arrives, and we are up and about, valiantly attempting to get out of the psychological doldrums and into an upbeat mental state, when we find ourselves reviewing a current magazine article regarding energy and the relationship between the price and the supply of oil and natural gas. As we scan this brief article, we begin to think about the influence upon us and importance to us of the energy policies of the government and where the energy path being charted by the government will lead. This is an issue of vital importance when you stop to consider the enormous extent to which we, in our daily lives, depend upon energy to function. To say that energy is integral to our lives is one of the all time understatements of understatements.

We are almost reluctant to delve into an area that we believe the government has so grossly mismanaged, and we fear nipping our fleeting feeling of optimism in the bud, but, gluttons for punishment that we are, we are more or less (a little more than less) compelled to examine the role that past and present administrations and lawmakers have played in forming and managing our use of energy. You might say we feel the "need to weed" -- in this case, weed the government's energy policy garden, so to speak -- of course, we will need a lot more than our hands to weed this particular garden, probably a gasoline-powered weed eater (maybe, in light of the subject matter, an electric weed eater would be preferable).

As we read through the article, we come to a discussion about the role the federal government has played in the price and availability of energy for our everyday use. The information is disconcerting at best and deeply disturbing at worst. In a nutshell, we would have to describe the last four decades of government energy policy as exemplifying management by crisis, which is to say a reactive rather than proactive approach.

In order to attempt to understand what likely lies ahead, in terms of energy, for us and our children and grandchildren, we first need to take a brief stroll with you down "memory lane" to find out how we arrived at the current state of affairs regarding energy -- one reason being that forgetting the mistakes of the past will doom us to repeat them. Or, perhaps, in viewing and reviewing the government's role vis-à-vis energy initiatives, it might be more fitting to conclude that the real reason we study history is to recognize the same mistakes each time we make them.

Now, when we talk about energy policy in the United States, we must first talk about it in relation to national security because the two are inextricably intertwined and "energy security," as it has come to be known, has had a direct and sometimes decisive impact on the cost and availability of energy. This concept of energy security, at least in America, is believed to have originated in 1912 when President Taft made a tactical decision about the importance of petroleum to our national defense by establishing the Naval Petroleum Reserve. Not much else about energy security made its way into federal policies until after World War II when the U.S. became a net oil importer for the first time and when, in 1950, oil consumption in the U.S. for the first time in American history exceeded that of coal as a source of energy.

After the Second World War, the U.S., having furnished the European Allies with most of their oil needs for the war, was left with enormously depleted reserves. This realization prompted President Roosevelt to meet with Saudi Arabia's King Ibn Saud in 1945, as the war was coming to a close, a meeting that laid the framework for a virtual trade agreement pursuant to which we would provide the Saudi government with military and other protection in exchange for privileged access to Saudi oil. And so began our tie to Middle East petroleum ("petroleum politics") for the next many years. Regarding the home front, however, it should also be noted that one of Roosevelt's "claims to fame," energy-wise, was the construction of massive dams to produce hydro-electric power, an incredibly expensive project in its day. The Grand Coulee Dam alone, completed in 1942, if priced today in an equivalent share of GDP, would have cost over $40 billion. Most of these dams are still operating today but satisfy less than 5% of the country's energy needs.

Roosevelt's successor announced the Truman Doctrine which let the world know that the United States would protect oil-rich Middle Eastern nations, like Iran and Saudi Arabia, from Soviet incursions. The Truman Administration was also instrumental in the adoption of a National Security Council Resolution (138/1) expressly designed "to secure oil resources for the Western world." Truman's energy strategy is partially credited with ushering in the "golden age of oil," which witnessed a ten-fold increase in energy consumption and exponential economic growth. Of course, the policies of "easy oil" (sort of like the Fed's "easy money" policies) would ultimately lead to quite serious national security (and just plain national) problems in the future. At the time, the big oil companies maintained that importing oil from abroad was conducive to energy security because it was cheaper and would slow depletion of domestic reserves so domestic supplies would be available if and when needed for national security purposes.

In the 1950s, President Eisenhower addressed foreign policy concerns by implementing domestic energy security policies. Forced to deal with dwindling supplies of oil at home and the potentially deleterious effect on security of supply and the crisis in the Suez Canal (after Egyptian President Nasser nationalized the Suez Canal in 1956, France, England and Israel invaded Egypt, vowing that the Suez Canal was too important a waterway to allow to be controlled by Egypt alone, an action that the United States vigorously opposed), President Eisenhower proposed the development of an emergency oil reserve. However, this idea was condemned by politicians and industry experts as impractical and unsound policy. Nevertheless, Eisenhower's suggestion eventually did become law, but not until 1975, 19 years later, after which it became a cornerstone of our energy policy.

An Eisenhower policy that was implemented during his term in office was the Mandatory Oil Import Program of 1959, which imposed quotas on amounts of crude oil and refined petroleum products admitted into the U.S. However, exceptions were made for Canada and Mexico (and later Venezuela), thus transforming the program into a quota system directed at imports from the Middle East. This action was one of the reasons for the formation of the Organization of the Oil Exporting Countries (OPEC), which was initially composed principally of Middle Eastern countries and which in turn precipitated years of problems for our energy policies, forcing an even greater connection between our foreign policy and energy policy.

Eisenhower is also credited with commercializing nuclear power with his "Atoms for Peace" address to the United Nations in 1953. Today nuclear power provides roughly 12% of energy consumed in this country, a number that is likely to grow with the administration's recent endorsement of the source and the industry's development of much cleaner, more efficient and safer nuclear reactors.

Eisenhower's legacy also includes the 1956 National Interstate Highway Act, which resulted not only in significant economic expansion but also helped trigger our nearly addictive dependence upon the automobile, which in turn fostered the rapid growth in oil consumption since more than 20% of our total oil consumption stems from highway use.

No national energy policies were instituted during the Kennedy or Johnson years because both were preoccupied with Vietnam and the Cold War (which may not have been a bad thing at all, given the poor results of future energy policies).

So we must skip ahead to 1973 and the first of several modern energy crises which resulted when King Faisal of Saudi Arabia embargoed oil exports to the U.S. thereby engendering the first major oil price spike. Nixon responded with his Project Independence, an ambitious (and totally unrealistic) plan to make America completely energy independent by 1980. In fact, however, our dependence on oil imports has more than doubled since then. Project Independence's claim to fame, if it has one, was raising national awareness and focusing national attention on the nation's need to increase domestic supplies, reduce domestic demand through conservation, and promote energy technology. Never one to shy away from pandering to the public, Nixon told the nation that he would take steps to ensure that "gasoline will never exceed $1.00 per gallon" (famous last words).

As part of his inflation-fighting plan, Nixon, in another moment of rank political opportunism, imposed price controls on domestic oil and gasoline, which contributed to supply shortages. The scarcity was then dealt with by rationing gasoline, which led to intolerably long lines at gas stations beginning in the summer of 1972 and increasing by the summer of 1973.

Nixon also proposed and signed into law as a fuel conservation measure the act that set the maximum highway speed limit of 55 mph, which soon became perhaps the most widely disobeyed law in our history. Its gross ineffectiveness in achieving its stated goal of significantly reducing gasoline consumption is demonstrated by the results -- the United States Department of Transportation reported fuel savings of about 1% stemming from the act but several independent studies found the savings to be a good bit less than half of that.

One of Nixon's signature energy policies was his authorization in 1973 of the $10 billion Trans-Alaska pipeline, which has since transported more than 15 billion barrels of oil, approximately 10% of total U.S. oil consumption since it became operational.

A Nixon energy footnote -- before the oil embargo, in 1970, Nixon proclaimed in an environmental message to Congress: *"I am inaugurating a program to marshal both government and private research with the goal of producing an unconventionally powered virtually pollution free automobile within five years."* But he failed to get the automobile companies on the same page, as they went on to build legions of large, fuel inefficient trucks, sedans and SUVs that today continue to represent the lion's share of our traffic and consume the lion's share of automotive gasoline. In fact, the largest gains in automotive sales of late stem from SUVs, with 3 of the top 10 gains coming from the SUV behemoths. It's not that we don't care about our reliance on imported oil and environmental degradation. It's just that we don't care enough to let those concerns get in the way of our lifestyle demands.

All in all, we would have to say that Nixon's government energy programs, in line with his penchant for government intervention, proved that too much government involvement in the free market is not efficacious in the energy field and may well operate as a setback to achieving energy efficiency and self-sufficiency.

Nixon's short-term successor, Gerald Ford, was more concerned with returning integrity to the office of the President than with energy, but he did sign legislation which created the Strategic Petroleum Reserve, an emergency oil stockpile with about two months worth of total imports. He also extended the target date for Nixon's import free policy to 1985 and signed the 1975 Energy Policy and Conservation Act, which set federal standards for energy efficiency in new cars for the first time.

President Jimmy Carter swept into office on a platform of change and made energy policy the centerpiece of his administration. He openly chastised the American public for failing to embrace conservation and for consuming too much of the world's energy resources and declared on April 18, 1977, that achieving energy independence was the *"moral equivalent of war."* In August of that year, Carter signed the law creating the United States Department of Energy, a Cabinet-level department, initially intended to manage America's ongoing energy crisis and deal with energy management issues on the federal level on into the future. However, our studies of the Department of Energy's history in establishing and implementing viable energy policies has led us to conclude that this federal department had contributed little of major or lasting value. Instead, over the past 33 years, its contributions to energy security and energy productivity have been sporadic, inconsistent, and inconsequential, for the most part, and more often than not, entirely ineffectual. This is not to say the Department has not earned any gold stars. It has, but they are few and far between. An early gold star was the Weatherization

Assistance Program which has provided weatherization services to more than 5.5 million families, enabling them to reduce, on average, heating bills by 31% and overall energy bills by over $360 per year at current prices.

President Carter also oversaw the completion of the Trans-Alaska pipeline which opened up the large energy reserves in Alaska and proposed adoption of a National Energy Act, a sweeping $142 billion energy plan designed to achieve energy independence by 1990 (adding another five years to Gerald Ford's timetable). There was significant Congressional opposition to the proposal, however, and Carter's "grand plan" for energy never became the law of the land. What emerged instead was five energy-related bills cobbled together to form the National Energy Plan (which was not really a comprehensive plan at all, but instead a series of separate energy-related measures, each of which paid lip service to a national security mandate for uninterrupted oil imports, yet none of which addressed environmental considerations or promoted the development of alternative energy sources). Carter himself, however, continued to push hard for alternative energy development, but was, for the most part, unsuccessful in his efforts due to strong resistance from Congress.

The Carter administration also was beset by the second great modern day oil shock, which occurred in 1979 in the wake of the Iranian Revolution. Amid massive protest, the Shah of Iran fled his country in early 1979, allowing the Ayatollah Khomeini to gain control. The protests served to stymie Iranian oil production. Although the new regime resumed oil exports, it was inconsistent and at a lower volume, forcing prices to rise. Saudi Arabia and other OPEC nations increased production to offset the decline, and the overall loss in production was only about 4%. However, a widespread petroleum panic resulted, driving the price far higher than would be expected under normal circumstances.

The second oil crisis also led directly to a Carter proposal that ultimately proved to be a bust -- his signature Synfuels energy project (synthetic production of oil, most notably from shale or coal), for which he originally secured a staggering $88 billion of funding (roughly $300 billion in today's dollars). Carter was able to ram his proposal through Congress with the help of the big oil companies and his dire predictions that oil was going to go to $200 a barrel. A few years later, when oil prices dropped dramatically during Reagan's tenure, the Synfuels projects were summarily abandoned and the government's expensive Synfuels support programs were dismantled, rendering the Carter plan a debacle and tarnishing his reputation in the energy area. In fact, the term Synfuels became such a dirty word (and not just because it produces dirty fuel in terms of greenhouse emissions and other pollutants) that it was replaced with the term "unconventional oil products."

Nonetheless, no matter what you may think of Carter's Presidency (and many are quick to label it an abject failure on foreign policy and economic fronts), Carter, in part due to global events beyond his control, felt he had no choice but to make energy policy a presidential priority and he became the first president to propose a comprehensive long-term national plan for addressing energy concerns. Unfortunately, most of his proposals went the way of "the best laid plans of mice and men" -- that would be "astray," as the great Scottish poet Robert Burns once penned.

But perhaps Carter is rightfully entitled to be considered ahead of his time in attempting to construct a detailed energy policy that would have liberated America from dependence on Middle East oil and vulnerability to Islamic extremism. When Carter took office, we were importing 8 million barrels of foreign oil a day, which was reduced to 2 million barrels by the time he left office, four years later. There was, to be sure, a good deal of "pain at the pump" in the interim, but nobody ever said an effort to wean the country from imported energy would be painless. Unfortunately, despite Carter's bold assurance that *this nation will never again use as much foreign oil as we did in 1977,*" we now import over 11 million barrels of oil every day (approximately 56% of our total national oil consumption of 19.5 million barrels daily).

When Ronald Reagan took over the presidential reins, his signature energy policy was focused on ending national fuel price controls and deemphasizing energy as a special or unique issue, preferring the *"native American genius, not arbitrary federal policy, to be free to provide for our energy future."* In other words, President Reagan took a *laissez faire* approach to energy policy, preferring to leave as much initiative as possible to the private market. Although he still espoused the goal of energy independence, he wanted it to be achieved with minimal government intervention, so he proceeded to cut direct federal spending for alternative energy sources and conservation programs and sought to remove what he perceived as unnecessary federal roadblocks to domestic oil exploration and production.

On the very day he became president in January 1981, Reagan ended the remaining federal regulations on domestic oil supplies and prices, allowing oil prices for the first time since 1971 to fall and rise with world markets. In December 1985, Reagan signed legislation dismantling Carter's U.S. Synthetic Fuels Corporation. What happened when all of these federal government efforts to direct and manage our energy supply were euthanized by Ronald Reagan? Well, surprise, surprise, oil prices dropped from their peak of $37 per barrel in 1981 to less than $14 per barrel in 1986.

Reagan understood that, for most Americans, lower gasoline prices and lower home electric bills were all the energy independence they really wanted or needed. His efforts to reduce the federal government's involvement in efforts to control energy supply and demand, which had grown appreciably during the Nixon and Carter years, even went so far as wanting to abolish the Department of Energy, an effort which was rejected by Congress (for, as we all have learned over time, paring back the federal bureaucracy is at the very least a daunting proposition and at worst an impossible task, even for a president so inclined, given that any such proposals rarely if ever find favor with our lawmakers).

In 1991, in the prelude to the First Gulf War (Desert Storm), the first President Bush tried to palm off a piecemeal set of proposals as a national energy strategy. To no one's surprise, one of his guiding principles was the one that both previous administrations had held near and dear, "reducing our dependence on foreign oil." For the most part, Bush's plan represented a continuation of Reagan's policy of reduced government involvement, coupled with increased reliance on the private sector to achieve energy independence. The main goal of the Bush strategy was to increase domestic production and there was some increase, but very little.

President Clinton's energy policies, as many expected, were in large measure a return to "yesteryear" and the policies of the 1970s. His administration focused on reauthorizing the Strategic Petroleum Reserve and securing financial incentives to promote energy efficiency and alternative energy technologies. Although Clinton himself vocalized a sense of urgency and importance to energy, his Secretary of Energy did not seem to share these views, as demonstrated when he noted in his introduction to the proposed 1998 Comprehensive National Energy Strategy as follows: *"We are not facing an immediate crisis. Our economy is doing well. Energy supplies seem ample. The environment is steadily improving."* With Clinton's own Energy Secretary seemingly not overly concerned about the state of energy and being viewed as a lukewarm champion of Clinton's proposed energy plan "makeover," it is small wonder that the President's proposals were largely ignored by Congress, especially when the Republicans took back control of Congress in 1994.

Many consider Clinton administration's signature energy policy to have been the Partnership for a New Generation of Vehicles, a government-industry partnership formed to develop an 80 mpg family car without sacrificing size, comfort, range or speed--and spending a few billion dollars -- which never happened of course. Clinton's energy policies were widely considered one of his presidential failures. A prime example was his attempt to impose a blanket energy tax, equivalent to $3 on the then $20 barrel of oil, which even the then Democrat-controlled Congress hurriedly voted down.

When he first took office, the second President Bush placed a renewed emphasis on energy security and echoed previous administrations in calling for an immediate increase in domestic energy supplies. In a speech before the U.S. Chamber of Commerce's National Energy Summit in March 2001, George W. Bush's Energy Secretary observed that *"the failure to meet the energy challenge will threaten our economic prosperity, compromise our national security, and literally alter the way we live our lives."* To address these challenges, President Bush established the National Energy Policy Development Group, selecting Vice President Cheney as its head (a choice which many viewed with more than a little skepticism and some likened to a wolf being asked to make sure the sheep were properly cared for, given Cheney's longstanding ties to the oil industry -- after all, he served as Chairman and CEO of Halliburton, one of the world's largest oilfield services companies with operations in 70 countries). This Development Group eventually crafted Bush's National Energy Policy. Written before the events of September 11, 2001, the Policy sought the establishment of a secure supply of energy, mainly oil, to American industry and commerce. Although it included some sections on efficiency, conservation, and alternative and renewable sources of energy, far more emphasis was placed on reducing energy dependence through expanding domestic production. And the Plan also sought to better secure access to dependable foreign sources of petroleum. Certainly the oil industry applauded Cheney's "no oil company left behind" plan -- during Bush's eight years in office, big oil raked in over $650 billion in profits (obviously not just due to the administration's avid support, but that was certainly a contributing factor).

The 9/11 incident focused a new and heightened importance on energy security and what was increasingly perceived as our increasingly dangerous dependence on foreign oil. In particular, the public viewed our dependence on Middle Eastern oil as a serious threat to national security. In fact, many have claimed that the Iraq Invasion was far more a result of the desire to secure access to Iraqi oil than a desire to secure democracy in Iraq or because Saddam Hussein had weapons of mass destruction or links to Al Qaeda. It was of course on W's watch that the world saw the third great oil price spike as the price soared to a record $147 per barrel in July 2008 (and gasoline at the pump hit a record $4.50 per gallon in some states like California). The Bush administration responded with attempts to lift the ban on offshore drilling and his signature energy policy -- corn-based ethanol.

When oil prices rose to dizzying heights, President Bush proclaimed that the United States should "get off oil" and "get on ethanol". To the surprise of many Washington "outsiders" (but not to the "insiders" who know full well that votes can be readily bought and sold by big business), a Democratic Congress passed the Bush "Energy Independence and Security Act" in 2007, mandating ethanol production to be doubled to 15 billion gallons by 2015, up from 6.5 billion gallons in 2007. Its passage was a giant victory for the corporate agri-business lobbyists and another telling defeat for true alternative energy advocates. How big a defeat? The ethanol industry received $3 billion in federal subsidies in 2007, $4 billion in 2008 and $8 billion in 2009 -- almost twice as much as solar, wind, geothermal and other biomass combined. Plus, according to a recent study by Rice University's Baker Institute for Public Policy, the average cost to the American taxpayer from these subsidies was about $82 a barrel or $1.95 a gallon on top of the retail gas price -- not to mention the big rise in corn prices and in turn food prices from the widely acclaimed ethanol "fix". And, as it turns out, ethanol is no more environmentally friendly than gasoline.

The widespread fears about oil prices subsided substantially when oil prices dropped by 50% from those anxiety-ridden days of nearly $150-per-barrel prices almost two years ago. However, that respite was short-lived and the energy anxiety was replaced by an even greater one -- economic anxiety resulting from the fear of a financial collapse which was and is the primary reason oil prices fell so dramatically in the first place. Let's be honest here -- petroleum prices fell and fell precipitously, not because there was an increase in new energy production, whether oil, corn-alcohol farms, nuclear plants or wind farms, but due to the global recession-driven collapse in demand..

So now we finally come to 2010 and the "change we can believe in" administration of President Obama. Ever the master of rhetoric, he has again talked a "good game" about energy security and the need for a comprehensive, multi-faceted energy strategy, but will we make real progress under his administration in the direction of less dependence on foreign oil and stable prices for the consumer? With so many ambitious plans on the table and so many pressing needs in this country, does his plate really have room for another portion of food (and would we better "served" in the long run if he left more of the impetus for change with the private sector).

After all, the meat, potatoes and bread and butter (with Iraq and Afghanistan on tap, some might lift a phrase from the Lyndon Johnson years and say "guns and butter") are taken up with health care reform, the economic recession and unemployment, and military deployment in Afghanistan (soon to include Pakistan if our tea leaves are accurate). Vegetable portions on the presidential plate are provided by Middle East foreign policy, the threat of atomic weapons in Iran, and relations with China and, to a lesser degree, Japan and South Korea. For dessert, there are dishes of financial regulation and enforcement, Wall Street bonuses, bailouts and bank failures, and of course the out-of-control federal budgets, state government money problems and record deficits and government (at all levels) debt. Energy, if it makes the meal at all, can only slip in as a quick intermezzo (clear the palate) course, a very light sorbet between the main courses. Yes, that's about where energy has fallen in the presidential pecking order -- on down the cafeteria line (to belabor the food metaphor a wee bit more) and dropping further by the day.

And let's be honest. Are we going to get anywhere near full value for the governmental energy programs we the taxpayers are paying for? You know we won't. Especially when you consider that, for fiscal year 2010, the budget of the Department of Energy is a jaw-dropping $65 billion, including $39 billion provided for energy programs in the American Recovery and Reinvestment Act of 2009. Besides keeping statistics of our nation's energy production, does anyone have a clue as to how they spend an amount greater than the GDP of 2/3 of all countries on earth? Well, a review of the energy budget request shows that a large percentage is allocated for the safeguard of our stockpile of nuclear weapons. In fact, about $16.5 billion is earmarked for nuclear energy and security programs. Now, we are all for nuclear energy and for the security of our weapons stockpile, but why do we need another multi-level department to administer and manage our nuclear assets especially when we have a defense department whose job it is to watch over nuclear weapons?

One other major job of the Department of Energy is to protect the American electricity grid and support modernization of the power grid. How is that working for the nation? Not so good. The power grid has been on the blink for years. Terrorists and hostile foreign governments are well aware of the grid's vulnerabilities. Further, it has been reported recently that either North Korea or China (or maybe both) successfully hacked into the grid to determine the ease in making it a first strike target in case hostilities were to erupt. Better yet, let's see what DOE itself had to say about the state of the power grid. In its recently published *Overview of the Electric Grid,* the Department had this to say: *"North America's world-class electric system is facing several serious challenges. Major questions exist about its ability to continue providing citizens and businesses with relatively clean, reliable, and affordable energy services."* The recent downturn in the economy masks areas of grid congestion in numerous locations across America. All is not well on our electricity front.

Obama's final chapter on energy is yet to be written. However, he has given us a preview of coming attractions (or detractions), from which it is reasonable to conclude that he would like for his administration to go down in history as transforming (and reforming) the nation into a "clean green machine" -- it would have been nice to be able to say "lean clean green machine," but, in terms of government involvement under his direction, nothing remotely resembles "lean." Take for example Obama's surprise overture to the Republicans to allow offshore deep water drilling for oil. Sounded good until a major catastrophe occurs such as the BP rig Deepwater Horizon exploding, resulting in billions of dollars of damage, loss of life, and untold environmental damage to Louisiana, Mississippi, Alabama, and Florida. Then Obama did an abrupt "about face" and implemented a moratorium on deepwater drilling in the Gulf. You might have thought, with all the furor over The Spill, the moratorium would be welcomed with open arms. But, no, because it is taking a toll in terms of adverse economic impact through lost jobs and revenue, especially in Louisiana. Sometimes politicians too get to suffer the *slings and arrows of outrageous fortune* and, at the end of the day, are simply damned if they do and damned if they don't. But damned they are and often should be.

Nevertheless, President Obama strongly supports the development of alternative energy sources (so have the last seven Presidents), particularly clean(er) energy, and, in yet another instant of 1600 Pennsylvania Avenue déjà vu, he has clamored for a substantial decrease in our dependence on foreign oil. This move has obviously been given new life by the oil spill. In his words, the President believes his "clean energy agenda" will serve to "reverse our dependence on foreign oil while building a new energy economy that will create millions of jobs." Although he has not reached his mid-term yet, his grade so far on his energy-related "courses" of action would have to rate no better than a "D" or maybe a "C-"). We do not deny that alternative, cleaner energy sources are in our future -- they must be for the sake of security and prosperity. We do quarrel with wasteful and frequently counterproductive actions by the government to remake the energy sector in its image of what's right and proper (the "Big Brother always knows best" approach).

Now you may ask: What has the President done (or not done, as the case may be) to deserve such a low grade? Well, in the first place, he began his presidency by endorsing George W. Bush's push for biofuels, ethanol in particular. The only possible reason Obama could have for lending his formidable presidential backing to an energy source for which the negatives have been shown to far outweigh the positives must be the considerable clout of the agro industry lobbyists. We say this because several scientific studies on alternative energy proposals now claim that bio-fuels -- particularly ethanol-- actually cause more air pollution, require more land to produce, generate less horsepower than regular gasoline, and cost consumers more, despite being priced less at the pump. Mark Jacobson, a professor of civil and environmental engineering at Stanford, who published the first truly comprehensive study of major alternative energy proposals in *Energy & Environmental Science* magazine, stated that *"Ethanol-based biofuels will actually cause more harm to human health, wildlife, water supply and land use than current fossil fuels."* His top rated alternative energy choices are, in order: wind, concentrated solar, geothermal, tidal, solar panels, wave, and hydroelectric. In last place, as with other more recent studies, is ethanol, which Professor Jacobson calls *"the most damaging choice we could make in our effort to move away from fossil fuels."*

And here's a startling fact: the energy legislation passed in 2007 originally capped maximum ethanol production at 2.35 million barrels per day by 2022, but Congress then realized that amount of ethanol production would consume the entire corn crop of the United States which of course would wreak havoc on corn-based food supplies and prices. So Congress reduced the maximum number of gallons of ethanol from grain to 15 billion gallons, which would still use more than half the entire corn crop of the United States.

An early Department of Energy study showed that ethanol from grain emits more carbon dioxide per mile driven than gasoline, so it is far from the "clean" fuel that both Bush and Obama would have us believe. Yet federal subsidies for the domestic ethanol industry are expected to top $5 billion this year. Obama renewed his commitment to ethanol earlier this year, citing more recent studies by the Department of Agriculture and the ethanol industry (self-serving to be sure) which concluded that corn ethanol, when produced with new, more advanced energy-efficient means, could produce 20 percent lower greenhouse gas emissions than gasoline.

In energy, it seems that what one presidential hand giveth, the other sometimes taketh away (although given the growth of the federal government over the past 50 years, there has been a lot more presidential giving than taking) -- and so the President has proposed funding the renewable energy subsidies in part by hiking taxes on the oil and gas companies by $45 billion. This move is not likely to facilitate the call for increased domestic production, but is likely to cost a fair number of jobs in the traditional oil and gas sector. Furthermore, another Obama proposal would eliminate the domestic manufacturing income deduction for U.S. refiners while allowing all other manufacturers (automakers, weapons makers, drug companies, etc.) to continue using it. Because refinery margins are at their lowest in decades, removal of this deduction would further reduce America's ability to produce its own gasoline and diesel fuel while giving an unfair advantage to foreign competitors who would not be affected by the proposal. We doubt that the oil and gas industry can look for much help from one of Obama's chief energy czars, Vice President Joe Biden. After all, he was only one of five Senators to vote against the Trans-Alaska pipeline (the final vote was 80-5 in favor) and he has had his gun sights trained squarely on the domestic oil industry for some time - although, to be sure, some of this has been brought on by the short-sighted, "gouging is good" mentality of the big oil companies.

One positive for the Obama administration may prove to be its endorsement of greater development of our plentiful natural gas as an energy source. However, the impetus for this action did not come from Obama at all, but rather from the private sector led by high-profile Texas billionaire T. Boone Pickens. Pickens had boldly predicted that Congress will pass key energy legislation, known as the Natural Gas Act, by this past Memorial Day. Unfortunately, a vote on the bill has been delayed and may not take place until next year. The legislation would dramatically expand the use of natural gas as a transportation fuel among heavy-duty fleets. House and Senate versions of the bill provide tax breaks for natural gas-powered vehicles and fueling stations. Pickens has been one of the most vocal advocates for using abundant domestic natural gas supplies in the transportation sector. And he has put his money where his mouth is -- since the summer of 2008, he has spent more than $65 million of his own money promoting his Pickens Plan, which also touts the importance of wind power. And his plan has evolved in recent months. He is no longer focused on natural gas as a fuel for everyday passenger cars and trucks, but instead has turned his attention to heavy commercial vehicles like garbage trucks and city buses, which account for a great deal of the petroleum used in the U.S.

The Pickens Plan makes sense in that one source of energy this country has in abundance is natural gas. Last year's discovery of the massive Haynesville Shale formation in northern Louisiana was big news indeed for the natural gas industry. Estimates are that the dense rock formation could hold 200 trillion cubic feet of natural gas -- the equivalent of 33 billion barrels of oil or 18 years' worth of current U.S. oil production. Some industry experts believe the field could be several times that size. Moreover, huge new fields have recently been discovered in Texas, Arkansas and Pennsylvania. Our research shows that the United States now has well over 2,200 trillion cubic feet of natural gas available to be pumped, enough to satisfy 100 years of current natural-gas demand.

Plus natural gas is the cleanest burning fossil fuel. Because the combustion process for natural gas is almost perfect, very few byproducts are emitted into the atmosphere as pollutants. Natural gas produces 70% less carbon dioxide emissions than other fossil fuels. Also, new technologies have enabled producers to significantly reduce the output of nitrogen oxide, a pollutant targeted by the Clean Air Act. Furthermore, for vehicles running on natural gas, the cost, on average, is 1/3 less at the pump than gasoline. Running exclusively on natural gas, the Honda Civic GX has been named "America's Greenest Car" five consecutive years -- and it boasts virtually no emissions. Natural gas vehicles also provide superior convenience and safety. While new technology allows Natural Gas Vehicle (NGV) drivers to fill their tanks at home, natural gas cars can run on regular gasoline if need be. Plus, in the event of an accident or leak, natural gas dissipates into the air, whereas gasoline and diesel pool on the ground, creating a fire hazard.

Some well-known environmental activists have embraced natural gas as a way to slow adverse climate change. Take, for example, Carl Pope, the executive director of the Sierra Club, the oldest and largest grassroots environmental organization in the country. He views natural gas as a good *"bridge fuel"* to help the U.S. burn less coal and oil until renewable sources of energy are ready to take over. Some municipalities are also getting in on the act. Cities like New York, Los Angeles and Atlanta have converted portions of their bus fleets to run on natural gas and the private market is also responding. Of the 372 power plants expected to be built in America over the next three years, 206 will be fired by gas and just 31 by coal. Plus, AT&T has launched a $350 million purchase of natural gas powered vehicles to add to its fleet.

Pickens also endorsed the use of wind power as a renewable source of energy to help reduce our dependence on petroleum. When oil was over $140 a barrel, the wind energy, well, caught the wind of public opinion and was flying high. But as soon as oil prices fell, so did the public's enthusiasm about wind energy and the proposals have languished in the energy mire, so to speak. Our haste may make waste - of a good alternative, that is. Europe has been on the wind bend for 10 years and it is starting to pay dividends. Last year, for the second year in a row, more wind capacity was installed in the European Union than any other power source. 39% of all new electricity capacity installed in the EU last year was wind power. Wind power now accounts for almost 10% of total installed power capacity in the EU, up from less than 2% in 2000, and many experts are predicting that wind power will satisfy 50% or more of the EU's total electricity needs by 2050. Additionally, wind-generated power produces negligible carbon dioxide emissions and, according to several studies, has significantly reduced the price of electricity to many consumers in Europe (and you can also add Texas to that list in the United States).

And now we come to the presidential proposal which has turned into something of a fiasco for the administration… I am speaking here of the "cap and trade" plan put forth by the administration. First let me take this opportunity to give a quick overview of Cap and Trade.

The goal of the plan is to reduce carbon dioxide and other greenhouse gas emissions economy-wide in a cost-effective manner over a period of years. The cap is as follows: Each large-scale carbon emitter, or company, will face a limit on the amount of greenhouse gas that it can emit. The firm must have an "emissions permit" for every ton of carbon dioxide it releases into the atmosphere. These permits set an enforceable limit, or cap, on the amount of greenhouse gas pollution that the company is allowed to discharge. Over time, the limits become stricter, allowing less and less pollution, until the ultimate reduction goal is met. This is similar to the cap and trade program enacted by the Clean Air Act of 1990, which reduced the sulfur emissions that cause acid rain (and at a much lower cost than industry or government predicted.

The trade is as follows: It will be relatively cheaper or easier for some companies to reduce their emissions below their required limit than others. These more efficient companies, who emit less than their allowances, can sell their extra permits to companies that are not able to make reductions as easily. This should create a system that guarantees a set level of overall reductions, while rewarding the most efficient companies and ensuring that the cap can be met at the lowest possible cost to the economy.

The President's proposal was passed by the House of Representatives last year. But the 219-212 victory for President Obama was a narrow one in which many Democrats defected to the Republican side. And most Washington observers now agree that passage in the Senate this year is unlikely, a prediction Obama begrudgingly admitted is probably accurate. The complex bill passed by the House, a 1200+ page document, mandates a 17% cut in greenhouse gas emissions by 2020, and a reduction of 83% by 2050. It mandates that 20% of electricity come from renewable sources and increased energy efficiency by 2020. And the legislation gives electric utilities, coal plants, energy-intensive manufacturers, farmers, petroleum refiners, and other industries special protections to help them transition to new, less-fossil fuel-intensive ways of doing business. But the real fly in the ointment is this: the cap and trade law would cost American taxpayers up to $200 billion a year ($1761 per household), the equivalent of hiking personal income taxes by about 15%, according to an analysis prepared by the Executive Branch's own U.S. Department of Treasury.

Of late, President Obama seems far less troubled by the prospects of his "cap and trade" measure going down to defeat in the Senate. Why? Because he has apparently decided to do an "end run" by having the Environmental Protection Agency issue old-fashioned command and control regulations for global warming gases. The Supreme Court has already ruled that carbon dioxide can be regulated as an air pollutant under the Clean Air Act, so the only thing that could prevent the EPA from handing down strict carbon emission restrictions would be Congress preempting the EPA by passing new climate legislation to amend the Clean Air Act to proscribe the EPA's powers. That would require a veto-proof (2/3) majority of both the House and Senate to prevail. And we all know that is not going to happen.

Finally, what about the multitude of green energy jobs the President promised? Sadly, the overwhelming majority of stimulus money spent on his highly-touted wind power has gone to foreign companies, according to a 2010 report by the Investigative Reporting Workshop at the American University's School of Communication in Washington, D.C.

Nearly $2 billion in money from the American Recovery and Reinvestment Act has been spent on wind power over the last year, funding the creation of enough new wind farms to power 2.4 million homes. But guess what? Eighty percent of that money, according to the study, went to foreign manufacturers of wind turbines and "most of the jobs are also overseas," according to Russ Choma at the Investigative Reporting Workshop. He analyzed the foreign firms who had accepted the most stimulus money and concluded: *"According to our estimates, about 6,000 jobs have been created overseas, and maybe a couple hundred have been created in the U.S."* Ouch.

So now you can see the reasons for the low grade we had to give Obama on his energy "course" (of action). And we are far from alone in our assessment. Thomas Pyle, president of the Institute for Energy Research, a 20-year old public foundation that conducts research and analysis on the functions, operations, and government regulation of global energy markets, gave this description of our current national energy positions: *"When it comes to paving the way for the responsible development of homegrown, job-creating energy resources, no administration in history has done more to ensure producers do less."*

Now, unfortunately, we are going to have to lower the President's grade even more due to the woeful government response to the BP oil disaster. The Government did too little, too late and, worse, took BP at its word in its grossly erroneous estimates of the size of the spill (in actuality the rate of the spill was, right from the beginning, about 20 or so times greater than BP's knowingly false claims of 1000 barrels per day) and its early predictions that the spill would have minimal environmental impact on the Gulf Coast and would be contained in relatively short order. However, it took BP 85 days to get a temporary cap which may stop the leak until the claimed permanent fix of relief wells are brought on line. And during that time, 185 billion gallons of oil has been spilled, almost 18 times the amount of the *Exxon Valdez* disaster.

Regrettable, the federal government failed to act in a timely manner on the State of Louisiana's plans for building multiple lines of defense (barriers) to the huge volumes of oil threatening its marshes and the beaches. The response of the federal government to the worst environmental disaster in American history was, well, nothing short of "obamanable." And even if the leak is stopped permanently, the electorate is likely to remember the debacle at the polls, proving costly to the President, if not the entire Democratic Party, in the 2012 elections.

Now, moving on, you have to ask, what really does the Department of Energy do? When you boil its functions down to their essence, they monitor the power grid (poorly), a petroleum reserve (inadequate), nuclear weapons and power plants (redundant and unnecessary), fossil fuels (poorly), alternative energy programs (poorly) and statistics gathering (redundant with other agencies).

The management of the power grid could be transferred to a private group headed by electrical power utilities, answerable to the Army Corp of Engineers. A private sector organization then could prevail upon the financial markets to raise enough capital to update the grid and pass the increased costs to its users, like a free market is supposed to do. This would create jobs, vastly improve our infrastructure, be done at a fraction of the amount the government will charge, and would be finished in far less time than would be the case with the government running the show. In energy, as with other government programs (except more so), projects invariably take twice as long and cost twice as much as private industry.

All this being said, we do not disagree with the thesis that we, as a nation, ought to wean ourselves from the use of crude oil (40% of our total energy consumption comes from petroleum), not only because of the foreign producer relationships (we import 60% of our oil), but also in order to reduce the negative effect of green house gases in our atmosphere. The oil companies have done their dead level best (in concert with the auto manufacturers) to keep us hooked on the use of crude oil and gasoline by manipulating the price structure and the convenience aspects and giving us a (false) expectation of perpetually low to moderate prices at the pump. The oil suppliers know their limits in setting prices (the auto companies, at least in this country, did not). They realize that, if prices and profits get too high too quickly, as they did in 2008, the masses become disgruntled, which could escalate to outrage. Democrats started talking about reinstating some sort of windfall profits tax, and then, mysteriously (not) shortly thereafter, prices started to drop. Lengthen your stroll down memory lane a bit and you will see this happening time after time.

Think about it, oil suppliers seek to keep the price at a level just low enough to keep the alternative energy wolves away from their doors, but high enough for them to keep raking in big profits. And they have a potent lobby to make sure they do not get hammered too badly with legislation or regulation. Look at Exxon -- in 2008, it generated over $400 billion in revenues and earned a profit of over $40 billion dollars, the most in history by any public company and yet it paid no corporate income tax!

One last point regarding crude oil and the financial markets. We all recall vividly the price of crude shooting to $150 a barrel and gasoline hovering around $4.00 a gallon (more in California). And many of us came to understand and realize that this spike was an example of commodity market manipulation. But you may ask, weren't energy futures regulated by the Commodity Futures

Trading Commission (CFTC), the commodities counterpart to the SEC? Yes and no. Yes, the CFTC was supposed to have oversight over energy futures manipulation. No, it took no action by claiming that the activity was "orderly" during the price escalation and that it had no regulatory authority over derivative trades and speculative trading due to Congressional legislation in 2002 spearheaded by former Texas senator, Phil Gramm (and aptly named the "Enron Loophole").

To add insult to injury, the trading was led by commodity trading desks operating from the major banks and brokerage houses, such as Bank of America, Citibank, Goldman Sachs, JP Morgan and Morgan Stanley (the "usual suspects"), plus a multitude of hedge funds, endowment, pension and retirement funds, among others. They all feasted on the speculative run up in crude prices, as did our oil-producing adversaries such as Venezuela and Iran. Some argued that the price increase was driven purely by the traditional market law of supply and demand - - i.e., the demand for oil outpaced the supply and therefore, quite naturally, the price moved up. We say "Baloney." The statistical evidence just does not support this rationale. So, then, if not supply and demand, what fueled the fuel price run up? The same *non sanctum tripéctorus* (unholy trinity) that worked its dark magic on the financial industry -- greed, speculation and the government's blind eye.

Of course we cannot close a chapter on energy without making a few more observations regarding the catastrophe in the Gulf. We cannot add much to the 24/7 news coverage of that unmitigated disaster, and the White House's "too little too late" reaction – shades of Hurricane Katrina, for goodness sake (although there is nothing "good" about it at present, especially when you consider that more than 3 million barrels or 12 times the *Exxon Valdez* spill had flowed into the Gulf by the end of June). If any good might come from this tragedy of epic proportions, it would be America going into an intensive oil addiction rehab program and drastically reducing its dependence on petroleum. We know that is much easier said than done, but perhaps the BP oil spill could become the straw that begins to break the OPEC camel's back.

And while we're on the subject, we know BP's highly publicized original "top kill" plan didn't work, but we believe another "top kill" plan should be implemented -- one in which the top brass from BP and Transocean Ltd. are, well, you can fill in the blank. Not literally killed, of course -- we are not the People's Republic of China, at least not yet (you may recall the Chinese Government's execution last year of two food company officials and its imprisonment of 19 others over violations of safety standards resulting in the production of tainted milk that made thousands of Chinese babies sick). Nevertheless, we could, through aggressive civil enforcement and criminal actions, terminate the top officials "corporately" by making sure they have to step down from their current positions and can never again serve as executives of any public company operating in the United States. Now that would send a message that would reverberate through a lot of corporate boardrooms around the world!

Furthermore, if the federal government can indict and convict them for criminal violations of environmental and safety laws, they would suffer what is known in the law as "civil death" -- the forfeiture of civil rights and privileges stemming from a felony conviction, certainly during, but also after, incarceration. And finding them guilty of criminal violations is not far-fetched, especially when you examine BP's track record and find that it and its management have been far and away the oil industry's worst repeat offenders of safety and environmental regulations. In fact, Jeanne Pascal, a former EPA attorney who led many of that agency's investigations of BP during her 18 years with the EPA, had this to say about BP: *"They are a recurring environmental criminal and they do not follow U.S. health safety and environmental policy."* Scott West, the EPA agent in charge of the criminal investigation division that investigated BP's miscues in Alaska agrees: *"They are criminals -- they have been convicted of several environmental crimes. They are serial environmental criminals, and that phrase comes out of the mouth of a federal prosecutor."* As a matter of fact, over the past few years, BP has been convicted of two felonies and one misdemeanor and paid over $730 million in fines and settlements for safety and environmental violations and manipulation of energy markets. Two of BP's refineries accounted for 97% of all flagrant violations in the refining industry over the past three years (an astounding 767 *"egregiously willful"* violations, according to OSHA). Although isolated violations may not create felonious conduct, persistent, deliberate violations over a period of many years can easily constitute a pattern and practice of unlawful activity and an institutional disregard for law which can in turn cause even the most senior management to face criminal charges. BP, good luck with all that!

A recent footnote worth mentioning is the rejection by Anadarko Petroleum Company, a 25% owner of the Deepwater Horizon operation, of BP's demands for it to share in the costs of the oil spill clean-up and containment, claiming that BP must take total responsibility for the disaster due to its "gross negligence or willful misconduct" during the drilling of the leaking well, according to Anadarko's CEO Jim Hackett. This may well be a little of the pot calling the kettle black, but it is nonetheless a rather scathing indictment by a fellow member of the petroleum industry and former BP partner.

Oh and one more black mark for BP has recently surfaced which suggests BP might have more than drilling mud – would you believe blood – on its unclean hands. The once proud company is now being accused by some United States Senators of having played a pivotal role in the release of the Lockerbie Bomber in order to secure a large drilling contract from the Libyan government from which BP could earn as much as $20 billion. Many of you will recall the early release from a prison in Scotland last year of Abdel Basset al-Megrahi, the notorious Libyan intelligence agent convicted of the heinous bombing of Pan Am Flight 103 in 1988 which killed 270 passengers, including 189

Americans. We find it a wee bit more than coincidental that BP signed the petroleum exploration memorandum with Libya in May 2007, the very same month that Britain and Libya inked a memorandum of understanding that paved the way for the bomber's peremptory release from prison to be hailed as a hero upon his return to Libya. There's a back room deal that will forever live in infamy, perhaps thanks in large measure to BP's behind the scenes work.

Finally, just as we were going to press, we learned that the once somewhat obscure, but now widely infamous Tony Hayward has tendered his "forced resignation" and is being banished to the wilds of Siberia – quite literally, as he will be working for BP's Russian joint venture whose operations are concentrated in Siberia. Continuing the thread from the "top kill" discussion above, we might look upon this "removal" from office as some form of board-assisted corporate euthanasia ("mercy killing", as it were), the "mercy" part coming from the benevolence of his fairly generous (all things considered) severance package. Of course, it may also be looked upon as the converse to the old saying that *"no good deed goes unpunished"* and reflect instead the new saying, at least in the world of big oil that *"no bad deed goes unrewarded."*

Well, now, we do have a really radical idea for an alternative energy source – how about we anchor a barge in the waters off the Gulf Coast and have round-the-clock political speeches, starting with President Obama and Vice President Biden, then the 15 executive department heads who make up the President's Cabinet, followed by Ben Bernanke and a few of his best Fed buddies, then White House Chief of Staff Rahm Emanuel and White House Press Secretary Robert Gibbs, followed by the members of the Senate and the members of the House (save those few who honestly believe in serving the public trust and deserve in return the trust of the public), then the chairmen of the Republican and Democratic parties, then the "talking heads" of the broadcast media, followed by the Big Oil executives, and last but far from least the magnates of Wall Street. By our reckoning, such an event should produce enough wind power and hot air to satisfy the energy needs of a few million households for many months, maybe a year.

Sadly, wee are now out of "energy" ourselves and so it is time to again find respite in sleep. We can only hope we do not dream tonight about the mess our lawmakers and "trusted" leaders have brought upon us as a nation, from energy and environmental perspectives. The more we study and learn, the more we come to understand how being disaffected leads to despair at first, only to be replaced by becoming engaged -- by going from passivist to activist. Our own history should teach those in power that power is fleeting and relies ultimately upon the support of the governed, not their alienation (think about that term because that is exactly what our leaders have made us into, as compared with our beginnings - an alien nation!

And so we close this Chapter with the same phrase we used at the end of Chapter 10, but this time it has even more significance in the context of energy policy -- *"Power to the People"*!

CHAPTER 13

HOUSING
'Please Come to Our House *Warning* Party'

"No real estate is permanently valuable but the grave."
- Mark Twain

"The basic point is that the recession of 2001 ... was a prewar-style recession, a morning after brought on by irrational exuberance. To fight this recession, the Fed needs more than a snapback; it needs soaring household spending to offset moribund business; it needs investment. And to do that ... Alan Greenspan needs to create a housing bubble. To be honest, a new bubble now would help us out a lot even if we paid for it later. This is a really good time for a bubble... There was a headline in a satirical newspaper in the U.S. last summer that said: 'The nation demands a new bubble to invest in.' And that's pretty much right."
- Dr. Paul Krugman, winner of Nobel Prize in Economics, from his pre-bubble 2005 commentary

We just got back from a conference in Atlanta where the Federal Reserve was the main topic and listened to a discussion regarding the monetary decisions taken by Alan Greenspan and Ben Bernanke, the dynamic duo, beginning in 2003 and continuing through today. Both have adamantly and repeatedly denied charges that the Fed caused or was even a factor in the housing bubble. However, the vast majority of the persons in attendance at the conference were not buying the Kool-Aid they have been selling. In all honesty, "plausible deniability" is misplaced when it comes to the Fed's role in the creation and subsequent puncture of the housing bubble.

The Fed is uncanny in its ability to engage in revisionist history and is always defiant in defending it actions (or inactions, as the case may be). Audacity is never in short supply at the Fed. Ben Bernanke claims that it was flawed mortgage underwriting that allowed the housing and mortgage markets to get out of control. Greenspan claimed in a television interview last year that the Fed did not dictate the artificially low mortgage rates and that, therefore, he and the Fed "had little or nothing to do with the housing bubble or credit crisis." Yes, and as everybody knows, Hitler had little or nothing to do with World War II.

The case against the Fed is pretty much ironclad: in an attempt to fast forward the economy out of the 2001 recession, Greenspan slashed the federal funds target from 6.5% in January 2001 down to a ridiculously low 1% by June 2003. Then, after holding rates at 1% for a year, the Fed steadily raised them back up to 5.25% by June 2006 (apparently he heeded the words of Paul Krugman quoted at the beginning of this Chapter all too well). The connection between these moves by the central bank, first pumping and then popping the housing bubble, are surely more than just coincidence. To the contrary, it looks a whole lot more like the classic theory of using monetary policy in the form of artificially low interest rates to stimulate investment and the economy, followed by an overheating (i.e., inflationary pressures) which in turn requires a recession as a corrective measure. The Fed always believes it can apply the brakes to bring about a "soft landing," but it almost never does. In addition, in this case, Greenspan (and later Bernanke) facilitated a "crash landing" (maybe they were driving one of those defective Toyotas).

Greenspan also added a great deal more fuel to the fire when, in 2004, he encouraged the use of adjustable rate mortgages, then in 2005, endorsed subprime loans to help marginal buyers get into houses (while, all along the way, rejecting out of hand calls for more oversight of the exploding mortgage markets and ridiculing those calling for oversight). Moreover, Greenspan apparently failed to recognize signs of the housing bubble in 2005, when he told Congress that a national housing bubble did not "appear likely," concluding that there was at most a little "froth" in local markets.

And Ben Bernanke was no better in his (mis)assessment of the situation. In testimony before Congress in 2005, just a few days before President Bush nominated him for the chairmanship of the Federal Reserve, Bernanke (then chairman of the President's Council of Economic Advisors) stated that he did not think the national housing boom was a bubble that was about to burst. Quite to the contrary, he testified that the two-year run up in housing prices by almost 25% was not indicative of a bubble but rather was a reflection of "strong economic fundamentals," such as major growth in jobs, incomes and the number of new households. Even as late as 2007, Bernanke showed himself out of touch with the ramifications of the housing debacle by declaring that *"we see no serious broad spillover to banks or thrift institutions from the problems in the subprime market."* Later of course, the spillover he did not see had become a full-fledged flood and he was forced to admit (grudgingly) that there was more of a housing bubble than he realized. However, to this day, he still stubbornly refuses to admit the Fed contributed in any way, shape or form to that bubble or its subsequent sudden puncture -- never let the facts get in the way of a good story!

Now there are, to be sure, plenty of other villains to castigate and be *Fed* up with. We have already identified the Fed as a facilitator and enabler of the housing boom and bust. But there is also "Fed No. 2," the Federal Government. One of the "bad actors" in the housing scene that played such a prominent role in the financial drama (some might say tragedy) was the Department of Housing and Urban Development, operating in accordance with the dictates of the White House. In a personal letter to Ben

Bernanke dated January 26, 2010 from Dr. Joseph R. Mason, Associate Professor of Finance at Drexel University's LeBow College of Business, a Senior Fellow at the Wharton School and former financial economist with the Office of the Comptroller of the Currency and Adjunct Assistant Professor of Finance at Georgetown University School of Business, Dr. Mason attributes part of the blame for the housing bubble to:

> *"...the National Homeownership Strategy [launched by HUD under Bill Clinton, and continued and expanded under George W. Bush] that tried to achieve record high homeownership rates by pushing homes on people who 'lack... cash available to accumulate the required down payment and closing costs,' or 'do not have sufficient available income to make the monthly* payments *on mortgages financed at market interest rates for standard loan terms.'*

> *...the Strategy's unbridled pursuit of 'Financing strategies,' fueled by the creativity and resources of the private and public sectors, to address both of these financial barriers to homeownership,' actively promoted the practices that expanded poor mortgage underwriting and servicing practices to those that contributed to the [housing] crisis."*

Far more damning of the Federal Government's role in the housing disaster and the resulting financial market meltdown is November 2008 commentary by Peter J. Wallison, a Harvard Law graduate, Arthur F. Burns Fellow in Financial Policy Studies at the American Enterprise Institute for Public policy Research, and a widely recognized specialist in financial markets deregulation:

> *"Many culprits have been brought before the bar of public humiliation as the malefactors of the current crisis -- unscrupulous mortgage brokers, greedy investment bankers, incompetent rating agencies, foolish investors, and whiz-kid inventors of complex derivatives. All of these people and institutions played their part, of course, but it seems unfair to*

blame them for doing what the government policies were designed to encourage. Thus, the crisis would not have become so extensive and intractable had the U.S. government not created the necessary conditions for a housing boom by directing investments into the housing sector, requiring banks to make mortgage loans they otherwise would never have made, requiring the GSEs [Government Sponsored Enterprises, mainly Fannie Mae and Freddie Mac] to purchase the secondary mortgage market loans they would never otherwise have bought, encouraging underwriting standards for housing that were lower than for any other area of the economy, adopting bank regulatory capital standards that encourage bank lending for housing in preference to other lending, and adopting tax policies that favored borrowing against (and thus reducing) the equity in a home.

Expansion of homeownership could be a sound policy, especially for low-income families and members of minority groups. The social benefits of homeownership have been extensively documented; they include stable families and neighborhoods, reduced crime and delinquency, higher living standards, and less depreciation in the housing stock. Under these circumstances, the policy question is not whether homeownership should be encouraged but how the government ought to do it. In the United States, the policy has not been pursued directly -- through taxpayer-supported programs and appropriated funds -- but rather through manipulation of the credit system to force more lending in support of affordable housing. Instead of a direct government subsidy, say, for down-payment assistance for low-income families, the government has used regulatory and political pressure to force banks and other government-controlled or regulated private entities to make loans they would not otherwise make and to reduce lending standards so more applicants would have access to mortgage financing."

That sums it up quite nicely, we believe (although we should probably be reluctant to use "nice" in connection with this assessment).

Now then, we come to the third of the great "Fedocracy," the notorious Federal Government Sponsored Enterprises or GSEs as they have come to be known. They were set up under the 1992 Federal Housing Enterprises Financial Safety and Soundness Act, also known as the Federal GSE Act. Pursuant to that Act's "affordable housing" requirements, Fannie Mae and Freddie Mac acquired more than $6 trillion of single-family loans over the subsequent 16 years (more than half of the entire domestic mortgage market), many of which proved to be "bad" loans (i.e., became seriously delinquent and on the way to or into default), leading to their being taken over (placed in conservatorship) by the United States Treasury Department in September 2008. The Fannie and Freddie bailout may ultimately prove to be the costliest of all, thus eventually awarding it the ignominious distinction of being the "granddaddy of all bailouts."

After all, to date, we the taxpayers have covered over $130 billion of losses for these two wards of the state. When the government first took over Fannie and Freddie, then Treasury Secretary Hank Paulson capped taxpayer aid at $200 billion ($100 billion for each). However, Paulson's successor, Timothy Geithner, raised the cap to $400 billion total. And then all bets were off, as it were, in December 2009, when Congress, at the behest of Geithner and Obama, removed the cap entirely, giving Freddie and Fannie a blank check to draw on taxpayer monies. That does not necessarily mean the sky is the limit, but pretty close -- even the Congressional Budget Office estimated that Fannie and Freddie added $291 billion to the federal deficit in 2009 and will cost an additional $389 billion to run over the next ten years, for a total of $680 billion. That's without taking into account those agencies, with the inexplicable blessings of Fed 1 and Fed 2, traveling right back down the same subprime, lax underwriting standards, "no too low (3.5% for FHA loans) down payment" road, ignoring yet again the flashing signs all along the road warning "road closed for repairs," "bridge out ahead," "stop" and "turn back now." And to make matters worse, they are trying to hide the ball from us once again by considering these costs of Fannie and Freddie "off budget" items, meaning the actual cost to run these agencies is not considered by or under the purview of the Office of Management and Budget. Are you kidding me?

We have all seen this movie before and sadly, we know how it ends -- badly -- so why are the powers that be filming a remake with the same cast, same directors, same producers, and same script? We guess because they can and they know they can and they do not care about the reviews of the critics or even the viewers at large, us. Moreover, all-too-recent history shows that they will ignore all warnings with complete impunity, expecting complete immunity. How do we know for sure we are heading "back to the future"? First, a August 2008 *New York Times* article reported that, all the way back in 2003, Richard Synon, the CEO of Freddie Mac, received a memorandum from David Andrukonis, Freddie's Chief Risk Officer, warning that Freddie Mac was financing *boatloads* of loans that *"would likely pose an enormous financial and reputation risk to the company and the country."* According to the article, more than two dozen high-ranking executives with Freddie and Fannie simply decided to ignore the warnings.

And everyone was simply oblivious to the "spot on" concerns expressed in September 2003 by Representative Ron Paul (R-TX) before the House Financial Services Committee, of which he was then (and remains today) a member:

> *"One of the major government privileges granted to GSEs is a line of credit with the United States Treasury. According to some estimates, the line of credit may be worth over $2 billion [quite a paltry sum compared with the $130 billion already drawn down today and another $500 billion expected to be needed]. This explicit promise by the Treasury to bail out GSEs in times of economic difficulty*

helps the GSEs attract investors who are willing to settle for lower yields than they would demand in the absence of the subsidy. Thus, the line of credit distorts the allocation of capital. More importantly, the line of credit is a promise on behalf of the government to engage in a huge unconstitutional and immoral income transfer from working Americans to holders of GSE debt. The Free Housing Market Enhancement Act also repeals the explicit grant of legal authority given to the Federal Reserve to purchase GSE debt. GSEs are the only institutions besides the United States Treasury granted explicit statutory authority to monetize their debt through the Federal Reserve. This provision gives the GSEs a source of liquidity unavailable to their competitors.

The connection between the GSEs and the government helps isolate the GSE management from market discipline. This isolation from market discipline is the root cause of the recent reports of mismanagement occurring at Fannie and Freddie. After all, if the federal government did not underwrite Fannie and Freddie, investors would demand Fannie and Freddie provide assurance that they follow accepted management and accounting practices.

Ironically, by transferring the risk of a widespread mortgage default, the government increases the likelihood of a painful crash in the housing market. This is because the special privileges granted to Fannie and Freddie has distorted the housing market by allowing them to attract capital they could not attract under pure market conditions. As a result, capital is diverted from its most productive use into housing. This reduces the efficacy of the entire market and thus reduces the standard of living of all Americans.

Despite the long-term damage to the economy inflicted by the government's interference in the housing market, the government's policy of diverting capital to other uses creates a short-term boom in housing. Like all artificially created bubbles, the boom in housing prices cannot last forever. When housing prices fall, homeowners will have trouble as their equity is wiped out. Furthermore, the holders of the mortgage debt will also have a loss. These losses will be greater than they would have otherwise been had government policy not actively encouraged over-investment in housing."

A prescient assessment, indeed, as all of us would learn just a few short years later, but Representative Paul was derided at the time as a "spoiled sport" and the mortgage industry and the "asleep at the wheel" mortgage regulators thumbed their noses at him and went right along with their "let the good times roll" mentality (and roll they did until, that is, they slammed into the wall at breakneck speed, taking us right along with them as unwitting passengers).

Other cautionary notes were sounded even earlier -- for example, in 2001, the late Federal Reserve governor Edward Gramlich warned of the risks associated with the rapidly growing subprime market. He later charged openly that Alan Greenspan not only failed to heed his warnings and similar concerns expressed by others, but went so far as to actively block all efforts to corral the rampant predatory lending practices.

Then, in June 2005, *The Economist* magazine gave its readers a dire prediction that also went largely ignored:

"The worldwide rise in house prices are the biggest bubble in history. Prepare for the economic pain when it pops."

Then there was this blunt assessment given in 2005 by Robert Kiyosaki, author of the best-selling *Rich Dad, Poor Dad* series of motivational books and CDs, in words so simple that even a cave dweller (or Congressman) could understand them:

"Lately, I have been asked if we are in a real estate bubble. My answer is, 'Duh.' In my opinion, this is the

biggest real estate bubble I have ever lived through. Next, I am asked, 'Will the bubble burst?' Again, my answer is 'Duh!'

The reason I write this alert is because this time, when the bubble bursts, I think it will be a monster. Never in my life have I seen so much money being made on such weak fundamentals. If you think the last recession caused by the bubble bust was bad, the coming recession will be at least twice as bad. It might lead to a depression."

Now surely you say we have contained the degree of potential damage from these agencies gone wild, right. Nope. Talk about "agencies gone wild" or "when agencies go bad," the sheer magnitude of the numbers is numbing and should make everyone afraid, very afraid. Today, Fannie Mae and Freddie Mac are by far the biggest U.S. borrowers after the federal government. In addition to $1.7 trillion in unsecured corporate debt, the companies have $5.4 trillion in mortgage bonds, for a total of $7.1 trillion, according to an analysis done by **Bloomberg** in March of this year... By way of comparison, $7.1 trillion is more, by over 40%, than the GDPs of the second and third largest national GDPs in the world, those of Japan and China, and is almost half the entire GDP of the country with the largest GDP, the United States of America. A take your breath away amount in anybody's book and it is still growing with no end in sight. If you add in the $1.25 trillion of mortgage-backed bonds owned by Fed No. 1, you get to a daunting $8.35 trillion, more than $26,000 for each and every man, woman and child in America.

The three "Feds" composing the "Fedocracy" were of course not the only stars in the housing and credit drama (tragedy). Other leading roles were played by the mortgage brokers with their predatory lending practices, the banks and other lending institutions with their lax underwriting standards and inadequate risk management policies, Wall Street firms and hedge funds with their opaque, complex and speculative mortgage-backed securities and other financial derivatives, and the rating agencies with their grossly deficient due diligence, and the homebuilders with their excessive overbuilding and aggressive marketing campaigns.

And last but not least is of course the man and woman in the mirror -- that would be the homeowners with their prodigious overleveraging -- buying far more home (and homes) than we could realistically afford (the average new home size in America in 2006 and 2007 ballooned to a record 2,600 square feet, an 86% increase from 1970, and downright *mansionesque* as compared with Canada at 1,350 square feet, Japan at 1,300 square feet and most of Europe at just over 1,000 square feet) and using refinancing and home equity lines to supply funds to satisfy our consumption binge or pay down high interest credit cards which we had already maxed out to satisfy our consumption binge (the statistics speak volumes -- cash used by consumers from home equity extraction more than doubled from $627 billion in 2001 to over $1.4 trillion in 2005 as the housing bubble grew). WE speak from painful personal knowledge here for we too are part of that community of former homeowners who refinanced ourselves right into foreclosure by going with the seductive easy affordability, "teaser" rates on adjustable mortgages that soon after became not so affordable when the reset button got pushed on the third anniversary date. So we have seen the face of one of the "enemies" on the financial front-line and, much to our chagrin, it was ours.

Now many in government and in private industry are saying the worst of the housing crisis is over. Try telling that to the record 2.8 million homeowners who faced foreclosure in 2009 or the 3 million homeowners facing foreclosure this year. And try telling that to the 11.3 million homeowners (one in four) who today are "underwater" or "upside down" on their mortgages (owe more than their homes are worth) -- with aggregate negative equity a staggering $1 trillion. And try telling that to the owners of the 60 million homes that have declined in value over the past 30 months by more than $5 trillion. And try telling that to families who need to sell their homes but are already hampered by competition from foreclosures on the market, a situation which will worsen as the "shadow inventory" of bank-repossessed homes and soon-to-be repossessed homes begin to hit the market like a tidal wave of Biblical proportions -- according to a March 12, 2010 report in the *Washington Post* entitled *New Round of Foreclosures Threatens the Housing Market,* "*5 million to 7 million properties are potentially eligible for foreclosure but have not yet been repossessed and put up for sale ... as these foreclosed properties add to the supply of homes for sale, they could undercut housing prices.*"

We also wonder how those "experts" who would have us believe the housing crisis is "under control" reconcile that assessment with the record low for new home sales in May.

To recapitulate, the housing implosion was the result of too much money too readily available pushing real estate prices too high too fast. And when the inevitable happened -- too many delinquencies, too many defaults and too few new buyers -- the walls came tumbling down. Everybody, from the home builder to the mortgage broker to the mortgage lender to the Wall Street financier to the rating agency to the hedge fund operator to the buyer of the mortgage securities to the homeowner, was raking in money hand over fist, but the frenzy could continue only so long as real estate values continued to defy the laws of gravity. Just as in the 1637 Tulip Mania collapse, in 2007, not enough buyers remained to pay the grotesquely inflated selling prices and the buyers who had sated themselves with mortgage indebtedness began to retch uncontrollably. Consequently, residential real estate prices began to decline, and then the door was not nearly wide enough to accommodate the stampede of sellers who attempted to unload their overpriced properties, the same properties that they were convinced could only go higher in price just a few months before, leading to a free fall in prices and a downward death spiral ensued.

However, the bankers and brokerage house executives had their fail-safe weaponry: Congress and the Bush administration. So who was their Superhero who would arrive on the scene just in time to save the day? None other than Henry (Hank) Paulson, Treasury Secretary and former CEO of Goldman Sachs. And what was his Superpower? A massive, unprecedented bailout plan. He gave it a fancy government name, the Troubled Asset Relief Program (TARP), and the Treasury, in concert with the Fed, worked fervently to create a scheme purportedly designed to save the country from financial collapse, but primarily to rescue their Wall Street buddies. Some failed to make it, such as Lehman Brothers, Bear Stearns, Wachovia Bank, Washington Mutual and Indy Mac (acceptable casualties for the "greater good"). A total of 40 banks and credit unions failed in 2008. Nevertheless, Congress rushed recklessly to approve the plan and provided $787 billion dollars of taxpayer relief to save private sector firms from their own greed, stupidity and irresponsibility.

The supporters of the plan convinced the world that, without TARP, the financial world as we knew it would crash and burn. Banks would close, checks could not be cashed, the ATM machines would be empty and panic and chaos would reign supreme in every nook and cranny in the land. The message was that, without TARP, we would be entering the *"End of Days"* (they called it *"catastrophic systemic failure"*). So they reached deep into our pocketbooks and pockets and enlisted the aid of the Fed and purchased many billions of dollars of non-performing ("bad") loans to save those *"too big to fail."* It may be the end of the world as they knew it, but they felt fine, yes, they felt (and came out of it feeling) just fine.

In this Chapter, we have attempted to demonstrate how the system failed us and how we failed ourselves with regard to the housing and credit debacle. Some readers will think that we are being overly critical or overly cynical (though sometimes we wonder if it is possible to be either, given the data). Nevertheless, our intentions are to inform and attempt to encourage the citizenry to understand its options. And we do have options. We do not have to sit idly by and do nothing if we disagree with the status quo. Our founding fathers certainly did not take a "wait and see" approach.

They had no such luxury and they knew it, so they put everything they owned, including their lives, on the line for their beliefs and for posterity. Don't we in turn owe posterity something better than the status quo?

When you're mulling over the points being discussed, remember not to forget that the proponents of the status quo and those who give but token dissent to the status quo (those who disingenuously *talk the talk* but do not *walk the walk*) have jobs, have not had their homes foreclosed, have not been forced to declare personal bankruptcy (unlike the more than 3,000,000 Americans who have gone into bankruptcy since the meltdown), and have not had their credit cards cancelled and lines of credit frozen or lost their life savings and retirement accounts. They have little or no appreciation for the genuine hardships that the disaffected majority is experiencing today in America. They say they sympathize, but they do not and cannot truly empathize. They would tell you they do, but they do not feel our pain, trust us. In fact, many of the proponents of the status quo characterize our woes as completely self-inflicted -- they claim that folks in financial distress have brought it on themselves by borrowing and consuming way, excessively much. Their view is "Hey, you made your beds, folks, now you need to lie in them" (well, one thing they do know all about is how to "lie").

Furthermore, they couldn't care less that our credit report scores have been ravaged and are now so low that many of us cannot get loans, cannot get insurance coverage at reasonable rates, are denied jobs, may be unable to have utilities turned on, and may be unable to rent a place in which to live. Their attitude is reminiscent of Ebenezer Scrooge's caustic rejection of the humble plea for alms for the poor and destitute. Mr. Scrooge suggested instead that those who are badly off should go to prisons and workhouses, which he supported financially. When told, *"Many can't go there, and many would rather die,"* Scrooge gave the classic response: *"If they would rather die, they had better do it and decrease the surplus population."* Well, that *"surplus population"* is growing daily and just might have the final word when all is said and done!

One final note worth mentioning: the commercial real estate bubble has yet to burst. A mortgage crisis like the one that has devastated homeowners is now beginning to envelop our office and retail markets. The residential foreclosure wave is soon going to swamp commercial properties across the country. According to Elizabeth Warren, Chairman of the TARP Congressional Oversight Panel, half of all commercial mortgages in this country coming due over the next three years will be underwater by the end of this year. That is over $700 billion in mortgage indebtedness. And Warren says commercial property values across the country have fallen more than 40% since the start of 2007. The long awaited other shoe may soon be dropping. Now that is a comforting thought for everyone who believed the worst was over!

Please be aware that what we see happening today in Greece and soon to happen in Portugal and Spain, regarding sovereign debt, may happen here as well. We have as much or more debt relative to GDP as the so-called PIGS (Portugal, Italy, Greece and Spain). And at least they are being forced to reduce their budget deficits to bring them into line with the EU mandate of no more than 3% of GDP (ours is approaching 4 times that). Perhaps we will be joining the PIGS and the new acronym will soon be US PIGS.

All then is not well on the home front, even if our stock market has reclaimed a major portion of its losses. Think of it this way, the Fed has a credit card with a credit limit. We are now at our spending limit and soon the Fed will be required to withdraw a material amount of the stimulus that it has pumped into the financial markets in hopes that it could jump-start the economy. So far, no good. In the meantime, the Administration has spent money it did not have as if there is no tomorrow. Unless we take action now to stop the madness there will not be a tomorrow with any degree of prosperity!

CHAPTER 14

CREDIT
'In God We Trust - All Others Pay Cash'

*"Beautiful credit! The foundation of modern society. Who shall
say that this is not the golden age of mutual trust, of unlimited
reliance upon human promises? That is a peculiar condition of
society, which enables a whole nation to instantly recognize point
and meaning in the familiar newspaper anecdote, which puts into
the mouth of a distinguished speculator in lands and mines this
remark: -- 'I wasn't worth a cent two years ago, and now I owe
two millions of dollars.'"*
- **Mark Twain**

*"I hate this shallow Americanism which hopes to get rich by
credit."*
- **Ralph Waldo Emerson**

The debate we have been watching on television now shifts to a
discussion on consumer credit in this country, which one of the
guest commentators refers to as the "mother's milk of capitalism."
Another guest commentator in a little box on the television screen
cuts off the first speaker and proclaims loudly and somewhat
proudly that "this milk has gone totally sour." A third "expert" on
the panel jumps in and opines that American consumers "simply
gorged themselves" on credit, bringing the "credit squeeze" on
themselves and now have to pay the price for the sin of gluttony.
The speaker in the fourth box on the screen responds with a tone of
indignation, accusing the banks and credit card companies of being

"credit traffickers" who encouraged the "credit binge" and actively fostered "credit addiction." She even goes so far as to suggest that the banks and credit card companies should have been forced to put warning labels on their "easy credit products," similar to the tobacco companies, to the effect that "consumer credit can be habit-forming" and "excessive use of credit can result in serious, even fatal, injury to your financial health and well-being." These comments trigger a mixture of loud cheers and jeers from her fellow experts on the panel.

Then the talk show host says the panel has to take a break, but they will be back for more "spirited debate" and the channel goes to a commercial. The commercial just happens to be a promo to tune in to *The Dave Ramsey Show* and learn how to get "debt free." Then the ad flashes to Dave Ramsey himself, one of the most popular self-help financial gurus on television and radio today and there is a clip of him saying to an audience:

> *"We are going to help you get out of debt and stay out of debt, but the first step you have to take is to put all of your credit cards on the table and take your scissors and literally cut them up and throw away the pieces."*

He tells us that using credit cards with all their fees and high interest rates and traps with so-called customer service is just stupid and will keep you in debt for as long as you live.

Then the channel switches to another commercial, an advertisement for a credit reduction and counseling service, with the announcer saying that his company has helped thousands of consumers get their credit card debt consolidated into one low monthly payment and stopped the annoying phone calls from creditors. He goes on to say that, his company will negotiate directly with the credit card companies and collection agencies to reduce your credit card debt by fifty percent and more. The ad closes with, "Call us right now to reduce or eliminate your debt. We will work for you to make your life easier." Our minds start turning and churning about this whole credit situation and the tremors still rumbling through our daily lives after the massive financial earthquake two years ago.

Well, for starters, the financial crisis did trigger the first reduction in consumer credit in 60 years, from $2.56 trillion in 2008 to $2.45 trillion in 2009, a decline of 4.2%. But consumer credit started inching up again at the beginning of 2010 and is now $2.5 trillion (excluding mortgage debt), about $8,100 for every man, woman and child in America (and the average credit card debt per household is almost double that, at $16,000). Even credit card debt, which declined $93 billion in 2009, or a whopping 9.3%, from $969 billion to $876 billion began rising again in February, after 16 straight months of declines. Moreover, those 16 consecutive monthly decreases were due far less to consumers paying down their credit card debt than simply walking away from it. In fact, only about $10 billion of the drop in 2009 (less than 11%) was due to payments -- the remaining $83 billion (almost 90%) came from charge-offs by the credit card issuers. And the bloodletting is not over for the credit card industry. *Moody's*, one of the leading credit rating firms (albeit one which freely grants credit grace to the federal government), expects credit card charge-offs to peak at close to 12% in 2010, eclipsing the earlier all-time high of 11.5% in August 2009.

How have the credit card companies responded to the situation? As you might expect, they have reduced available credit to consumers by over $1.6 trillion and tightened standards considerably on the issuance of new credit cards. In 2009, there was a reduction of new credit card accounts from 2008 of over 40%. And their rapid-fire delinquency reporting to the credit rating agencies has resulted in the average consumer credit score falling to an all-time low. According to recent statistics, almost 45 million American consumers now have credit scores below 600 (thanks not only to the Great Recession but also the frequently flawed and sometimes arbitrary and capricious reports of the credit bureaus), which makes it unlikely they can get credit cards, auto loans, bank loans or home mortgages (and some even jobs, given the growing number of employers who require credit checks for all job applicants).

How have we, the consumers, responded? Some of us have resorted to bankruptcy to wash out crushing debt. Some of us have hired credit reduction services to negotiate reduced payments. Some have cut up their credit cards and vowed never to use them again -- in fact, almost 30% of consumers surveyed last year confirmed a shift away from credit cards to debit cards, a move which many attributed to helping them control their spending; in addition, 2009 also witnessed a reduction of almost 50% in the number of credit cards held by the average consumer from a record nine cards in 2008 to five cards (which is still 3 or 4 too many) this year. An almost perverse result of a reduction in the use of credit cards is a greater difficulty in building a higher credit score. Debit cards do not help consumers' credit scores at all. Credit scores of consumers without a credit card are, on average, 126 points lower than consumers who have at least one card with a monthly balance. In effect, the credit card issuers have worked in concert with the consumer credit reporting agencies to penalize consumers who do not own or use credit cards.

Of course, any discussion of credit has to include mortgage credit. According to Freddie Mac, the total household mortgage debt in this country stands at approximately $11.8 trillion or about $153,000 for each of the approximately 77 million homeowners. The aggregate value of homes with mortgages is approximately $11.6 trillion, which means that the average home in America today has no or negative equity, a scary thought for those who were led to believe that the equity in their home would provide for their retirement. This is consistent with reports of 11.5 million homes now being underwater relative to their mortgages (i.e., mortgage debt exceeds fair market value). The amount of negative equity was in excess of $800 billion at the end of last year and may reach $1 trillion sometime this year. These numbers, astonishing in their own right, do not tell the completely sad story: on the foreclosure front, for example, there is a new foreclosure filing in America every 12-13 seconds, and delinquencies are running at about 10 percent.

And how have these problems affected housing-related credit (after all, the vast majority of folks must have a mortgage to be able to buy a home)? In today's housing market, the rules imposed for purchasing a home are radically different from the rules of just three years ago. Today, probably less than half of our working population can meet the stringent mortgage requirements mandated by the lenders. The point here is not that improved underwriting guidelines are not warranted; rather the revised guidelines have been instituted to limit who qualifies for a mortgage. According to many in the industry, the lenders have simply stepped back in time and re-imposed the standards that preceded the "easy money" days leading up to the housing debacle when "anyone who could fog a mirror" could get a mortgage and buy a house.

Not so today -- in order to qualify for a mortgage now, a successful applicant must have verifiable employment and income, his or her debt to income ratios must meet new lower standards, he or she must have a verifiable down payment (in many instances equal to 20% of the purchase price), appraisals are scrutinized like never before (no more "drive by" appraisals), and credit scores must meet higher standards. As late as 2008, a credit score of 680 was considered acceptable in order to qualify, whereas today the mid-score requirement has increased to 720 for most lenders and some lenders require 740 or 750 scores. Consider this in the context that a perfect credit score is supposedly 850 and the average score today is well under 650. Long gone are the days when the ability of the average person "on the street" (unless it is Wall Street) to qualify for a mortgage was relatively simple or easy.

Amazingly, as late as 2006, there were over 2,500 mortgage lenders operating throughout the country. Today, that number has been cut by more than 90%, to fewer than 200. And, of the 200 or so lenders still in operation, over half of the mortgages are being originated by less than 10% of the remaining lenders, primarily the big Wall Street banks, JP Morgan Chase, Bank of America, Citibank, and Wells Fargo. Now, what does all of this mean to Main Street America? Simply (and sadly) that most of us, for many years to come, will not be able to qualify for a new mortgage and thus will be out of the home buying market. Consider these sobering facts: if you have a foreclosure or short sale on your report, you will have to wait a minimum of 5 years before you can even be considered for a mortgage and if you have declared bankruptcy, your wait will be 5-7 years minimum.

Credit card defaults and delinquencies will so damage your credit score that you will be unable to qualify for a mortgage for years. And there are new "credit debilitating" repercussions from failing to make student loan payments and in having tax delinquencies. Any negative item on a credit report must now be addressed and rectified before a prospective borrower will be considered for a mortgage. Oh, and, lest we forget, today's loan requirements mandate a down payment in the 10-20% range, seller-assisted financing is frowned upon and frequently disallowed, and borrowed down payments from credit lines or family members are verboten with the exception of FHA loans that still allow the down-payment (3.50%) to be gifted from a non-profit organization for a fee. Undoubtedly, though, as more and more FHA loans become delinquent or are foreclosed this provision will also be eliminated. The trend is for borrowers to have more skin in the game (equity injection) in order to limit the number of walkways.

Why the abrupt change? In the first place, the securitization market that Wall Street created by which it bundled up mortgage loans and sold them off to pension funds, non-profits, foreign governments, bond funds, state and local governments, etc. is no longer functioning since the housing bubble popped and the subprime mortgage market melted down. Consequently, the only buyers of mortgage loans today are the Fed, Fannie Mae, Freddie Mac and Ginnie Mae (FHA and VA) -- all government agencies using taxpayer money. And we have already made note of the Fed's buying up $1.25 trillion of otherwise unmarketable mortgage-backed securities (some of which will prove to be quite toxic, rest assured).

Now, then, think how mortgage financing has been turned on its head: those who bailed out Wall Street, Fannie and Freddie, the taxpayers, now are advised, time and time again, that they do not qualify to borrow to buy a home themselves. Why so they ask? The "one size fits all" answer to this and other questions regarding the adverse consequences to the consumer from the financial meltdown: this is a necessary "byproduct" of the new (and "improved") changes which Congress, the administration and the Fed "had to" impose upon lenders. In other words, they took our money to bail out their buddies, but now these "buddies" slam the very doors our money kept open in our faces. Their actions literally took the shirts off the backs of many folks and now those same folks find signs posted by those same institutions saying "no shirt, no service."

So let us get this straight (although the result seems about as far toward "crooked" and as far from "straight" as possible) -- it is okay to take gobs of money from the taxpayers, without their consent (most certainly without their or their legislative representatives' "informed" consent), under the pretext that Fed 1 (The Fed) and Fed 2 (the Federal Government) were acting to save the taxpayers from a financial cataclysm, and yet scads of those same taxpayers are the ones now being taken, financially speaking, behind the woodshed (which, coincidentally, is now where they have to live, since they cannot get financing to buy a home). But the "powers that be" conveniently neglected to let the public know, at least in the early days when the bailout was being rammed through Congress and crammed down the public's throat) that the root cause of the credit crisis which resulted in the bushel baskets of bailout money was none other than Wall Street's Cerberus (three-headed dog who guarded Hades in Greek mythology): greed, arrogance and stupidity.

Unfortunately, however, it almost certainly would not have changed the outcome, given the longstanding incestuous relationship between Fed 1, Fed 2 and Wall Street. For all the hue and cry afterwards about the dire need for transparency, during that time, when the bailout potions were being brewed in the darkest recesses of the Federal Reserve, the Department of Treasury, the White House, and the offices of Goldman Sachs, J.P. Morgan, Morgan Stanley, and AIG, transparency was viewed in about the same light as exposure to smallpox -- to be avoided at all costs, including extreme quarantine (in this case, an "informational quarantine").

As we noted above, more and more consumers are changing their ways when it comes to the use (and abuse) of credit. This must happen in order for the financial system to change for the better in the future. Otherwise, there will be another financial meltdown and the next one could easily be the Second Great Depression. We, as a society, are addicted to credit. For reference, take a little time to read about the buying habits of our parents, grandparents and great-grandparents, if they were products of the Great Depression. There was a simple, hard, and fast rule that was written on the hearts and minds of those who lived through those times -- if you could not pay cash for something, then you did not buy it. Why? In the first place, they did not trust a system based on credit -- many had just lost anything and everything being financed because they could not make the installment payments. In the second place, they had to learn to live without credit because there was virtually no credit available (does not that realization give you a blinding flash of déjà vu).

Today we have drifted far from the maxim of pay as you go (buy). Today our anthem is (or at least was until recently) "do not put off until tomorrow what you can purchase today on credit." We have been shown the land of "milk and money" that we supposedly could enter through the gates of credit -- "no money down and no payments for the first year," "90 days, same as cash," "zero percent interest financing for 60 months." "Come buy with me," say the credit card companies and so we did. We have allowed ourselves to become indentured servants to the purveyors of credit. The Good Book (in **Proverbs 22:7**) says it this way: "The rich rule over the poor, and the borrower is servant to the lender."

And who supplies the credit? The Fed and Wall Street -- the Fed through its monetary and regulatory policies and Wall Street through the issuance of credit and credit-based securities. We bought into the whole shebang (the operative word here being "bought") and thus we have become a nation of debt and debtors. Many are as or more concerned about credit scores than their physical and mental health. We have convinced ourselves that our children must have more material goods than we did when we were growing up or we will have failed as parents. Until recently, we had to purchase a bigger house or a better vehicle or take vacations to far away destinations or join a private club, and many of us did all of these things and more by tapping our readily accessible credit facilities. We were living large on charge and our consumption was limited only by our available credit lines and our ability to meet each month's minimum payment. We don't know about you, but we began to feel like the ghost of Jacob Marley, with chains forged of credit instead of past sins, but, like Marley's, of our own doing (and undoing).

We blame lawmakers and Wall Street for poor decision-making and greed, but we, hailed as Main Street America, allow the lawmakers and greed seekers to implement their nefarious scheme of keeping us in debt. Remember the earlier discussions comparing lobbyists to drug dealers -- well, the same analogy is equally applicable here, only here the "dealers" traffic in credit instead of narcotics. Today they have us in a particularly bad spot by indiscriminately and abruptly reducing or freezing our lines of credit, increasing interest rates to near usurious levels, eliminating any ability to borrow on our homes, leaving us on a financial tightrope without any safety net.. The people we vote into office and the Wall Street greed mongers that we reward each time that we pay their exorbitant interest rates are squeezing us mercilessly.

Moreover, we have to listen to the big banker's whine that it is, at the end of the day, Main Street America after all who the real cause of the credit problems is today. We compound the problem by electing lawmakers who take monies year after year from the financial institutions they are supposed to regulate. President Obama has publicly lambasted the banks, but his presidential campaign gladly accepted millions in contributions from them and don't kid yourself for a moment -- he will not go too far in damning them, for fear the contribution spigot will be turned off for him and his political cohorts.

Credit purveyors cannot continue to operate in the manner that they do unless we, as the consumer, allow it to happen. Unbelievably, we, the consumer, have ultimate power over the credit creators and contractors, but we have not exercised that power. Until we decide to curtail our use of credit -- to stop being "creatures of credit" -- they will continue to hold us in bondage. They will continue to feed our addiction and the price will be financial debilitation. Withdrawal, as is true with any addiction, will be painful, but it is the only way to attain and maintain lasting financial sobriety.

Have you ever noticed that lenders always tend to employ the admonition that you have a moral obligation to pay your bills if you get behind in making your payments? Legally, there is nothing in a credit contract that stipulates a moral obligation to do anything. The law does not consider moral obligations as a principle of law, a legal right or legally actionable. Morality is an ethical or spiritual interpretation of right or wrong, not a legal interpretation of right or wrong. Consider this: when you signed up for a credit card under the bold face banner that the interest rate would be 3.99% or 4.99% and went out and charged up to your credit limit and then were informed by the credit issuer that your 3.99% or 4.99% percent interest rate was merely the introductory or promotional rate and has been raised to 14.99% or 15.99% and then, subsequently, all the way up to 24% or higher, do you truly think that the credit seller is concerned about its moral obligation to you? Not in this lifetime! No more so than the drug dealer who gives out "samples" of his "product" to get the junkie-to-be hooked, after which the price is ratcheted up rapidly and repeatedly.

To make matters worse, the legal system protects the credit grantor and punishes the credit grantee (us) if we fail to pay on time, even though the credit grantor is allowed to change certain of the fundamental contract terms after credit is granted. Talk about the "fine print." Nobody really reads the fine print (a/k/a the *terms and conditions*) on credit card agreements. The wording is abstruse, confusing, and filled with "boilerplate legalese" designed to be unintelligible to the nonprofessional (and most lawyers). And the size of the print requires a magnifying glass. That is all by design to bury the time bombs, which allow them to rape and pillage with impunity, financially speaking.

Remember, credit cards belong to the issuer, not to the user. The courts have held that your credit cards may be cancelled at any time for any reason or for no reason. Further, credit lines may be reduced or frozen at any time for any reason or for no reason. It is the issuer's property and you have only a limited license to use it. Moreover, even if you find yourself in a position to consider bankruptcy because your debts are well beyond your means -- if you have a job, then you still must repay a portion of your credit card debt. This provision became effective in 2007 in the revisions of the personal bankruptcy rules, known as either a Chapter 7 or Chapter 13 petition. Before the revisions (which the credit card companies won through an intense lobbying effort), there was no requirement to repay any credit card debt, which is not true today.

We have addressed some critical components in our society, housing and credit. We now know that many of us will not be allowed to purchase a home or secure credit for the near future if we have been unable to meet our past credit obligations. We, as a society, need to engage in an honest and open debate regarding the financial future of our children and grandchildren. Do we want them to follow our example and become indentured servants? No matter how one looks at it, most of us work for the credit companies, to some degree (some, sadly, full-time) and not for ourselves. If we do not pay, the credit purveyors are allowed to seize our property, garnish our pay, and even take our retirement accounts, whereas, individually, we are essentially devoid of any defense against the credit grantors because the lawmakers, the laws, and the courts protect them. The simple, most basic change that we can make in our financial lifetime, to protect the financial future of our children and grandchildren, is to teach them not to be addicted to credit. We need to teach future generations that credit is to be used sparingly, only for emergencies, or for purchases which can be repaid without interest. And they will not learn if we do not walk the walk (i.e., it is not going to work if we fall back on that old saw, "do as I say, not as I do").

Yes, it will be difficult and it will entail a radical departure from all we have been encouraged to do as the "ultimate consumption generation." We must no longer be ruled by debt, but must instead liberate ourselves from the financial bonds of credit. Only then can we, to paraphrase from the late Martin Luther King *I Had a Dream* speech, cry from our mountain tops, *"I'm free from debt, thank God Almighty I'm free from debt at last."* Think about making this your dream so future generations can live a life of financial freedom. That would be a truly worthy gift to posterity. And take this message, not as a denouncement of capitalism, but rather as a prayer of sorts for our children's and their children's future happiness.

Moreover, should we not teach our children to save at least as much as they spend? As a society, America has one of the lowest savings rates in the world. After all, if we are living in glass houses (those of us fortunate enough to still have houses), we have to be careful about throwing stones at the lawmakers who spend us and our heirs into financial servitude. We have the power to rid ourselves of the system of greed and deceit, but do we have the strength of character to throw off the chains, including those self-imposed?

CHAPTER 15

HEALTH CARE
'Health is Wealth'

"In nothing do men more nearly approach the gods than in giving
health to men."
- Marcus Tullius Cicero, Roman orator and statesman

"America's health care system is second only to Japan ... Canada,
Sweden, Great Britain ... well, all of Europe. But you can thank
your lucky stars we don't live in Paraguay!"
- Homer Simpson

It is timely that we are writing this chapter as we prepare to witness the vote in the United States House of Representatives on the hotly contested health reform legislation, lauded by some (mostly Democrats) and denounced by others (mostly Republicans). The vote is being called "historic" by almost every commentator and journalist ("histrionic" might be more apt) and, for the past week, has been called "too close to call." This evening, however, the broadcasters are reporting that Democrats have the 216 votes needed to pass the measure; however, it is extremely doubtful that many of the Representatives know exactly what they are being asked to vote on since they will be voting first on the 2400-page bill passed by the Senate last December and then on a 153-page reconciliation bill designed to "fix" provisions in the Senate bill they don't like -- which means it would take the average reader more than 50 hours of serious concentration to plow through the measures (moreover, the text of the 10-title act cannot be meaningfully read from front to back as printed because the tenth title is a list of amendments to the previous nine titles, which must be applied to the titles and sections to which they refer before the bill can be properly interpreted). Not that any of the Democrats (or Republicans for that matter) would take the time to read and study the bill. That sort of mundane work is left for the staff and, of course, their lobbyist comrades, who will tell the Representatives what the bill says. Not that there is time to read and understand the bill. This piece of work was put on the fast track and steamrolled through Congress for fear the Democrats may not (likely will not) have the votes come November to prevail on any legislative initiatives.

Passions are running extremely high particularly with the opponents, as many are disgusted with talk of "back room" deals and worries over the cost of the reform measure and the "fine print" of the bill (they know the devil is in the details and they are pretty sure there is more than one Satanic figure lurking in the health care legislation, and they're probably right). Strong feelings have caused some of the protests to turn ugly, even vicious, with some reports of racial epithets hurled by some Tea Party protesters at three black Congressmen, House Majority Whip Jim Clyburn (D-South Carolina), Representative John Lewis (D-Georgia) and Representative Andre Carson (D-Indiana), all of whom support the health care bill. Representative Emanuel Cleaver, another Afro-American Congressman (D-Missouri) who supports the proposal, reported being spit upon by demonstrators from the Tea Party. Representative Henry Waxman (D-California) was surrounded by a group of protestors at the House Office Building who angrily called him a "liar" and a "crook" and some resorted to more abusive (i.e., profane) terminology. Of course, the Democrats and some news media are seizing on a few nasty incidents to indict the entire Tea Party movement. They are hoping to cast the movement as a radical fringe element that decent, God-fearing folks should not want to be associated with. That is always one of the first lines of attack on any third parties, as we noted in the Chapter on Term Limits.

In truth, protesters who do resort to violence and obscenities do no good for themselves or their politics. Vituperations laced with expletives and sprinkled with random acts of violence only serve to (i) divert attention from a fair and responsible examination of a proposal on its merits, (ii) undermine otherwise valid and reasonable arguments against a plan, and (iii) discredit and bring into disrepute an entire organization with those of the voting public who might be on the fence regarding the proposed legislation under review. It also allows certain segments of the media to portray the protesters as a radical, potentially dangerous, "out there" element, undeserving of being taken seriously by mainstream America. We can understand, appreciate and even sympathize with, a need to vent and even express a degree of rage, but vindictive, vile, tasteless and cruel personal attacks are not going to "win friends and influence people" on such an important issue -- in the long run, such behavior is more likely to drive away than attract moderates in both parties and independents who will ultimately decide future political contests in which this legislation may prove a decisive issue.

For all of the extreme divisiveness and partisanship the debate on health care has engendered on both sides of the aisle and with the public, there is one thing that pretty much everybody seems to agree upon -- the current health care system is broken and not sustainable as it now stands. The late, great Walter Cronkite, anchorman for the *CBS Evening News* for 19 years (1962-1981) and often called "the most trusted man in America" during his tenure with CBS, observed many years ago that "America's health care system is neither healthy, caring, nor a system." Since those words were spoken, however, the situation has not improved -- in fact, it has grown noticeably worse.

According to the latest statistics, 15% of the population in this country, more than 45 million Americans (including more than 8 million children), have no medical insurance at all and can receive only emergency treatment at hospitals. Another 64 million

Americans (21%) are underinsured and thus not able to cover the costs of their medical needs.

Researchers from Harvard Medical School attribute the lack of health insurance coverage to 45,000 deaths per year in the United States. The Harvard study estimated that people without health insurance have a 40% higher risk of death than those with private health insurance because of their being unable to obtain necessary medical care. The cost of uninsured health care to every American family is more than $1000 per year. And more than 60% of personal bankruptcies in this country are linked to medical bills, making medical bills the primary cause of bankruptcy filings in America (remarkably, in 78% of the personal bankruptcies attributed principally to medical costs, 78% of the filers had health insurance).

More money per person is spent on health care in the United States (more than $8,000) than in any other nation in the world, and a greater percentage of individual and family income is spent on health care in the U.S. than in any United Nations member state except for East Timor (if you know where that island country is, you are not at all geographically challenged). World-renowned billionaire and financial expert Warren Buffett told CNBC earlier this year that health care costs are "a major drain on U.S. businesses" and act like an "economic tape worm." He observed that America's health care system needs fundamental reform to attack costs because it's impractical to continue devoting 17% of the nation's gross domestic product ($2.5 trillion), to health care, especially when, by comparison, "much of the rest of the world is paying only 9% of their GDP on health care and yet have more doctors and nurses per person." At the current rate of increased spending, in five years, the U.S. will be spending $4 trillion on health care, or 20% of our GDP (a staggering $12,600 for every man, woman and child in the country). It is well known that Medicare will go broke without major reform. Already the Medicare Hospital Insurance Trust Fund (also true for Social Security) is paying out more in hospital and other benefits than it receives in taxes and other dedicated revenues. Moreover, the insolvency issue is going to get much worse as more and more Baby Boomers reach retirement age, throwing the ration of retirees to workers further out of whack. If nothing is changed, the growing deficits are projected to completely exhaust the Medicare Trust Fund Reserves by 2018 at the latest.

Well, we have been told all of our lives that you get what you pay for, right? So, then, it stands to reason that our paying the most in the world for health care must also mean that we have the best health care in the world, right? Afraid not. A 2009 survey of primary care physicians in 11 countries, conducted by an 18-member expert committee commissioned to study international measures of high quality health care by the Commonwealth Fund, a non-partisan health care foundation, concluded that *"the United States lags far behind its peers in key measures of access, quality, and use of health IT -- undermining doctors' efforts to provide timely, high-quality care."* The U.S. was not the top scorer in any of the international indicators of health outcomes, quality, equity or efficiency, despite our spending double the amount spent by Canada, France, Japan, and the U.K., all of which rank higher on these measures of health care. The study further ranked the U.S. last among industrialized nations for infant mortality and last on performance measures such as life expectancy and preventable mortality.

There are other disturbing statistics concerning the state of health care in America. Twenty-five percent of us do not visit the doctor when we are sick because we cannot afford it. Twenty-three percent of Americans were found to have skipped a test, treatment, or follow-up recommended by a doctor due to affordability issues. Another 23% were unable to fill a prescription. And almost 17% of cancer survivors (2,000,000 people) skipped necessary care because of costs. No other country is close to this sort of income-based rationing. In Canada, only 4% skipped a doctor's visit, and only 5% skipped care. In the U.K., those numbers are even lower, 2% and 3%, respectively. More than 20% of Americans are unable, or have serious problems, paying medical bills. No other country surveyed was even in double digits.

Americans are by far the likeliest people on earth to report spending more than $500 out-of-pocket on prescription drugs annually. That is a big problem, as higher out-of-pocket costs mean more of us going without prescriptions, which means less maintenance of conditions and, thus, greater cost when our chronic illnesses become catastrophic health events. Indeed, 42% of Americans with chronic conditions -- the exact same percentage who report paying more than $500 for drugs -- report skipping care, drug doses, or doctor's appointments due to cost. Along with Australians, we are the most likely to report a medical, medication, or lab error, with about 20% of us experiencing one of these yearly. For those Americans with chronic diseases, the rates are even higher.

The Commonwealth Fund report also dispelled several popular myths about health care. One is that the other countries have all socialized medicine. The report determined that many wealthy countries, such as Germany, The Netherlands, Japan and Switzerland provide universal health care coverage using private doctors, private hospitals, and insurance plans. What about the claim that waiting periods for medical treatment are much longer outside the Unites States? Well, the study found that in Japan waiting times are so short, most patients do not bother to make an appointment. And, although Canada is plagued by long waits for non-emergency services, other countries, including Germany, Great Britain and Australia actually outperformed the U.S. on waiting times for elective surgeries.

The report also took issue with the popular claim that, in comparison with America, the foreign health care systems are very inefficient, bloated bureaucracies. The fact is that our health insurance companies have the highest administrative costs in the world, spending 20-30 cents of each health care dollar on non-medical costs, such as paperwork, claims review, marketing, and profits. According to the AMA, the American health care system spends $210 billion annually on claims processing. By contrast, France, which has one of the best health care systems in the world, spends four cents of every dollar on administration.

Another popular misconception is that cost controls in the medical industry will stifle innovation. In fact, in the U.S., an MRI scan of the neck region costs about $1,500. In Japan, the identical scan costs $98. France pioneered the latest techniques in hip and knee replacement, and many of the modern "wonder drugs" promoted so aggressively on American television were developed in British, Swiss, Japanese and Israeli labs.

Not all the news on the American medical system is negative and has us bringing up the rear. We do have slightly better survival rates for a few common cancers than several of the European countries and Canada and we do have somewhat better access to treatment for chronic diseases than patients in many other developed countries (of course, that may also be due to the fact that we have much higher incidence of chronic disease than other countries).

There is one aspect of the health system in which there is and can be no comparison with the rest of the world -- the cost of "defensive medicine" in this country adds billions of dollars (as much as $200 billion annually) in unnecessary expensive diagnostic testing to protect doctors from frivolous lawsuits, a cost that simply does not exist anywhere else in the world. Medical malpractice premiums have become unaffordable in many states, particularly Florida, Nevada, Michigan, Illinois and D.C.

The House voted in favor of the first health care bill (the Senate Bill) by a slim margin of 219-212. Not one Republican voted for the measure. The conservative talk show hosts began in short order to have a field day with this.

The House subsequently voted 220-211 to pass the House measure to amend the Senate legislation to change certain provisions in the Senate bill passed earlier that the majority voting for health care reform did not agree with. The President signed the first measure (the Patient Protection and Affordable Care Act) into law earlier today. The Senate must also pass the second bill under a budget process called reconciliation that requires a simple majority vote. Battle lines were quickly drawn for a fierce battle in the Senate as the Republicans are planning a "no holds barred" "last ditch" effort to derail the legislation. Republicans hope to force major changes to the reconciliation bill, some that could set up a political nightmare scenario for Democrats. If certain unpopular provisions of the Senate's version of the bill -- like special carve-out deals for individual states -- are not corrected, the Democrats risk being branded as supporters of the dreaded "back-room" deals. And if Republicans manage to scuttle reconciliation language that would delay the implementation of new taxes on high-value (the so-called "Cadillac") insurance plans, union groups who are counting heavily on that change will be incensed. Because the House and Senate must pass the same bills -- word for word -- even a minor tweak would send it back to the House for another vote. In the 22 times that reconciliation has been used, only once has the Senate bill not been changed and sent back to the House.

After running through a gauntlet of Republican amendments and procedural objections, the Senate finally approved the reconciliation bill passed by the House. So it is now official -- Congress has passed the most far-reaching social legislation in nearly half a century. The vote in the Senate was 56 to 43, with the Republicans unanimously opposed. Three Democrats opposed the measure: Senators Blanche Lincoln and Mark Pryor of Arkansas and Ben Nelson of Nebraska. The reconciliation measure also included a broad restructuring of federal student loan programs to pay for billions of dollars in government-sponsored school initiatives. The vote came after Senate Democrats defeated more than 40 Republican amendments aimed at delaying or derailing the legislation. Few measures in history have so polarized the citizenry. As we expected, the conservative talking heads went into an absolute "feeding frenzy," and as usual, are fanning the flames of protest with routine rhetoric involving claims of "righteous indignation" (more likely, self-righteous indignation), with some reaching for and finding new heights of histrionics.

Let us check in first with the Ronald "Muck" Donald of conservatism, Sean Hannity. On national television, he compared the passage of the health care act to "giving the American people the middle finger." Might be right, but he could employ a better use of the "king's English," if you ask us.

Next, we tune in to self-proclaimed political profit and well-known author and radio host Glenn (sometimes a "brain wreck") Beck. Never one to shy away from preposterous or irresponsible analogies, he compared the health care reform legislation to Flight 93 on 9/11, Pearl Harbor, Chamberlain meeting Hitler, and the Hindenburg. According to Beck, *"Yeah, providing health care insurance for millions of uninsured Americans is just like horrific and violent attacks that leave thousands of Americans dead."* He dismissed the CBO report that the health care reform bill would result in a $130 billion deficit reduction in its first ten years by saying, on air no less: *"Well, that's a party in my pants!"* What did Beck have to say about the supporters of the bill? Before the vote was taken, he said, *"Here is a group of people that have so perverted our faith and our hope and our charity, that this is an affront to God."* Heaven help us if Glenn Beck speaks for God. Again drawing on his frequent "holier than thou" claims (not to mention his penchant for borderline bigotry); he added on his radio show that *"Jesus Martinez"* might support the health care bill, but *"not the Jesus of Nazareth I know."*

Moreover, how about nationally-syndicated radio talk show host Neal Boortz (whose self-given (not God-given, as he might like to believe) nicknames include "The Talkmaster," "Mighty Whitey," "The Mouth of the South," "America's Rude Awakening," and the "High Priest of the Church of the Painful Truth")? He denounced the health care measure with this flight of fantasy: *"Obama Care will do more damage than a successful terrorist bombing of an airliner... and kill more people as well."*

Of course, we cannot overlook the formidable force of Rush Limbaugh, the icon of neocons, the king of right wing, and the man the Democrats love to hate (which I am sure causes him to cry all the way to the bank -- after all, he makes over $40 million a year and has the highest-rated talk radio show in the United States). One of health care reform's fiercest opponents, Limbaugh claimed, in one of his less zany moments, that *"human beings will die earlier than normal"* under the *"freedom killing"* and *"life threatening"* plan, and called for it to be *"aborted."* He compared the plan to the *"policies of the Nazis"* and said that as a result of the legislation, *"America is now hanging by a thread."*

Limbaugh even went so far as to vow to move out of the country as a result of the health care bill (a "leave not lead by example" tactic, and a promise which some have argued is reason enough to vote for the bill). When asked where he would go, he responded, *"to Costa Rica."* An interesting choice by Rush since Costa Rica has a longstanding universal health insurance system. Costa Rica's public health insurance system, commonly known as the "Caja," is available nationwide to all citizens and legal residents. There are ten major public hospitals – four in San Jose, including the Children's Hospital – affiliated with the Caja. For non-emergencies and everyday medical care, small clinics, known as EBAIS (pronounced ay-vy-ice), are located in almost every community. His uncanny ability to speak without the benefit of a factual basis was also at work after his recent emergency room visit in Hawaii for chest pains. He survived, and he says that proved that America does not need health care reform. What Limbaugh failed to mention is that Hawaii has already instituted many of the reforms that are included in the federal health care reform bill before Congress. Therefore, I guess that what Limbaugh was really saying is that health care reform works.

A recent poll shows that many Republican listeners are 'drinking the same Kool-Aid' as their iconoclastic mouthpieces. According to a new Harris Poll released after the health care vote, 57% of Republicans believe that Obama is a Muslim and 38% of

Republicans believe that Obama is like Hitler. Perhaps most disturbing of all, a quarter of Republicans believes Obama to be "the Antichrist."

It is high time to move on to a discussion of the health care plan itself. But before we summarize the "benefits," let us take a brief look at the anticipated costs associated with implementation of the plan. The plan is projected to cost approximately $940 billion over the next 10 years, financed by Medicare cuts to hospitals and fees or taxes on insurers, drug manufacturers, medical-device companies and Americans earning more than $200,000 a year. A new report from the Congressional Budget Office estimates that enacting the Senate-passed measure (H.R. 3590) and the reconciliation package would reduce the budget deficit by $143 billion through 2019 and $1.2 trillion over the second 10 years. However, many place little stock in the CBO estimates. After all, when Medicare was passed in 1965, the projected cost was $10 billion over the subsequent 10 years, the actual cost was more than 10 times that amount, and the costs of that entitlement program have of course continued to spiral out of control.

But the real $64,000 question (more like the $6 trillion question, since that is where annual healthcare expenditures are heading in the next 10 years) is whether this act will cause a real reduction in our health insurance costs or health care expenditures? President Obama said at a rally for the bill in Ohio (only 200 people of the more than a thousand expected actually turned up) that, under his plan, employees *"would see premiums fall by as much as 3,000%"* and added that such a big reduction *"means they could give you a raise."* Right, and the moon is really made of blue cheese. The White House quickly corrected the gaffe and said the President meant to say the reduction could be up to $3,000, not 3,000%.

But is this even accurate? Not according to Keith Ashmus, chair of the National Small Business Association, who said the bill is likely to increase insurance premiums because it eliminates caps on benefits and requires insurers to cover children on their parents' policies until they turn 26. *"Premiums will go up under this bill faster than they would otherwise,"* he says. *"Some of that will be offset by subsidies for some small businesses but only for a limited period of time."* As it turns out, health insurance premiums are indeed going up after passage of the reform measure and even faster than before. According to several sources, health insurance premiums in 2010 are increasing at an annual rate of 20%.

David Cordani, CEO of CIGNA, agreed that the reform will increase the price of health insurance and he cited several reasons. First off, the bill adds $70 billion in taxes on insurers that will be passed along to consumers. Additionally, the so-called cost-shift from Medicaid to private insurance will worsen as millions of eligible people are added to the Medicaid rolls. The program's low reimbursement rates to doctors and hospitals will mean higher medical prices for people with private insurance, according to Cordani.

The Kaiser Family Foundation estimated that a family with private insurance last year paid an average of $1,850 to cover low reimbursement rates from Medicaid, he said.

Cordani added, *"Without any change in the system, healthcare costs will go up, so, premiums will go up. ... And in an environment where emergency-room utilization and costs have quadrupled in five years, use of MRIs has doubled in the last five years, biomedical utilization is growing rapidly, the costs will continue to grow."*

Insurers do stand to benefit from the provision in the law, which requires citizens to have health insurance and theoretically offer tens of millions of new customers, including healthy young adults who now choose not to buy insurance. But insurers continue to be skeptical about that mandate, contending there is little incentive for a person to pay thousands of dollars for insurance each year compared to hundreds of dollars in penalties.

The industry trade group, America's Health Insurance Plans, offered only a single statement after the bill passed the House: *"The access expansions are a significant step forward, but this legislation will exacerbate the healthcare costs crisis facing many working families and small businesses, "* said the group's president, Karen Ignagni.

Some groups, such as the National Federation of Independent Business, see the bill as a potential job killer that will only serve to exacerbate the coverage problem the bill is supposed to help solve. They have voiced serious concerns that the legislation will discourage businesses with fewer than 50 employees from expanding their payrolls. *"The tax credit itself is limited by a firm's size and wages, so if you want to remain eligible, you need to remain small and not pay high wages, "* says Amanda Austin, the trade group's Director of Federal Public Policy.

Others have argued that the legislation, which will create state-based exchanges through which companies can purchase coverage, does not really do a thing to address a chief concern: the spiraling costs of health insurance.

So, then just what exactly is the plan going to deliver to the American people in the form of "reforms" and how far-reaching are those "reforms"? Let us address the second question first. According to many of the opponents, the plan spells the end of capitalism in America (in point of fact, however, pure capitalism, if we ever really had it, ended many decades ago) and usher in socialism, communism, bolshevism, or fascism (choose your "ism" poison) and thus is anathema to all "right-thinking" and "freedom-loving" Americans. A quick footnote is in order. Many Americans honestly believe that plans such as the health care act are a strong step in the direction of socialism (more than 40% believe this to be the case, more than two-thirds of Republicans, according to some polls). We were somewhat flabbergasted when we heard Al Sharpton say a couple of days ago on national television that "the American people overwhelmingly voted for socialism when they voted for President Obama -- that is news, and not good news, to us!

Now the health care plan's proponents counter the opponents with contentions that the plan is essential to preserving and protecting the most basic and most fundamental of human rights, the right to life (you all remember that one, the very first of the three "inalienable rights" listed in the Declaration of Independence). The proponents also claim that, without a right to medical care, the American people will also be effectively denied the third of those inalienable rights, the right to "the pursuit of happiness." As usual, both are playing to their respective audiences and are too "political" and too extreme in their assessments.

As long as we are talking about "rights" in connection with this legislation, we need to make note of the fact that a scant 7 minutes after the President signed the legislation, 13 Attorneys general from 13 states sued the federal government in Florida, claiming the bill is unconstitutional on the basis that *"the Constitution does not authorize the United States to mandate, either directly or under threat of penalty, that all citizens and legal residents have qualifying health care coverage."* The lawsuit also claims that the bill infringes on the sovereignty of the states by requiring them to expand eligibility for Medicaid without providing sufficient funds to cover the costs at a time when many states are already facing severe budget shortfalls.

Florida Attorney General Bill McCollum is taking the lead and was joined by attorneys general from South Carolina, Nebraska, Texas, Michigan, Utah, Pennsylvania, Alabama, South Dakota, Idaho, Washington, Colorado and Louisiana. All are Republicans except James "Buddy" Caldwell of Louisiana, who is a Democrat. According to McCollum, the suit *"should put the Federal Government on notice that we will not tolerate the constitutional rights of our citizens and the sovereignty of our states to be trampled on."*

Virginia sued separately to overturn the legislation and 6 additional states followed *suit*, bringing the total number of states seeking to overturn the health care legislation to 20. Virginia even went so far as to pass state legislation which effectively seeks to

218

nullify the federal law by declaring the federal mandate requiring Virginians to purchase health care insurance illegal.

The Justice Department, which is responsible for defending U.S. law in court, pledged to fight any challenges to the new healthcare law. *"We are confident that this statute is constitutional and we will prevail,"* said Justice Spokesman Charles Miller. The White House, as should be expected, agreed with the Department of Justice. Many legal experts have joined in the opinion that the law is constitutional and will survive the judicial challenge. University of Washington law professor Stewart Jay said that Congress has the authority to act and that the courts have supported lawmakers in similar efforts, including farm subsidies and Social Security. He commented: *"I don't think there is any basis to challenge the legislation constitutionally. The grounds that have been raised strike me as frivolous."*

Yale Law Professor Jack Balkin agreed that the legislation is likely to survive the states' challenges, as did Timothy Jost, Washington and Lee University School of Law professor, who called the lawsuits nothing more than *"political theater."* In a similar vein, Robert Sedler, a constitutional law professor at Wayne State University said the effort of the attorneys general *"isn't going anywhere"* and referred to the challenges as *"pure political posturing."* Tulane constitutional law professor Keith Werhan opined that the lawsuit has no legal legs to stand on. *"The federal government certainly can compel people to pay taxes and can compel people to join the Army,"* noted Bruce Jacob, a constitutional law professor at Florida's Stetson University. How then, he asked, *"can this law be declared unconstitutional?"*

Now back to the law itself. Many on both sides would have us believe the bill will affect virtually every man, woman and child in the United States in some way, from the twenty-somethings who constitute one of the largest uninsured groups to poor, childless adults who don't qualify for Medicaid in most states to well-paid professionals who could see their benefits shrink. Sounds pervasive, does it not? But is it really as revolutionary and radical as it might appear at first glance? Not so much. In fact, it is an expansion of care that most people will not notice in 10 years. According to the Congressional Budget Office, the bill signed into law will change the insurance of about 40 million people by 2019, about 30 million of whom would have been otherwise uninsured. The other 10 million will come from the employer or individual markets in search of more affordable options. About 23 million people will still be uninsured, many of them illegal immigrants. Therefore, according to this analysis, 90% of Americans will be exactly where they would have been anyway if this reform had never passed.

To be sure, though, there are some significant changes and it is a worthwhile exercise to describe the changes wrought. Many of the provisions included in the healthcare reform legislation signed into law -- and the bill that adds fixes to that measure that was sent to the Senate -- would take place not immediately, but along a 10-year timeline through 2020. Here is a summary of how that timeline rolls out. But bear in mind that several of the provisions do not apply if at variance with union (collective bargaining) provisions in place, as the unions were accorded special dispensations (no surprise there).

2010

- ❖ Adults with pre-existing conditions who have been uninsured for at least six months can enroll in a temporary high-risk health insurance pool and receive subsidized premiums -- beginning three months after the bill's passage. (The pools expire when exchanges are implemented in 2014.)

- ❖ All health insurance plans are to offer dependent coverage for children through age 26; insurers are prohibited from denying coverage to children because of pre- existing health problems.

- ❖ Insurance companies can no longer put lifetime dollar limits on coverage and cancel policies -- except in cases of fraud.

❖ Tax credits will be provided to help small businesses with 25 employees or fewer to get and keep coverage for these employees.

❖ The Medicare "doughnut hole," in which beneficiaries had to pay full cost of their prescription drugs, begins narrowing by providing a $250 rebate this year to those in the gap, which starts this year after they have spent $2,830. The doughnut hole fully closes by 2020.

❖ Indoor tanning has a 10% sales tax.

2011

❖ For Medicare beneficiaries reaching the Medicare doughnut hole, prescription coverage will be available with a 50% discount on brand name drugs.

❖ A 10% Medicare bonus will be provided to primary care physicians and general surgeons practicing in underserved areas, such as inner cities and rural communities.

❖ Medicare Advantage plans would begin to have their payments frozen -- and then lowered in 2012. The plans would have to spend at least 85 cents out of every dollar on medical costs, while leaving 15 cents for plan operations, including overhead and salaries. Reductions would be phased in over the next three to seven years.

❖ A voluntary long-term care insurance program would be made available to provide a modest cash benefit for assisting disabled individuals to stay in their homes or cover nursing home costs. Benefits would start five years after people begin paying a fee for coverage.

❖ Funding for community health centers would be increased to provide care for many low income and uninsured people.

❖ Employers would be required to report the value of healthcare benefits on employees' W-2 tax statements.

❖ Pharmaceutical manufacturers will have a $2.3 billion annual fee that will increase over time.

2012

❖ Nonprofit insurance co-ops would be created to compete with commercial insurers. Hospitals, physicians, and payers would be encouraged to band together in "accountable care organizations."

❖ Hospitals with high rates of preventable readmissions would face reduced Medicare payments.

2013

❖ Individuals making $200,000 a year or couples making $250,000 would have a higher Medicare payroll tax of 2.35%—up from the current 1.45%. A new tax of 3.8% on unearned income, such as dividends, capital gains, interest, and other investment income, is also added.

❖ Medical expense contributions to tax sheltered flexible spending accounts (FSAs) are limited to $2,500 a year—indexed for inflation. In addition, the thresholds for claiming itemized tax deduction for medical expenses rise from 7.5% to 10% of income. People age 65 or older can still deduct medical expenses above 7.5% of income through 2016.

❖ Medicare device makers would have a 2.3% sales tax on medical devices; devices such as eyeglasses, contact lenses, and hearing aids would be exempt.

2014

❖ New state health insurance exchanges would be created. Income based tax credits will be available for many consumers in the exchanges. The sliding scale credits phase out for households that are four times above the federal poverty level (about $88,000 for a family of four).

❖ Medicaid would be expanded to cover low-income individuals up to 133% of the federal poverty level -- about $28,300 for a family of four.

❖ Insurers would be prohibited from denying coverage to people with pre-existing conditions, or charge higher rates to those with poor or chronic health conditions. Premiums (with limitations) can only vary by age, place of residence, family size, and tobacco use.

❖ Insurers will be required to cover maternity care as they do other medical procedures.

❖ All legal residents would be required to have health insurance—except in cases of financial hardship—or pay a fine to the IRS. The individual penalty starts at $95 each in 2014—rising to $695 in 2016. Family penalties are capped at $2,250; penalties will be indexed for inflation after 2016.

❖ Employers with more than 50 workers would be penalized if any of their workers get coverage through the exchange and receive a tax credit. The penalty is $2,000 times the total number of workers employed at the company. However, employers get to deduct the first 30 workers.

❖ Health insurance providers will begin paying an annual fee of $60 billion.

2018

❖ A tax would be imposed on employer-sponsored health insurance worth more than $10,200 for individual coverage, and $27,500 for a family plan. The tax is 40% of the value of the plan above the thresholds, indexed for inflation.

2020

❖ Doughnut hole coverage gap in Medicare prescription benefit is phased out. Seniors continue to pay the standard 25% of their drug costs until they reach the threshold for Medicare catastrophic coverage.

We just learned that the health care legislation has a loophole that allows insurers to continue denying coverage to children with pre-existing conditions until 2014 rather than later this year. Health and Human Services Secretary Kathleen Sebelius claims this will be fixed through executive rule making, but that is far from a given, and the enforceability is questionable in the extreme. Regardless, the legions of high-priced attorneys representing the health insurers will undoubtedly find ways for the insurance companies to circumvent most of the supposedly tough regulations in the new law.

Now, then, we must address a very important question: Who is going to enforce the health care requirements? None other than the most feared and despised agency in the federal government, the IRS. You heard right, the *Infernal* Revenue Service has been tapped to function as the federal government's chief enforcement arm for the health care reform measure, and will be charged with monitoring both businesses and individuals to certify whether they have the insurance coverage the government requires.

Although that minimum level of coverage will be defined later by the Department of Health and Human Services, it will be the responsibility of the IRS, beginning in 2014, to monitor individuals and employers and to punish those who do not comply.

The IRS would monitor the health insurance status of individuals and businesses through the mandatory reporting the Act requires. Under the law, every individual and most businesses are required to report to the IRS, on their tax returns, whether they have purchased or provided the required level of coverage and disclose to the IRS which months, if any, in which they failed to do so. Using this information, the IRS will then determine whether an employer or individual falls under the mandate, which contains exceptions for religious conscience, hardship, incarcerated persons and members of Indian tribes.

If either individuals or businesses have failed to comply with this mandate for any month during the year, they are required to pay a separate tax to the IRS. For individuals this is a maximum of $750 per person (up to $2,250 per household) and $750 per uncovered employee for businesses. Because these penalties would each apply on a monthly basis, individuals and employers would have to pay $1/12^{th}$ of the maximum penalties for each month they failed to comply with the mandates.

In order to carry out its new monitoring and enforcement duties, the Congressional Budget Office estimated that the IRS would need $10 billion in additional funds -- funds that, by the way, were not made available under the Act. An analysis done by Republicans on the House Ways and Means Committee estimated that this $10 billion could go to fund an additional 16,500 new IRS agents and other personnel to monitor and enforce the new mandates.

The IRS will also be in charge of collecting the new taxes on high cost insurance plans and the so-called "unearned income" from couples making over $250,000 per year and single filers making over $200,000 per year. Because these new mandates and taxes are under the purview of the IRS, taxpayers and businesses could incur additional penalties normally reserved for normal income tax cheats, paying fees over and above those for not complying with the new health care mandates.

The IRS currently charges potentially hefty penalties for, among other things, filing false or fraudulent returns, filing late returns, and failure to pay a tax on time. Taxpayers and businesses could be saddled with these extra penalties because they are required to use their tax returns to prove to the IRS that they are complying with the mandates and because they will have to pay any tax penalties to that agency as well. And do not expect much leniency from the "kinder and gentler" IRS. We know they have "Service" in their name but it's not really in their governmental DNA, trust us on this one.

Now the involvement of the IRS is just one relatively small piece of a much bigger bureaucratic pie that will have to be baked for this expansion of the role of the federal government. You know that any government intrusion into the private sector has to be accompanied by scads of "red tape" which means scads of "red tape dispensers." This is no different and may prove worse than most, as it creates about 160 new boards and regulatory agencies to oversee various elements of health care, and creates one big new agency just to oversee the overseers.

So, each side can argue *ad infinitum* about the merits of their respective position, but in the end, the results will be the same: in the future, without real cost containment, health care costs will grow even higher and will ultimately make the cost of care unaffordable for most of us. The primary reason is that neither side is willing to roll up its sleeves and tackle head-on the problems plaguing the entire health care system today. One main issue is that our health care delivery system is grossly inefficient. Approximately 30 cents of each dollar spent on health care today is spent on administrative costs. Government-run health care programs claim much lower administrative costs, fewer than 5%, but these claims are inaccurate and misleading. Government programs do not have sales and marketing expenses, nor do they have shareholders to answer to, but profits are part of the insurance companies' pricing schemes. Interestingly, some lawmakers may claim the efficiency of government controlled health programs but in reality the programs are not paid for as advertised, because each administration since Lyndon Johnson's has borrowed the trust fund monies earmarked for Social Security and Medicare and never repaid the Social Security Administration, instead, as we have discussed previously, the Fed just prints more money and takes back worthless IOU's.

On the other hand, for the private insurers, profits are the name of the game. So drug companies, medical equipment manufacturers and suppliers, care providers, hospitals and the like just keep increasing their prices for services provided because that is the way the system works. Moreover, never forget that the insurance industry provides mega-millions of dollars to their lobbyists (bag men) in order to influence their lawmakers of choice in order to ensure favorable votes for beneficial legislation and votes against what they perceive as detrimental legislations. This goes back a long way. 60 years ago, the insurance industry secured passage of legislation that exempted them from the antitrust laws, an exemption that stands tall today. In addition, the health insurance companies do not have to worry about competition from across state lines.

Oh, then there is the black market segment of the health care industry, those that rip off the government with bogus Medicare claims for services and products -- to the tune of over $70 billion dollars annually! And, remember now, this is the same outfit that wants to take over the private health care market and run it with less waste and greater efficiency. When have you ever seen government run a service more efficiently than the private sector? We believe the staggering deficit speaks directly to this point. If a company or a household ran that far in the red, either would be out of business and out of luck.

The bigger question we need to address is not who is better qualified to provide health care services, rather, should health care providers profit from the care of an individual's health? We can thank former President Nixon for the injecting the profit motive in spades into the health care industry. We need to hold a national referendum and let the people decide the answer to this question. It could be accomplished by adding the issue as a separate item to a general election ballot or it could be made part of a new constitutional convention. If the answer is yes, then the private sector needs to furnish the services and products and the government needs to stay out of the health care arena in its entirety, except for the VA, and some form of Medicare and Medicaid, but nothing like the millstones around the neck of the general public those programs have become and are becoming.

Conversely, if the citizens of this great country decide that health care providers should not profit from the health of others then our health care system needs to be revamped.

We might even look at a hybrid system like that of Singapore for some ideas. Singapore has a universal health care system, but it is not like the ones in Europe or Japan. The Singapore government ensures affordability, largely through compulsory savings and some price controls, but the private sector provides most of the care. Overall spending on healthcare in Singapore amounts to only 3% of annual GDP (compared with our 17% which is approaching 6 times higher than Singapore's). Of that amount, 66% comes from private sources. And Singapore currently has the lowest infant mortality rate in the world (equaled only by Iceland) and among the highest life expectancies from birth, according to the World Health Organization.

Singapore has *"one of the most successful healthcare systems in the world, in terms of both efficiency in financing and the results achieved in community health outcomes,"* according to an analysis by the 130-year old global consulting firm **Tower Watson**. Singapore's system uses a combination of compulsory savings from payroll deductions (funded by both employers and workers), a nationalized catastrophic health insurance plan, and government subsidies, as well as active regulation of the supply and prices of healthcare services in the country to keep costs in check. Many citizens of Singapore also have supplemental private health insurance (often provided by employers) for services not covered by the government's programs.

However, until the people answer the question, the current health care debate is premature and will produce ill conceived and haphazard (not to mention inordinately expensive) approaches like the current legislation. Some may argue that Obama's election is a clear mandate for government run health care. We do not believe that the majority of folks who voted for Obama also voted to create another mammoth government bureaucracy. Supporters of the President may well be proponents for health care coverage for all those who seek coverage, the elimination of pre-existing condition clauses in insurance contracts, insurance portability, and competitive pricing for health care products and services, and still strongly defend their right to see the caregiver of their choice and at their election.

If we hold a national referendum on health care, and the mandate is for a private health care system to provide services and products to individuals at a profit, then the health care and health insurance industries need to do a better job of providing products and services at competitive and affordable prices. Profits need to take a backseat to patient care.

Now, provided we do hold a referendum and the choice is for government to be the provider of health care services such as provided under Medicare and Medicaid then the private sector insurance companies need to stay in place for those who prefer not to be covered under a government plan. In addition, under the national plan, and in order to ensure efficiencies, the private sector would be the health care provider, certainly for the next generation and subsequent generations, not Medicare and Medicaid, which would be phased out. The cost of the national plan could be borne by way of an employment tax such as collected today. For Medicare and Medicaid recipients, the cost could be paid by instituting a national gaming lottery akin to state lotteries used to finance primary and secondary programs for education. Further, Medicare and Medicaid as separate operating programs would be eliminated with oversight and guidance provided by existing state insurance departments and agencies. In addition, to reduce the cost of "defensive medicine," legal awards for malpractice claims would be capped as with Louisiana's Medical Malpractice Act, which limits recoveries to $500,000. Additionally, attorneys' fees should be capped at no more than twenty-five percent (25%) of the award.

One of the major players in the health care debate is the drug companies and a major concern is the ever-increasing price of their products. On average, the retail price for prescription drugs escalates by 8% annually, resulting in a doubling for prices every twelve years. In addition, price escalation is pervasive for both drug retailers and medical equipment providers. The question is not if the drug or device is beneficial to society, but how to address the constant price creep. To further complicate the issue, consumers are allowed to purchase the same pharmaceuticals from outside the United States, most notable Canada or Mexico, at prices substantially lower than their stateside counterparts, resulting in a deleterious dichotomy that allows pharmaceutical manufacturers marketing privileges to sell their products under the Medicare Part D program at higher prices to Medicare (Health and Human Services) than other federal agencies such as VA. We can thank former Congressman Billy Tauzin (R-LA) for this privilege for he steered the bill through the House only to leave shortly afterwards and take a $2 million a year job with the Pharmaceuticals Research and Manufacturers of America, the pharmaceutical manufacturers' main industry lobbying (bag men) group.

Then we have the medical equipment providers who also exploit the system. One prime example is medical scooters. We have all seen their ads on television (*ad nauseum*) during which a senior citizen tells the story of how his or her life has been made so much better because of the scooter. Then the company announces it will take care of all the billing through Medicare. Well, these equipment providers pay, on average, $1,200 for each scooter, but then turn right around and bill the federal government in excess of $4,300, a 358% markup! Yet droves of Democrats would have us believe that a federal agency can do a better job in achieving health care savings for taxpayers - not in this lifetime!

Next, we have care providers such as hospitals, health clinics and the like. The cost for a night's stay in a hospital is simply unconscionable. For example, depending upon the services received, a one-night stay can range from $800 all the way to: brace yourself, $5,000. In addition, have you ever wondered about the pricing model that a hospital uses to price their services? We attempted to uncover their secret after having the misfortune of being confined in one for several days. Sadly, the secret is as well guarded as the formula for Coca Cola. However, this much is known -- the model is based on a tiered pricing model with the tiers based upon whether the patient has private insurance, government coverage such as Medicare, state coverage such as Medicaid, or is not insured. And, of course, staffers will inform you that prices are high because there are those who do not pay. However, they fail to discuss reimbursements received from government agencies such as Medicare and Medicaid or various federal and state agencies providing infrastructure financing for hospitals and health clinics at below-market rates. The inescapable conclusion though is grim -- prices will continue to escalate not decrease for there is no mechanism in place today, even with Obama Care, which will act as a deterrent to rising prices.

And, what about the personnel who provide the health care services -- physicians, nurses, technicians, administrators, and the like? The cost to employ them also increases year after year. Since there is enormous need today for health care professionals, a need, which will only increase with the "graying" of America, the demand for health care services will continue to outpace the supply of available service personnel far into the future, thereby eliminating any possibility of holding labor costs in check. Therefore, we can expect to see a continual swell in personnel costs for health care workers. However, the answer for controlling spiraling health care costs is not in instituting rigid price controls or infusing other artificial government-crafted deterrents into the system. Rather, if allowed to work as intended, good, old-fashioned, free market competition can keep prices in check.

Private health providers will now accelerate the rate and size of increases in individual health plan premiums to take from our hides the money they will need to pay for the impositions for the new health care legislation. Bet on it. If we have learned anything from the past growth of government, we know that, in the end, the more government interference, the greater the price increases -- one reason being the need to establish a contingency fund to take care of unknown risks associated with government mandates. The bottom line is that the insurance carriers have until 2014 before many of the provisions that they perceive as more onerous kick in so you had better believe they would use that time to build a storehouse of cash through higher premiums (they will follow in earnest the adage of *"making hay while the sun shines"*).

We the people, not the politicians holding hands and playing "kissy face" with the medical lobbyists and the bureaucrats, need to develop a cohesive plan to manage growth in the health care industry and find methods to improve the delivery of health services while containing costs. It is a tall order but we have the shoulders of our forefathers to stand on and give us the height we need. Future health care needs will be ever increasing as our population ages, stretching the industry's ability to provide care. We have a crisis on our hands, but if we do not take the rope, we will end up hanging by it, as the crisis becomes catastrophe. Nothing stops the citizenry from forming working groups throughout the nation, holding conventions, establishing better plans, and informing lawmakers what we want passed into law. Too many times, we sit on our collective hands and do nothing but complain. But we, the people, have the power to change the status quo by informing the elected the kinds of legislation that we want passed, not the other way!

Unless we desire health care to become ration care, material changes are mandatory. Irrespective of the type of profit motive, government needs to step aside, allow, and encourage the private sector to manage our health care system. Efficiency is not a hallmark of government bureaucracy but government can provide needed assistance in the areas of financing, training of personnel, and the elimination of unnecessary and often burdensome regulation and oversight to help mitigate rising health care costs. The bottom line is this: creating a new health care system managed and administered by the federal government will eventually result in another huge un-funded entitlement liability for the taxpayer with no means to pay for it. If we are and want to stay a market-based economy operating on the tenets of true capitalism, then we should reject the notion that government is the answer to our health care problems and, instead, recognize that government is more a cause of our health care problems than a solution to them. As for health care and the government's role, we may have to dance with the devil, but that does not mean we have to marry him or her!

A final note, when President Obama spoke to the Democrats who supported Obama Care, he thanked them profusely and publicly for doing *"the right thing."* He then said he had heard that the Republicans are planning to run in the mid-term Congressional contests on a "repeal the bill" platform. His response: *"Bring it on!"* Be careful what you wish for, Mr. President. According to a Washington Post poll taken a few days after the health care bill was signed into law, only 46% of those polled said they support the changes made by the new law, while more than 50% oppose them. Furthermore, 26% said they are very angry about the changes enacted by Congress, whereas only 15% said they are enthusiastic about the new measure. And a poll from Bloomberg News taken just after the vote revealed that only 38% of Americans favor the plan passed by the Democrats, whereas 53% of those polled said they totally oppose the overhaul, claiming that the Act amounts to a government takeover of the health care industry which will result in higher costs and a reduction in the quality of care. A survey by Rasmussen released this May indicated that 54% of the public favor the repeal of the health care law and only 42% oppose revocation legislation. Remember that old saying about the devil being in the details. Well, if the details end up demonstrating that the legislation costs the taxpayers a boatload of money in return for precious little, if any, improvement in health care, then that particular devil will show up, horns, trident, forked tail and all, in the mid-term congressional elections and the Democrats will have, to coin a phrase, *"hell to pay."*

CHAPTER 16

THE STOCK MARKET
'A Place to Feed the Need for Greed'

"Wall Street people learn nothing and forget everything."
- **Benjamin Graham, creator of Value Investing and Warren Buffet investment mentor**

"October: This is one of the peculiarly dangerous months to speculate in stocks. The others are July, January, September, April, November, May, March, June, December, August and February."
- **Mark Twain**

"The main purpose of the stock market is to make fools of as many men as possible."
- **Bernard Baruch, famous American financier/ economic advisor to Presidents Woodrow Wilson and Franklin Roosevelt**

As we listen more carefully to the "war of the words" between the political parties regarding the upcoming mid-term national elections, we begin to equate the rhetoric to a boxing match with equally skilled (or unskilled, depending upon your point of view) opponents. At times, the gloves have come off and the match has become bare knuckled. Each side goes back and forth with various combinations of jabs, crosses and counter punches, each scoring points, but no knockout blows are delivered. Remember, it is not about eliminating the other party from competition, rather it is about taking control for a while from the other party (each gets its "turn in the political barrel"). Each side actually needs the other (Democrat "yin" needs Republican "yang" or vice versa to complete the whole in their world of party politics) in order to continue their control over the American people. And, as noted before, one of the principal suppliers of the funds that enable the lobbyists and lawmakers to continue to perpetuate perhaps the greatest scam known to man is Wall Street. Wall Street helps the powers that be remain the *powers that be*, not only with campaign and other contributions, but also by continuously seeding key government positions from their own ranks.

Wall Street functions in a manner not dissimilar from Las Vegas and other casino communities. Better yet, think of Wall Street as the granddaddy of the casino kingdom, and the stock markets as the largest roulette wheels on earth. Understand that the Wall Street "houses" (rather interesting that, like the big casinos, they are called "houses") take a cut from each transaction -- each buy and sell order for a bond, stock, mutual fund transaction, etc. Further, the "house" makes even more when it makes a market in the security being bought or sold or takes the other side of the trade. It is not dissimilar to placing a bet with a bookie. The bookie charges a percentage of the bet as the "bookie fee" or the "juice." The bookie can then "lay off the bet" to a larger bookmaker (maybe his boss) or he can take the bet himself and, if you lose (and you surely will over time), he pockets the full amount of your wager plus the fee. Only it is an even better deal for Wall Street houses because they have access to much greater and higher quality information than the typical investor (or even bookmaker, for that matter).

Alternatively, the Wall Street house may decide to play both sides of the transaction such as with certain credit default swaps or other derivative trades or engage in an arbitrage transaction (buying a stock, bond, currency, or commodity in one market and simultaneously selling the same security or instrument in another market at a higher price), where it can make money on one or sometimes both "legs" and charge transaction fees to one or sometimes both parties to the transaction. Even if the fees and the transactional profits are relatively modest for any one transaction, they add up rapidly and become big in the aggregate when you consider that millions of transactions are handled every day.

Consider this: Goldman Sachs currently trades over one billion) shares for its own account in a typical week. Even if it made only a single penny per share, it would total $10 million and you know that Goldman is reaping more than one cent per share (it is not named Gold Man for nothing). So, in order for Goldman Sachs to have been able to report net revenues of over $45 billion and net earnings of over $13 billion dollars for 2009, you can "take it to the bank" (they are one - or at least were one - so that's pretty easy to do) that it participated in an almost incomprehensible number of trades from which it earned transaction fees and profits. In addition, it had the luxury of being able to use taxpayer capital for a while and it enjoyed reduced competition after the timely elimination of Lehman Brothers and Bear Stearns (by the way, its fingerprints have been found all over those liquidations).

As most everybody knows by now, Wall Street is largely a closed shop, a very exclusive private club. Membership is by invitation only and you have to have a sponsor. Wall Street is fiercely protective of itself and its membership and holds regulators and lawmakers (other than its own offspring) in utter disregard. However, it also realizes that, in order to play its game (that would be its version of "Three-Card Monty"), it must placate the lawmakers and regulators to some degree and so it does, first by outmatching the regulators with its "silk stocking" Wall Street lawyers, second, by hiring away the best and the brightest from the regulatory ranks, and third, by buying off the lawmakers using its high-priced lobbyists and political contributions.

John Q. Public looks upon Wall Street as the bastion of avarice and greed and the typical Wall Streeter as Mr. Ebenezer Scrooge (prior to his ghostly encounters). Wall Street looks upon retail investors (that would be us) as the "suckers" P.T. Barnum claimed are born "every minute". We are the sheep to be sheared and they are darn handy with the clippers.

The Street, as it is affectionately termed by Wall Street insiders, is able to trade on material information much more readily than the retail community because it has constant access to material information or, when necessary, can create the material information. The retail investor is usually the "last to know" for a reason and the big trading profits have usually been made by the time the retail investor trades on the information. And how can you compete with the sophisticated computerized (programmed) trading vehicles used by the big houses to take care of themselves, as principals, or their big customers, as brokers. Wall Street can trade at speeds which are literally orders of magnitude faster than the man on the street (Main Street that is). The Street is no two-way road, on which we can drive safely along with the Wall Street sleek and speedy "trading vehicles." No, it is a one-way street and they are granted the "right of way" at all times and in all places.

Have you ever wondered why The Street pushed for the way retirement accounts, such as the 401(K) and IRA, are treated under the tax laws? Because they get to use the money (your money) for longer periods, charging you fees and commissions for the privilege of having your money kept under their watchful eye. And, with the repeal in 1999 of the Glass Steagall Act (which prohibited commercial banks from owning or operating investment banks), the commercial bankers, formerly risk averse, have now become just as risk tolerant as their broker counterparts. Many use your checking and savings account money to make plays in the derivatives market or to buy crude oil or crop futures. In turn, they make huge profits and pay you virtually nothing for the use of your money. And many were able to use TARP (taxpayer) money to make such speculative investments.

Lawmakers have given The Street virtually unbridled use of depositors' monies to use how and when they see fit and, incredible as it may seem, Wall Street is not required to pay you anything for the right to use your money for their betterment.

Moreover, unbelievably, you do not have the right to opt out or demand a participation fee, nada, zilch, zero. The only right you have is to move your money elsewhere. This, in sum and substance, is what the latest Capitol Hill argument is about: should The Street be required to separate your money from their money when it comes to their investing in high-risk transactions. The Obama Administration believes that The Street should not be allowed to use your money to fund their stake in their high-stakes poker games, whereas the Republicans in Congress (and a few Democrats), not wanting to bite the hand that feeds them, favor keeping the status quo intact. In the end it probably will not be much of a battle -- the Republicans and the few Democrats, with Wall Street whispering sweet nothings (that would be sweet "do" nothings) in their ears will most likely derail Obama's proposal or end up with some watered down version of the original proposal.

During the process, you may bear witness to some wailing and gnashing of teeth by the White House and some of the Democratic leaders in Congress, but it will be primarily for show, a lot of sound and fury signifying nothing. It will undoubtedly prove to be yet another example where the Democrats are no match for their more battle-hardened and remorseless Republican brethren, who can fight with equal aplomb a guerrilla war, a war of attrition, or a pitched battle. In addition, they have the resources to launch massive air assaults (political *"shock and awe"*) and the will to use tactical nukes if need be. However, Democrats have shown they are they are adept at one type of attack -- the Kamikaze (suicide) mission.

In addition, let us not forget the recent *"too big to fail"* debacle. Another example of lawmakers taking care of their Wall Street *"familia"* (or *"familiars"*, as the human enablers are often referred to in popular vampire and witch mythology) and using our hard-earned money to do so. Moreover, this bears repeating: former Treasury Secretary Henry Paulson and current Fed head Bernanke used our money to bail out bankrupt financial institutions under the banner that the failure to do so would shut down Wall Street AND

Main Street. Not true. But the hoax was on us! If Paulson and Bernanke were so determined to save Wall Street at all costs (that happened to run into the hundreds of billions of dollars), why did they not save Bear Stearns and Lehman Brothers? Were they expendable for the greater Goldman and J.P. Morgan good (or greater Goldman Morgan greed)? Surely, this did not have anything to do with Goldman and J.P. Morgan making obscene profits in 2009!

If you recall, the concern was that the banking system would fail utterly and the "man on the street" (Main Street) would be unable to cash his paycheck or withdraw money, which would trigger a worldwide Depression to rival or exceed the Great Depression. Fear mongering at its best (and worst). What about the thousands of credit unions and community banks that took no part in the "Big Boys" game of craps (that name sounds about right)? We were intentionally kept in the dark as the "high priests" of corporate finance, Paulsen, Bernanke, Geithner, and their cadres of elite Wall Street bankers, "divined" from on high the "one true" way out of the wilderness -- the bailout plan.

Maybe, in retrospect, it should have been called the "Baal" Out Plan ("Baal" being pronounced the same as "bail," but referring to one of the seven princes of Hell in the Old Testament). In fact, these institutions should have failed along with the auto manufacturers and the rest of the companies that the taxpayers "saved" if we, as a nation, believe in the fundamental tenets of free market capitalism -- with risk sometimes comes failure. You cannot save the biggest players and allow the little guy to be reduced to rubble. This approach will not work because the little guy, who is the backbone of American business, will ultimately disappear either by being gobbled up by the big guy or growing so weary of the charade that he will close shop or become an activist and work to bring down the lawmakers who have given their support and favors to the big guys. In order for the system to work, it must be perceived to be fair and equitable -- ***"too big to fail"*** is grossly unfair and inequitable!

Oh, one more "dirty little secret" regarding Paulson, Geithner, Bernanke and Goldman. Bet you did not know that Barclays, a large UK banking conglomerate, offered to purchase a majority of Lehman Brothers prior to its bankruptcy petition. To complete the deal, Barclays wanted a guarantee from the Fed that it would stand behind the transaction and make Barclays whole in case of losses. Secretary of Treasury Tom Geithner, then head of the New York Federal Reserve Bank, and Ben Bernanke said no go. However, Barclays did end up buying Lehman's brokerage business for a song which Lehman is now challenging in bankruptcy court on the claim of price manipulation allegedly orchestrated by Paulson and Geithner.

Furthermore, the self-avowed financially sacred trinity of Paulson, Geithner, and Bernanke also convened in their high finance inner sanctum and prayed together (*ala* Nixon and Kissinger right before Nixon resigned the presidency) and decided it had been revealed to them that they must save AIG by infusing $180 billion dollars of our money – that's $180 billion to save a bankrupt company that through its trading subsidiary, AIG Financial Products, helped facilitate the subprime debacle and credit bubble through its issuance of specious and speculative credit-default swaps. Those instruments it sold were valued in the trillions of dollars and they were sold to organizations attempting to hedge against enormous levels of risk who knew or should have known that AIG was not in a position to cover if there happened to be a spate of defaults (which of course happened).

AIG failed to cover its bets by collecting adequate premiums. In fact, AIG collected only a fraction in premium dollars of the amounts needed to cover its exposure; and yet here was one of the premier insurance companies in the world, supposedly the crème de la crème when it came to understanding and evaluating risk and setting the premiums to be commensurate with risk. Yet, lo and behold, when one of the world's largest financial fans was hit with monumental amounts of ripe fertilizer, the Government quickly directed AIG to pay off its guaranties to the counterparties 100 cents on the dollar, not even bothering to attempt to negotiate a reduction (it could have paid nothing if it had been placed into bankruptcy, as it should have been). And who were the recipients of this $62 billion payoff? The big banks, with Goldman leading the pack at (hold on to your hats) $14 billion, $5.6 billion in direct funds and $8.4 billion in collateral it was permitted to confiscate. So then the "saving" of AIG was hardly the dispensation of financial grace to save AIG as a repentant financial sinner (the financially damned if you will). Instead it was a clever and at the time clandestine use of monetary dispensation to save the august college of financial cardinals a/k/a the big Wall Street banks.

Another example of the special favors bestowed by the aforementioned financial trinity on the chosen ones was arranging for Bear Stearns, a competitor to Goldman Sachs, to be acquired by Jamie Diamond at JP Morgan Chase, for pennies on the dollar. Having friends in high places never worked so well (except for the taxpayers of course)

Now, would it not have made infinitely more sense for the Fed to have saved Lehman by guaranteeing the Barclays offer, telling the various AIG counter parties that their credit-swap contracts were void, and directing AIG to go into bankruptcy? We mean -- is it not the rule of thumb in business that along with great reward must come great risk? This market rule was suspended, however, if you happened to be the former CEO of Goldman Sachs, as was Hank Paulson -- he had a set of new rules: eliminate the competition, maximize profits, and make sure your former firm is made whole, dollar for dollar, even if the money had to come from the "none-the-wise" public. The Paulsen rule was even better than the adage about having cake and eating it too -- in this case, they did not even have to bake or ice the cake, as that was all done by Treasury.

There is an additional point about AIG that the "talking heads" at CNBC and Fox Business will not raise with Paulson, Bernanke, Geithner or lawmakers. The "party line" for saving AIG was the fear that an AIG failure would wreak havoc on account holders of retirement accounts and insurance products under AIG's aegis, plus cause untold financial damage to the counter parties of the AIG credit-default swaps estimated in excess of $60 trillion dollars. But look a little closer and the arguments begin to fall apart. If AIG had been immediately put into receivership, the court would have made the retirement accounts of consumers priority one so those accounts would have been protected against any loss not covered by assets or other governmental protection programs, and the states, which regulate the capital reserves insurance companies must maintain in order to issue life and property policies, had already passed on the adequacy of AIG's insurance reserves.

The real issue then was the credit-default swaps. A bankruptcy court would have had the legal authority to unwind, cancel, and/or sell these financial instruments. Remember, the problem was that AIG Financial issued these swaps to almost anyone who paid the premium, undertaking little or no due diligence in its risk assessment of the possibility that they might have to cover the swaps. It was all about risk assessment and the financial assumptions, which AIG Financial assigned to these instruments. From a pure greed perspective, the less risk assigned to the possibility of having to make good on the swaps, the greater the profits and bonuses that could be generated. And, of course, we now are aware which avenue was taken - the one that was paved with indiscretion and led to ever-higher profit and bonuses! Yet how many times did we hear that AIG had to honor its contractual commitments required under these swap contracts? So, let us try to understand this: General Motors and Chrysler did not have to honor the contractual agreements it had entered into with its employees or retirees or vendors, but AIG did. Talk about preferential treatment. But of course, when you put a fox in control of the hen house and he throws a barbeque, you know who is going to be invited to the meal and, worse, which is going to end up as the meal!

Then we have the mouthpieces, the "lip jockeys", for the Wall Street elite, CNBC, Fox Business News, the Wall Street Journal, and all the rest of those who regularly march in the Wall Street parades. To tell you the truth, we are surprised that the gang on CNBC does not wear cheerleading uniforms when they do their broadcasts (we often get this vivid image of each person in his or her little on screen boxes holding up a letter, which, when seen together, spells out W A L L S T R E E T or, alternatively, each using his or her arms and legs to spell it out in the same way as the *Village People* did for the song "YMCA"). By way of comparative illustration, CNBC is as biased in their reporting for the Wall Street crowd as Fox News' reports are for the Republican Party. Just obscenely biased! For all practical purposes, their broadcasts are mostly commercial advertising for various public companies being promoted by The Street at any given time. Only they make it sound like they are "reporting" something of interest and value to John and Jane Q. Public, when anyone else wanting that kind of "coverage" would have to buy ad time to get it. They must think the viewing public is dumb as dirt if they believe they are palming off their purely promotional dialogue as "news."

The stable of CNBC commentators, including Kudlow, Francis, Leisman, Cabrera, Kneale, and others are skewed so far to the right that their comments lack any semblance of objectivity, just as Cavuto, Asman, Buttner, Varney and most of their guests who appear on Fox. It is not about news, but rather about their opinions. Neither one should be permitted to claim any connection to "news". Instead, they should be required to state, as are infomercials, that the broadcasts are "promotional" in nature and purely "editorial" in content. They are required to do so for the *Mad Money* segments of Jim Cramer, but the "prime time" broadcasts are not dissimilar. And we could care less about their opinions!

Seriously, if these programs are truly interested in presenting facts and not just opinions or "free" advertisements for Wall Street, then why not go after the facts instead of glossing over the facts.

We are not asking them to be *60 Minutes* all the time, but for goodness sake, do they have to be such rank sops and sycophants to The Street day in and day out? Does not one of them have a real investigative journalist's bone in his or her body? If they did, a condition of their hiring must have been that it had to be surgically removed.

When lawmakers come on these cable-babble programs, why not challenge them with unminced words for repeatedly voting for more and more deficit spending. What would be so egregious about challenging them regarding the national debt -- you would not keep an employee on your payroll who failed to do his or her job, especially after being put on notice, so why should you expect to get re-elected? Would you not be doing a greater service by not running for another term, or, better yet, resigning right here right now? Why treat Paulson as the savior of our financial markets when he helped to destroy them when he talked Christopher Cox, then head of the Securities and Exchange Commission, and other bank regulators, into changing the rules to facilitate the huge expansion in the use of financial leverage. In addition, all of them worked in concert to ignore the elephant in the room (and not just any elephant, but a Jumbo size elephant) -- the frenzied trading in Wall Street's Frankensteinesque creations, the CMOs, CDOs, CBOs, credit default swaps and other exotic, esoteric, speculative, high-risk derivatives.

Before 2002, the maximum use of financial leverage did not usually exceed eight to ten times an asset or debt valuation. With Paulson and his toady Cox at the helm, leverage was allowed to increase to forty times the asset or debt valuation. And Paulson asks how the credit bubbles could have come about! Please! The greed that knew no bounds finally hit a wall at full speed, but their airbags installed by Paulson and Friends deployed (that would be the bailout money from us) and away they walked with hardly a scratch. And instead of taking Paulson to task for his egregious conflicts of interest regarding Goldman and horrendous decisions in allowing AIG to stay in business, directing them to pay counterparties dollar for dollar, rejecting the Lehman offer, increasing the use of leverage in financial markets, etc., Congress and the "talking heads" hailed him as a hero. We are surprised they did not place a bust of him in the White House (and "bust" would truly be the correct terminology, given what we now know and should have known even then).

For example, if one watched Steve Liesman of CNBC during a recent interview of Paulson, part of Paulson 's promotional "book tour" for his new book, you would think that Paulson, along with Bernanke, literally, not just figuratively, saved the world from economic and financial annihilation. Liesman was so fawningly biased that he treated Paulson as if he was royalty. It is a good thing for us that the interview did not air right after lunch, because we would have lost it (lunch, that is). Never watch CNBC or Fox News if you have a weak stomach and are prone to retch. If so, we fear you will end up spending as much time in your bathroom as your living room.

There are thousands of events, which the so-called business news commentators could explore from a true journalistic perspective instead of their "entertainment" bent. But this would not do at all since it would necessarily entail scathing critiques of Wall Street and the lawmakers who protect and preserve the status quo for Wall Street. We cannot keep track (nor would we want to) of the number of times Kudlow has clamored for government to do more to serve the business interests of his monied friends and supporters, whether it is tax cuts or letting the banks and financial institutions run hog wild (like most Wall Streeters, Kudlow has acute short-term memory loss). If Kudlow would spend as much time denouncing government spending, the national debt, and the lawmakers whose actions helped get us in this mess as he does looking for ways to make himself and his friends richer, he might actually do some good for John and Jane Q. Public. Nevertheless, let us face facts -- he cannot relate to and does not care about the common man. If it came right down to needing to rip up some of Main Street to repave or repair Wall Street, Larry Kudlow and his friends would be right there directing the demolition and construction crews -- you can all "bank" on it.

We are surprised the "talking heads" do not blame the unemployed for being unemployed or the foreclosed for losing their homes (actually they do hint at such from time to time). If they had to walk in the shoes of those unemployed or face foreclosure or have their credit lines frozen or terminated, they might be a little less cavalier, a little less arrogant, a little less condescending, and a little less "ho hum" about the people out there for whom the world has been transformed into a harsh reality by the very institutions slavishly worshiped by Kudlow and Company. They need a dose of reality at ground zero instead of looking at it at 30,000 feet from the comfort of their luxuriously appointed Gulfstreams. We believe they just might hear a different tune, don't you?

Remember this; financial markets are neither fair nor forgiving. They take advantage of the misinformed, the disinformed and the ignorant. Their purpose is to use your money and return the least possible to the consumer. Consider this quote from a preface to a biography of Warren Buffet published in 2001 entitled *The Essential Buffet: Timeless Principles for the New Economy*:

> *"With each passing year, the noise level in the stock market rises. Television commentators, financial writers, analysts, and market strategists are all overtalking each other to get investors' attention. At the same time, individual investors, immersed in chat rooms and message boards, are exchanging questionable and often misleading tips. Yet, despite all this available information, investors find it increasingly difficult to profit. Stock prices skyrocket with little reason, then plummet just as quickly, and people who have turned to investing for their children's education and their own retirement become frightened. Sometimes there appears to be no rhyme or reason to the market, only folly."*

Now this observation may have been a revelation in 2001 when written, but in the past nine years, it has become almost a cliché. But the public continues to ignore the truth and be fleeced by the stock hucksters. We guess it is the same mentality that keeps billion- dollar casinos and bookies in business year after year. This is particularly so today when we just completed a decade in which the S&P 500 suffered the worst performance in 200 years of recorded stock-market history. It was the very first time the Standard & Poor's 500-stock index finished a decade with a negative total return -- a $1 investment in the S&P 500 at the end of the 1990s would have been worth just 90 cents at the end of 2009 -- and that includes investment income. Even the dismal performance during the 1930s was better, posting a paltry, but positive, total return of 1.0%.

The average investor is no match for the Wall Street bully boys (a/k/a traders) who can trade in such volume that they can move (manipulate) the securities markets, rendering them far from the pristine paragons of free market capitalism in which we have long been led to believe. Joe Saluzzi, an equities trading expert, stated on Bloomberg television that the big Wall Street trading houses act in tandem through their notorious high frequency programmed trading strategies to artificially inflate or deflate the stock market. Unless you can trade high volumes in milliseconds, says Saluzzi, you have no business trading for your own account. He estimated that 60-70% of the stock market volume at any given time is fictitious. He said the market is a big boy's game and the typical retail investor is, for the most part, clueless and a dupe.

Here is part of what Ben Stein, noted actor, writer, attorney, intellectual and commentator on political and economic issues wrote in the New York Times about Wall Street traders in 2008:

"I have come to believe in the theory of what I would call 'financial realism,' or what might more accurately be called 'trader realism.' Under this theory, on which I have an imaginary patent, traders can see masses of data any minute of any day. They can find data to support hitting the

'buy' button or the 'sel'" button. They do not act on the basis of what seems to them the real economic situation, but on what is in it for them. Just as a tiny example, years ago a close friend, now deceased, was a trader in London for a big financial house. As he told it, one day I.B.M. came out with stellar numbers. The boss of the trading floor said, 'O.K., the guy who's getting the prize is the one who can make us money selling I.B.M. short.' So the traders grabbed for their phones and started to put out any bad thoughts they could dream up about I.B.M. They called journalists, retailers, anyone. They sold huge amounts of I.B.M. short. Soon, they had I.B.M. on the run, made money on their shorts and went to Langan's to drink champers.

As I see it, this is what traders do all day long — and especially what they've been doing since the subprime mess burst upon the scene. They have seized upon a fairly bad situation: a stunning number of defaults and foreclosures in the subprime arena, although just a small part of the total financial picture of the United States. They have then tried — with the collaboration of their advance guards in the press — to make it seem like a total catastrophe so they could make money on their short sales. They sense an opportunity to trick other traders and poor retail slobs like you and me, and they generate data and rumor to support their positions, and to make money.

MORE than that, they trade to support the way they want the market to go. If they are huge traders like some of the major hedge funds, they can sell massively and move the market downward, then suck in other traders who go short, and create a vacuum of fear that sucks down whatever they are selling. Note what is happening here: They are not figuring out which way the market will go. They are making the market go the direction they want.

I know this because I know traders. They've told me that they love to sell into fear because fear is bottomless —

you can make money selling all day, while buying eventually slows because enthusiasm has limits. The amount of money available to large professional traders is so large that they can overwhelm the market, at least for a while, anytime they want. And they like to do it when the market least expects it.

So when you see the market gyrating wildly downward and hear some pundit saying it's because of this or that data or this paradigm or that ratio, remember   trader realism. The traders move the market any way they want, any way they think they can make money, and then they whisper a reason to journalists later in   the day. Then the journalists print it or say it on television, and the amateurs believe it. And the traders snicker.

These traders, not economists or securities analysts, can turn the world upside down, make governments tremble, give central bankers colitis and ruin the lives   of ordinary men and women saving for their children's college education or their own retirement. In America today, it is the traders, not the politicians or the generals or the corporate bosses, who have the power.

This is what has become of the America of Thomas Jefferson. Lucky for the traders. Sad for the rest of us."

We couldn't agree more.

Wall Street, as Mr. Stein intimated, made a bundle on the short side as the market tumbled in 2008 and 2009. Recently they decided it was time to go long again and start making money from a market rise. So they put their "operatives" to work to ensure the "bulls" would be large and in charge for a while. So now, tune in almost any day to Fox Business or CNBC or their ilk and listen to the predictions of a bull market and the accompanying raucous rah-rahs by the host and the vast majority of their guests. Same goes for the investment print media such as *Barron's, Investor's Business Daily, The Wall Street Journal,* and *Business Week.*

And it is certainly no problem for Wall Street to draw support from the analysts who, although supposedly objective and independent in their investigations into companies, are now recommending buy orders over sell orders by a ratio of 9 to 1. Small wonder since the analysts are employed, for the most part, by the investment banking community, many of whose clients are the same companies being reviewed by their analysts. The broker-dealers would have you believe they have impenetrable firewalls between their analysts and their brokers and traders. Right you are and we can sell you the Brooklyn Bridge for a mere $10,000, but you have to pay us in cash today. If an attorney engaged in such arrant conflicts of interest, he or she would be disbarred forthwith. So, if you doubt the legitimacy and integrity of analysts' recommendations you are right to do so. Case in point: Investors who followed the **Enron** recommendations of most of the analysts in the large national brokerage firms rode the stock all the way down to zero. And the analysts knew or should have known what was happening but they were being paid at that time not to "rock the boat" (even though it had capsized and was breaking apart).

In short, the message is loud and clear from those who most benefit from a healthy Wall Street: *"I won't lie, it's time to buy"; "if you snooze, you lose"; "he who hesitates is lost"; "there is a stampede of bulls and if you don't stay ahead of it, you will be trampled"; "this train, the Wall Street Express, is leaving the station and if you're not on it, you will be left behind"; "if you are a day late, you will be many dollars short."* If you are tempted to get caught up in this so-called "money making mania," first ask yourself this question: when a commentator tries to convince you that now is the time to put your hard-earned money (what little you may have left) back into the market, does the commentator stand to gain? Follow the money and you will find that most of these self-ordained experts have a vested interest as they attempt to sell their "book" (stocks or bonds they own or broker). We believe it is safe to say that you never see the talking heads interview a Main Street guy who just lost his life savings because he or she followed the investment advice of a Wall Street guru, and you never will. When the current financial crisis was unfolding over the past two years, did the commentators interview Wall Streeters who lost their clients millions of dollars -- do not think so.

The point here is not that you cannot make money in the stock market because some of you do (a few folks also make some money from time to time at the roulette wheel, the craps table, the Blackjack or poker table, or even playing the slots), however, most do not (and most of those who do make some money generally only do slightly better than break even over time). Let us ask it this way: what chance does the average poker player have against the professional card shark? Something about a snowball's chance of surviving in the netherworld, we think. And please etch this truth indelibly upon your memory (i.e., remember this if nothing else) The Street is able to make money, and much of it is yours, during bull markets and bear markets (in good times and bad, for better and worse, until your money do you part). During the last ten years, although the final tally shows it at about the same level now as then, in the interim, we have witnessed all manner of wild and wooly swings, and yet, during all this time, fortunes were made by Wall Street and lost by Main Street.

And if you doubt for a second there is manipulation by the traders, just watch the stock market the last hour of trading. Is it not remarkable how often the traders can take it up so many points in the last hour of trading, many times in just the final ten or fifteen minutes? And watch how their cheerleaders on CNBC and Fox work themselves into a frenzy cheering the market on. Folks, the market movement is by choice, never chance.

Hold the presses (and we did), this in from the major news services: **"Goldman Sachs Charged with Fraud by SEC."** The Securities and Exchange Commission has charged Goldman Sachs with fraud, deception and conflicts of interest in connection with its marketing collateralized debt obligations (CDOs) tied to subprime home mortgages. The SEC has evidence that Goldman failed to disclose that one of its clients helped create -- and then bet against -- subprime mortgage securities that Goldman sold to other investors. In essence, the SEC is going after Goldman for facilitating the perpetration of fraud on one customer to benefit itself and another. You will recall we referenced and condemned this practice earlier in this book. Damages resulting from the allegedly wrongful conduct are claimed to be in excess of $1 billion. The suit has also proven that the long (and hairy) arm of party politics reaches into the heart of the most important regulatory and enforcement agencies, like the SEC, as the vote of the commissioners to bring the Goldman action split 3-2 along party lines. The two votes against the suit by the two Republican Commissioners could very well come back to haunt the Republican Party, and, in all honesty, it absolutely should!

State enforcement agencies are also joining the party. Connecticut Attorney General Richard Blumenthal said his office has begun a preliminary review of the Goldman case. *"A key question is whether this case was an isolated incident or part of a pattern of investment banks colluding with hedge funds to purposely tank securities they created and sold to unwitting investors,"* according to Blumenthal. If Connecticut is "on the case," can the New York Attorney General be far behind? No, never.

And the SEC's action has already led to the filing of a class action lawsuit by investors in the CDOs sold by Goldman. Others will likely follow suit (literally). And Goldman will almost certainly not be the only Wall Street defendant.

And the SEC action against Goldman could prove to be merely the opening salvo in a full-scale enforcement assault by the SEC against other large financial institutions and perhaps Goldman for other instances of investment misconduct. "We are looking very closely at these products and transactions," Robert Khuzami, head of the SEC's enforcement division, commented in connection with the filing of the fraud suit against Goldman. "We are moving across the entire spectrum in determining whether there was fraud."

Apparently the Department of Justice, through the Manhattan U.S. Attorney's Office, is investigating Goldman and others for possible criminal wrongdoing. We predict that this investigation will end up with the same result of the criminal investigation against AIG's executives – being dropped, apparently under the doctrine of "too big to jail."

As you might expect, Goldman denied any liability and vowed to aggressively defend itself to its last breath. And the $1 billion at stake means Goldman will be willing to pay millions in legal fees to defend itself and its (tarnished) reputation. However, some folks on Main Street are saying this action proves there is a God and that His name is in fact G O D, and not G O L D.

After the announcement regarding the SEC suit, Britain and Germany also announced that regulatory authorities in those two countries would also be launching investigations of possible wrongdoing by Goldman Sachs.

It is also of note that Goldman is also under investigation in Europe and by the Federal Reserve in this country for its role in helping the Greek government hides its massive debt through the clever use of credit default swaps created by Goldman bankers. Some European officials have hinted that Goldman's charter to do business in the EU should be revoked. That result is highly unlikely, but the imposition of some sanctions is not.

And we recently learned that the SEC is investigating whether Goldman Sachs and the other big Wall Street banks used their own and their clients' money to bet in financial markets against municipal bonds they had sold. Even if those actions are not *per se* illegal, the banks might be found liable for failing to properly disclose their short selling activities to buyers of the municipal bonds. In a similar vein, the State of California is looking into Goldman's urging some of its big clients to place investment bets (through the purchase of municipal credit default swaps from -- *ta-da*-- Goldman of course). So Goldman was, yet again, making money from all angles. First, it collected tens of millions of dollars in fees for bringing the bonds to market and finding the initial investors. Then it marketed credit default swaps -- an insurance policy against a bond default -- and collected millions more in fees. Goldman touted a shorting strategy (betting on a price decline in municipal bond markets in California and other states) to clients in a 58-page report. Officials in California believe the strategy contributed to credit fears in the bond market, which in turn helped drive down the price of California bonds, drive up the interest rate the state and local governments had to pay to borrow money (an increase of a single percentage point on a $1 billion bond issue would cost taxpayers an additional $10 million a year in interest) and increase the value of the credit default swap investments for Goldman clients. Smacks again of the inappropriate conflict of interest which has become habitual for Wall Street, particularly over the last decade.

One quick aside worth noting. We turned on the television right after the news broke on the filing of the SEC action against Goldman. The commentators on *CNBC* looked as though they had just gotten news that a close relative had been in a terrible accident. And you might have thought the *Fox Business* commentators had just seen a ghost (maybe the Ghost of Things Yet to Come, to borrow from Charles Dickens).

But wait, the news just broke that Goldman has agreed to settle the SEC civil action for $550 million. This of course is a pittance (many in the financial press have called it a *"drop the bucket")* to Goldman as the firm makes this much in profit in less than a month. In addition, the stock value of Goldman, shortly after the announcement, rose by $3 billion, showing the settlement was welcomed with open arms (and open pocketbooks) by the investment community. Moreover, the company did not have to admit it committed fraud and it was able to insulate its executive officers from any individual admissions of wrongdoing. So, all in all, we would have to say Goldman got off easy, proving perhaps that its long arm of influence was able to reach into the very highest heart of the agency charged with responsibility for insuring the integrity of securities operations. Most feel this settlement will also serve to abort any possibility of criminal charges, at least at the federal level.

One positive upshot of the action against Goldman was a renewed impetus for financial "reform" legislation. Consequently, in May of this year the Senate passed the *Restoring American Financial Stability Act of 2010* (with some differences in the House and Senate versions being worked out in conference). We tuned in as the Senate passed the so-called "historic" measure (really more "histrionic" than "historic"). You would honestly have thought, from all the "high fiving," backslapping and self-applause going on, that a Congressional rapture of sorts was taking place before our very eyes and only those who had voted for the bill were to be numbered among the "elect." The sponsors of the bill hailed it as revolutionary legislation, the most sweeping in scope in the last 75 years, and claimed it will reign in Wall Street, really. Would that the legislation lived up to its grand and exalted title, but it doesn't. We hate to rain on the political parade, but, in truth, the legislation is profoundly more noteworthy for what if fails to do than what it does. Senator Russ Feingold of Wisconsin, one of only two Democratic Senators to vote against the bill, had this to say:

> *"The bill does not eliminate the risk to our economy posed by "too big to fail" financial firms, nor does it restore the proven safeguards established after the Great Depression, which separated Main Street Banks from big Wall Street firms and are essential to preventing another economic meltdown. The recent financial crisis triggered the nation's worst recession since the Great Depression. The bill should have included reforms to prevent another such crisis. Regrettably, it did not.*

The only other Democrat to have the courage of conviction and vote against the bill, Senator Maria Cantwell of Washington, voiced similar and other concerns:

"While this bill takes much needed steps to help prevent a crisis of this magnitude from ever happening again, it fails to close the very same loopholes in derivatives trading that led to the biggest economic implosion since the Great Depression. Throughout this debate I have fought hard against efforts to weaken this legislation as well as to pass language to strengthen it further. But the fact of the matter is, without key reforms in derivatives trading, this bill does not safeguard America's economy from a repeat of this crisis."

"It sets up a process for responding the next time we have a financial crisis, but it doesn't prevent this kind of thing from ever happening again. We have to stop these types of dangerous activities. We need stronger bans on banks gambling with depositors' money. We need bright lines – like Glass-Steagall – that separate risky activities form the traditional banking system. We need to refocus our financial system away from synthetic bets and get more capital into the hands of job creators and Main Street businesses. There are good, strong provisions in this bill and I'm proud of the work we did to get them in there, but I fear that without closing the loopholes primarily responsible for this economic meltdown, we are missing the entire heart of the matter".

Even Senator Dodd, the principal architect of the Act, admitted that his bill "*will not stop the next crisis from coming.*" What's that you say??? Moreover, a gaping hole in the Senate bill is the exclusion from regulatory reform of Fannie Mae and Freddie Mac, the two Government Sponsored Enterprises that have already cost the taxpayers $150 billion in bailout monies and may, according to the Congressional Budget Office, cost us an additional $240 billion in federal subsidies by 2020. Even officials in the Administration have freely admitted that Fannie and Freddie were at the core of the financial meltdown (but surely President Obama's having received contributions from the two entities when he was in the

Senate in an amount second only to "line my pockets" Chris Dodd had nothing to do with the Democrats voting repeatedly to block proposals to include Fannie and Freddie in the Act). The "sacred cow" treatment of the mortgage giants in the bill, along with the failure of the legislation to install a reliable, anti-lock braking system on Wall Street's propensity for excessive risk have prompted many critics to dub the new legislation "pseudo," "quasi" or "faux" financial reform. Take your pick, but what it really boils down to is flawed financial reform.

And now we learn that provisions which sought to stop the conflicts of interest, which are rife within the credit-rating agency industry, were stripped out in conference. Never mind that the credit-rating agencies contributed to the meltdown by assigning ridiculously rosy ratings to Wall Street's dubious debt offerings – even former Fed Chairman Alan Greenspan, a staunch defender of the rating agencies, referred to their AAA ratings of mortgage-backed securities as *"grossly inflated"* and *"inaccurately high"* in testimony before the Congressional Financial Crisis Inquiry Commission (of course that did not stop him from defending his longtime buds in the ratings agencies by saying that their errors were *"honest mistakes"* – uh huh and so were BP's and former Illinois governor Rod Blagojevich's).

At the last minute, a provision was included in the new law which would make ratings agencies liable for the quality of their ratings when used in selling documents for debt securities..The response of the ratings agencies? As you might expect, rather than stand by their ratings (for which they are paid very handsomely) they are refusing to allow their ratings to be used in connection with bond sales, which has brought the bond market to a standstill because federal regulations will not allow the bond offerings to be registered for sale without ratings. The ratings agencies are not going to play ball if they cannot play by their rules of having their cake and eating it too (getting paid for their ratings but having no liability if their ratings are bogus). The lobbyists have now shown up in droves and the word on the *Street* is that the law will be quickly amended to *fix* the problem or the financial regulators (under Geithner's friendly hand) will *fix* it through the issuance of corrective interpretive rules.

Nouriel Roubini, one of the most respected economists in the world and one of the first experts to accurately predict the 2008 collapse three full years before it happened, has called the financial reform bill merely "cosmetic" and warned it will not impede the next crisis at all. After the legislation was passed and sent to President Obama to sign, *Forbes* has this to say about it: *"So Unlce Sam didn't lead us out of the woods; he led us deeper into the woods. While he (temporarily) saved Wall Street, he may have gravely endangered Main Street."*

And the legislation may also do some serious harm by expanding the power of the Fed, which already has too much power and too little accountability. It really does nothing to force into the light the future operations of the Fed and instead essentially endorses the Fed's clandestine workings. Shockingly, the bill even places the Bureau of Consumer Protection, designed to oversee consumer financial products, under the control of the Fed. Go figure.

Not only does the bill do too little to reign in the big financial institutions, it does too much to restrict capital-raising by entrepreneurs and small business owners. The bill preempts state exemptions from costly federal securities filings and needlessly toughens the federal exemptions, to the point of making it unreasonably difficult to raise money from "angel" investors (including friends and family) who have served in the past as the lifeblood of entrepreneurs and small businesses for equity capital. According to some angel investment groups, the new restrictions may render 70% of current angel investors ineligible to invest. This would deal a major blow to capital formation for small businesses which are, let's not forget, the mainstay of job creation in this country.

Additionally, we now know it was not so much the lack of regulation that allowed Wall Street to almost shut down Main Street in 2008. Rather, it was a failure of the regulators to enforce laws and regulations already on the books, followed by the government's intervention to save them from their mistakes. The free market would have taken care of the offending Wall Street institutions had they been allowed to fail, as should have been the case.

As we were finalizing this chapter, the financial reform legislation was enacted (the final name being the ***Dodd-Frank Wall Street Reform and Consumer Protection Act of 2010***) and sent to the President for his signature. Again we had to witness the spectacle of highly animated self-adulation and cross-congratulation for an extended period of time -- plenty of "hip hip hooraying", dancing in the aisles and raucous cheers (nevertheless, we did detect some hearty Bronx cheers from a few Republicans). We were honestly surprised not to see the halls of Congress blanketed with confetti. Many of the major print media were somewhat less laudatory, however, in their view of the financial reform legislation which was approved first by the conference committee and then both houses. Consider these headlines:

"Banks Dodged a Bullet as Congress Dilutes Rules" **(Bloomberg)**

"Financial Reform Package Wouldn't Change Wall Street Much" (***Los Angeles Times***)

"Reform Without Punishment" **(Newsweek)**

"In Financial Reform, Rules Made to be Broken" **(Time)**

"Disjointed Risk Watchdog Reforms will Fail to Stop Financial Crises" **(The London Times)**

"Don't Bank on this Bill"
(**National Review**)

"Financial Reform? Not so Much"
(**Forbes Magazine**)

"Financial Deform"
(**Investor's Business Daily**)

"Financial Reform, R.I.P."
(**Forbes.com**)

The legislation deserved such critical responses in the press mainly because it fails miserably to get anywhere near the heart of the problems with the large financial institutions. It doesn't tackle Fannie and Freddie. It doesn't do away with the *"too big to fail"* doctrine. It doesn't bar many of the most dangerous Wall Street practices which helped fuel the meltdown, such as rapid-fire, high volume programmed stock and bond trading. It doesn't address the packaging of trillions of dollars of complex and highly speculative securities to hedge opaque investment bets. It doesn't touch Wall Street's bonus-oriented pay system which rewards higher risk activities and makes short-term trading profits the principal focus. Unfortunately, however, it does scale back drastically the provisions in the Senate bill which struck at derivatives, a principal culprit in the meltdown and it gives the big banks a dozen years to cut their stakes in in-house hedge funds and private equity units (by contrast, when Glass-Steagall was enacted in 1933, it gave commercial banks only one year to get out of the underwriting business). It also establishes a mind-boggling 533 new regulations, many of which will not be fully understood for years (plus this does not include the hundreds or perhaps thousands that will be issued by the regulatory agencies in charge of implementing the new legislation). And doesn't it speak volumes (literally and figuratively) that the new financial reform legislation is a mind-boggling 2,319 pages,(16 titles and 383,000 words) whereas the mighty Glass-Steagall Act was a mere 100 pages, less than 1/20 in length? Glass-Steagall stood the test of time for 70 years and kept the system intact and mostly prosperous during that entire period. The same will never be said of its "replacement" legislation, bet on it.

We like the characterization of the financial reform legislation by one commentator as nothing more than a *"fig leaf"* (the reference being to Adam and Eve covering their nakedness with fig leaves after eating the forbidden fruit and hence the phrase coming to mean a mere token covering for an act or behavior that is considered shameful or embarrassing).

The new law also gives the Street's old friend Timothy Geithner vast powers to determine the final form of the new rules to be drafted to implement the legislation. That is a sad commentary indeed. Remember this is the same Geithner who, as head of the New York fed, directed AIG to use taxpayer dollars to pay off the big bank trading partners 100 cents on the dollar (to the tune of $46 billion). In fact, it does not take an FBI forensic specialist to find Geithner's fingerprints on every bank bailout over the last 15 years. Might this be one reason we are hearing so little protest from Wall Street over the passage of the act? You tell us.

And transparency, the highly touted hallmark of the financial reform legislation took a hit in the final passage. Under a little-noticed provision of the legislation, the Securities and Exchange Commission no longer has to comply with virtually all requests for information from the public, including those filed under the Freedom of Information Act. The real reason behind the blatant undercutting of transparency? Apparently the SEC induced Congress to buy into its desire to shield future failures from the public. It would seem the publicity surrounding the recent spate of SEC shortfalls on the enforcement front, such as the Bernie Madoff miscues, were becoming too painful for the once proud agency that is supposed to protect the public from such schemes and artifices. They want to keep their dirty laundry well hidden from public view from now on -- what we don't know can't hurt them, although it can do us harm.

We have one final thought on this topic we want to share with you. We are confident that research studies in the not-too-distant future will demonstrate that most Wall Street bankers (and probably most politicians and lobbyists to boot) have an overdeveloped or overactive *striatum*, the part of the human brain which has been shown in recent scientific studies to promote greed. Similarly, along the lines of the **Grinch** whose *"heart was two times too small"*, they will also be shown to have *"two times too small" amyglada*, the part of the brain that controls (limits) risk-taking behavior. What will really be interesting will be whether these parts of the brain are shown to be genetically or congenitally abnormal and serve to induce afflicted individuals to seek careers on Wall Street or as politicians or lobbyists, where such behavior is the accepted norm, or whether such abnormalities are actually developed over time as a result of working in such environments. We predict this discovery will also popularize a new slang terminology for people who exhibit foolishly risky financial behavior as having a *"banker's brain."*

CHAPTER 17

THE JUDICIARY
'Guilty as Charged'

"All the rights secured to the citizens under the Constitution are
worth nothing, and a mere bubble, except guaranteed to them
by an independent and virtuous Judiciary."
- Andrew Jackson

"Judges are the weakest link in our system of justice and they are
also the most protected."
- Alan Dershowitz, American lawyer, jurist, political commentator and
Harvard Law School Professor

With our background in law, we take a special interest in our judicial system. Given the sad (as in ethically impaired and morally bankrupt) state of our lawmakers and law enforcers (our legislative and executive branches), we worry a lot about the integrity of our judicial system. Judges, after all, are supposed to be, like Caesar's wife, above reproach and suspicion (in this case, above even the slightest hint of political influence) -- this is the very reason that Lady Justice who adorns most courthouses and courtrooms in our country, holding the scales of justice, is depicted as wearing a blindfold, to signify that justice should be dispensed with complete objectivity and is (or should be) blind to money, power, or political influence. Or might it be the case that Lady Justice is deliberately blindfolded to keep her from seeing the way justice (or the lack thereof) is meted out today in our courts.

Let's start with the highest court in the land which one would believe should exhibit, without question, the highest degree of integrity and non-partisanship. Unfortunately, recent Supreme Court decisions serve to erode the validity of this belief. Let's turn first to **Citizens United v. Federal Election Commission**, handed down in January of this year. In this landmark ruling, a bitterly divided Supreme Court, by a 5-4 vote (strictly along ideological or "party" lines), overturned federal laws, in effect for decades, that prevented corporations from using their profits to buy political campaign ads, thus clearing the way for corporations and unions to spend enormous sums of money on direct political advertising.

The case began when a conservative group, Citizens United, made a 90-minute movie that was highly critical of Hillary Rodham Clinton as she sought the Democratic presidential nomination. Citizens United wanted to air ads for the anti-Clinton movie and distribute it through video-on-demand services on local cable systems during the 2008 Democratic primary campaign. But federal courts said the movie looked and sounded like a long campaign ad, and therefore should be regulated like one.

The majority opinion (along with Chief Justice Roberts' concurring opinion) went well beyond the issues presented, well beyond the relief the appellants had asked the court to rule on, thereby contravening the Chief Justice's repeated declarations that it is not a judge's role to legislate (I guess his reference to "judge" did not include "Justice").

In a contentious, sometimes scathing, 90-page dissent, read in part from the bench (in a pointed departure from court protocol), Justice Stevens claimed that the ruling "threatens to undermine the integrity of elected institutions around the country." He continued: The difference between selling a vote and selling access is a matter of degree, not kind. And selling access is not qualitatively different from giving special preference to those who spent money on one's behalf."

President Obama, speaking for the Democrats, called it "a major victory for big oil, Wall Street banks, health insurance companies and the other powerful interests that marshal their power every day in Washington to drown out the voices of everyday Americans." Indeed, but that will likely not stop him and other Democrats from tapping the pipeline of corporate and union money in the upcoming mid-term elections." He warned that the decision gives "a green light to a new stampede of special interest money in our politics." The public seems to agree. According to several bipartisan polls, voters oppose by a more than a 2 to 1 ratio the court's ruling.

Republicans, for the most part, lauded the ruling. The Senate Republican leader, Mitch McConnell of Kentucky, effusively praised the decision from the Senate floor right after it was handed down. Not too surprising in light of the revelation that Senator McConnell has received substantial funds from a subsidiary of a big foreign defense contractor currently being investigated by the Justice Department for bribery. This year alone he has requested $17 million in earmarks for its Louisville facility. As noted American journalist and public commentator Bill Moyers quipped on one of his weekly PBS programs, "Yes, the sun, and the dollar signs, shine bright in Senator McConnell's old Kentucky home." Amen.

And how about the landmark decision in **Bush v. Gore** in which the Court, again voting along "party" lines, overturned the Florida Supreme Court and ruled 5-4 that the Florida recount was unconstitutional, thus effectively resolving the presidential race in favor of George W. Bush? Surely this was one of the most brazen examples of the Supreme Court "playing politics" in its storied 221-year history, of judicial activism (decisions based more upon personal and political considerations than existing law) at the highest level, literally. It was a decision of truly historic importance since, as a result, George Bush was able to secure his election by only the narrowest of margins, 271 electoral votes (270 votes representing the minimum required for election) to Gore's 266 (and Bush actually lost the popular vote to Gore).

Perhaps the most famous and most politically polarizing (controversial) decision of the Supreme Court is the epic 1973 decision of **Roe v. Wade**, a remarkably audacious example of the High Court legislating from the bench, but this time reflecting the will of the more liberal Justices. The court deemed abortion a fundamental right to a woman under the United States Constitution, thereby subjecting all laws attempting to restrict abortion to the standard of strict scrutiny. But the court did not stop at striking down, as unconstitutional, a Texas law that made it a crime for a woman to have an abortion unless it was deemed medically necessary to save the mother's life. Instead, the Court, in a majority opinion authored by Justice Blackmun, held that a woman's right to an abortion is determined by her current trimester of pregnancy:

> *"In the first trimester, the state cannot restrict a woman's right to an abortion in any way. The Court stated that this trimester begins at conception and ends at the point at which the fetus becomes viable.*
>
> *In the second trimester, the state may only regulate the abortion procedure in ways that are reasonably related to maternal health.*
>
> *In the third trimester, the state can choose to restrict or proscribe abortion as it sees fit when the fetus is viable (except where it is necessary, in appropriate medical judgment, for the preservation of the life or health of the mother)."*

If that is not a piece of judicial legislation, we do not know what is. Justice Rehnquist, in his dissenting opinion, apparently agreed, as he observed:

> *"The decision here to break pregnancy into three distinct terms and to outline the permissible restrictions the State may impose in each one partakes more of judicial legislation than it does of a determination of the intent of the drafters of the Fourteenth Amendment."*

Put simply, the court was cutting out of whole cloth, making the means fit the end, manufacturing the result to conform to the Justices' more liberal leanings in 1973. The decision has come under extreme criticism and subsequent decisions of the High Court have sought to limit its scope somewhat, but it has not been overturned and remains the law of the land today, 37 years later.

History is replete with periods of judicial activism by the Supreme Court. However, even though judicial independence is a fundamental element of our republic, we can find nothing in Article III of the Constitution whereby the framers bestowed upon the judiciary the power to make law, only the power to interpret law.

Moreover, in earlier times, the court, more often than not, labored mightily to reach more of a consensus before its decisions were handed down. Not so today, it would seem. In recent years, the Supreme Court's decisions tend to be rendered strictly along "party" or ideological lines, with the barest of majorities, 5-4, deciding for the court a good 60% of the time. Another example in an increasingly long line of examples of such judicial division occurred in late June when the Supreme Court decided the case of **District of Columbia v. Heller**. In this historic ruling, the Court declared that the Second Amendment's guarantee of a right to *"keep and bear arms"* means that the government cannot enact an outright ban on certain commonly held weapons or otherwise prevent citizens from having a gun at home for personal protection or other lawful uses. The landmark constitutional pronouncement came as the court struck down a 32-year ban on private possession of handguns in Washington, D.C. The court also invalidated two other strict gun-control measures in the district requiring rifles and shotguns to be kept disassembled or secured with a trigger lock at all times. Justice Samuel Alito, writing for the majority, said the Second Amendment right *"applies equally to the federal government and the states."* The court was split along familiar ideological lines, with the five conservative-moderate justices in favor of gun rights and the four liberals opposed.

Next we turn to the important issue of length of service of the judiciary. Article III, Section 1 of the Constitution, relating to the length of service for federal judges, provides that federal judges *"shall hold their offices during good behavior."* Neither the framers nor Alexander Hamilton in *The Federalist*, Essay No. 78, in describing the role of the Judiciary, quantified such service as a lifetime commitment. However, it was well established precedent by the time of the writing of the Constitution that the term "good behavior" meant tenure for life unless the jurist was brought up and removed on a charge of misbehavior. Even though options for more limited tenure were available to the framers, it has long been settled law that federal judges, sitting at the supreme, circuit, or district levels serve for life or until voluntary retirement or involuntary removal for wrongdoing.

Now, the reason most often cited in support of life tenure is to ensure juristic independence from either the executive or legislative branches of government. Unfortunately, some of the more obviously biased Supreme Court decisions were based solely on political affiliations or to placate a particular constituency. One early example was the historic 1803 decision of **Marbury v. Madison**, in which the Court held a portion of the Judiciary Act of 1789 unconstitutional and thus invalid, thus establishing the Supreme Court's right to exercise judicial review of legislation and nullify legislation which it deemed unconstitutional. Although the decision itself benefited newly elected president Thomas Jefferson, he vehemently disagreed with the reasoning of Chief Justice John Marshall, writing for the Court, observing that if this view of judicial power became accepted, it would be *"placing us under the despotism of an oligarchy."*

Although the Constitution does not explicitly grant a right of judicial review, the decision became the accepted law of the land and also set the stage for the High Court veering away from a strict construction of the Constitution to a more expansive reading of the great document, when such liberality of review was necessary to find support for "political" or "arbitrary" decisions. And so the

Court on occasion has referred to rights being in the "penumbras" (a favorite judicial concoction from law school days) of the Bill of Rights (ala **Roe v. Wade**) -- the term "penumbra" being, by definition, an unreliable element of law inasmuch as it is defined as "an area in which something exists to a lesser or uncertain degree." Or sometimes the Court, finding naught to its liking in the actual words of the Constitution, decides to drill right through the words to find support for its position in the "interstices" of the Constitution -- another highfaluting word (to quote Steve's father) which the Justices use to justify using the Constitution to say what they mean and mean what they say, even though the true meaning of the term "interstice," "a small or narrow space between things or parts" would seem to make the Court's use of it to expand the Constitution inappropriate. And then the Court has even stretched the fabric of the Constitution to the point where it hardly resembles the document as written by drawing on, almost in sorcerer-like manner, those mysterious "emanations" from other provisions to create new rights, such as the right to privacy conjured up by Justice Douglas in 1965 in **Griswold v. Connecticut**, later used as the underpinning for an expanded privacy right in **Roe v. Wade**.

One of the more shameless (and, as it turned out, shameful) Supreme Court decisions driven purely by the politics of the day was the **Dred Scott Decision** of 1857 which held blacks, either free or slaves, were not citizens, much to the liking of Southern slave owners and then President James Buchanan. In a similar vein was **Plessy v. Ferguson** (1896) which upheld the constitutionality of racial segregation even in public accommodations under the court-created doctrine of "separate but equal," irrespective of the Thirteenth and Fourteenth Amendments. This decision held sway for 58 years until overturned in 1954 (when the political climate had shifted a bit) by the Court's landmark decision, **Brown v. The Board of Education**, which declared state laws establishing separate public schools for black and white students and denying black children equal educational opportunities unconstitutional.

There are many more examples of judicial activism based upon jurist political affiliations and ideologies in the Supreme Court and the other federal courts, but the point is clear -- even though the concept of judicial independence free from political or other types of influence is noble in concept, in practice it is honored more in its breach than in its adherence. Consequently, the primary reason for bestowing life tenure on members of the federal judiciary is largely eviscerated by practice.

Therefore, do we, the electorate, allow for the continuation of an honorable abstraction to stay in place or do we demand that our lawmakers effectuate change through the initiation of term limits for federal jurists? We have already made a strong case for term limits on the Supreme Court in Chapter 6 on Term Limits. The rationales enumerated there apply with equal weight to all life-tenured judges. And so we believe strongly that lifetime tenure needs to be eliminated for federal jurists. They should not be entitled to drink from some juristic Holy Grail.

Look, we are talking about a group of middle-aged judges, mostly white men, usually well off, who have longstanding political and bar connections. Each administration that enjoys the right to appoint judges does so for the sole purpose of influencing future legal decisions to reflect the political beliefs of the party in power at the time of the appointments. The main objective, then, in appointing jurists is the attempt by one party to stack the deck against the other party for as long as possible. And with the increased life spans and the reluctance of judges to step down from their judicial thrones, that can prove to be a very long time indeed. Most federal judges today do not resign until they are 70 and even then they simply move to Senior Judge status and continue to hear cases, but with a reduced workload, albeit at full salary and with a staffed office, including a secretary and law clerks.

Also remember this, when the framers first considered the concept of a grant of lifetime tenure for federal jurists, the role of political parties as it has developed today had not come into play. Nevertheless, by the time of the federal elections in 1801, political influence in all three of the then nascent branches of government was commonplace, even though the framers apparently failed to conceptualize that judicial thought would be so heavily influenced by political leanings or affiliations. In fact, when Chief Justice John Marshall first took his seat on the bench, he continued to serve as acting Secretary of the Treasury for President John Adams until Jefferson was sworn in. Can you imagine the inherent conflict of interest that created? The framers were really more concerned with the concerns of their English predecessors -- personal wrongdoing by jurists including bribery and graft to influence rulings rather than their judgment and judgments being politically influenced.

And let's not overlook the fact that we have precedents even within the current federal court system for limitations on terms. For example, federal bankruptcy judges are appointed to 14-year terms, federal magistrates serve 8-year terms and federal tax court judges serve 15-year terms. Litigants appearing before these courts surely have no less an expectation of fair and impartial treatment, free from ideological or partisan influence, from these jurists than from other federal judges. And thus the argument for life tenure for federal judges would seem to us to fall from the application of constitutional grace. Certainly we see virtually daily examples wherein the grant of lifetime tenure fails miserably to erect an insurmountable wall against the might of political influence.

Plus there is also a considerable cost, in terms of dollars and cents, associated with lifetime tenure for 866 federal judges. We spend annually almost $6 billion to support our federal court system, of which a full $150 million goes to support the grand concept of lifetime tenure; even though this amount seems relatively small, over time. More importantly, it's both unwarranted and wasteful. The simple solution would be to limit the terms of federal jurists to no more than fifteen years.

Since many more people are impacted by the state court system than the federal system (98% of all lawsuits in this country take place in state court), we would be remiss if we neglected to discuss the state judiciary. After all, there are more than 12,000 state judges, more than 14 times the number of federal judges. In 39 states, some or all of the judges are elected rather than appointed. The election of judges at the trial level is more common than at the appellate level. At the state appellate level, 25 states and the District of Columbia use blue ribbon panels with a Governor (or in South Carolina, the legislature) permitted to choose among several nominees from the panel, 13 states use non-partisan elections, 8 states use partisan elections, 3 states have judges appointed by the Governor (in California, this power is unilateral, while Maine and New Jersey follow the federal model), and 1 state, Virginia, has judges appointed by the legislature without blue ribbon panel input. Altogether, 58 state high court justices (18 in Texas alone) are elected to office in partisan elections, which represents about 17% of all 338 state Supreme Court justices.

There is developing a trend of increased campaign contributions in state court elections which may further erode the public's confidence in the impartiality of state judges and instead promote the perception that judgeships and justice can be bought. This disturbing trend was given even greater wing by the Supreme Court's **Citizens United** decision discussed above. As Supreme Court Justice John Paul Stevens wrote in his lengthy dissent: *"At a time when concerns about the conduct of judicial elections have reached a fever pitch... the Court today unleashes the floodgates of corporate and union general treasury spending in these races."* States that elect their judges, he said, *"after today, may no longer have the ability to place modest limits on corporate electioneering even if they believe such limits to be critical to maintaining the integrity of their judicial systems."*

This concern was also voiced in rare public remarks earlier this year by U.S. Supreme Court Justice Ruth Bader Ginsburg to the National Association of Women Judges. She said the money involved in electing judges remains one of the most pressing concerns facing the American court system. And she joined her former colleague, Sandra Day O'Connor, in calling for reform.

Former Supreme Court Justice O'Connor (the only living current or former Supreme Court member to have been an elected state court judge) told a group of Georgetown Law students that the flow of money into judicial elections has become *"a threat to judicial independence. If both sides unleash their campaign spending without restrictions,"* O'Connor cautioned, it will *"erode the impartiality of the judiciary."* She has called for states with judicial elections to switch to a system of merit selection.

In the past decade, candidates for state judgeships raised more than $206 million, more than double the $83 million judges raised in the 1990s, according to the soon-to-be released study by the Brennan Center for Justice at NYU School of Law and Justice at Stake, two non partisan groups that advocate for reforming the judicial selection process.

Three of the last five state Supreme Court election cycles topped $45 million. And judges shattered fundraising records in all but two of the 21 states with contested Supreme Court elections in the last ten years.

Concerns about the expanding role of money in judicial elections achieved widespread attention two years ago when information surfaced documenting contributions from West Virginia mining executive Don Blankenship to fund an advertising campaign for a candidate for that state's high court. Blankenship, the CEO of the country's fourth largest coal company, helped raise more than $3.5 million for ads aimed at getting a new judge elected, all while his company was appealing to the State Supreme Court a $70 million judgment against it. The justice elected cast the deciding vote in a 3-2 West Virginia Supreme Court decision which overturned an earlier verdict against Blankenship's company. That decision led the U.S. Supreme Court to intervene and cry foul, holding that a justice should step aside from a case if one of the parties has given so much money that the probability of bias would not be *"constitutionally tolerable."*

Another highly publicized compromise of judicial integrity was in Wisconsin, where a business group made up of utilities, insurance carriers, investment houses, and others began supporting candidates in judicial elections. Wisconsin Manufacturers & Commerce spent $4 million on ads that blanketed the airwaves in contests for two seats on the Wisconsin State Supreme Court, according to research by the Wisconsin Democracy Campaign, a non-partisan group that tracks political giving in the state. The most controversial ad in a 2008 campaign was produced by Michael Gableman, the business-backed challenger to Justice Louis Butler. The ad accused Butler of setting a child molester free to rape again, and showed a photo of Butler, who is black, next to the mug shot of the rapist, who is also black. The Wisconsin Judicial Commission called the ad misleading, but Gableman nonetheless won the election and now sits on the court.

After Wisconsin Manufacturers & Commerce spent $2.2 million to help elect conservative candidate Annette Ziegler in 2007, its lawyers filed a friend-of-the-court brief on a major corporate tax case and Ziegler authored a 4-3 decision in the case that, not surprisingly, ruled in the group's favor.

The 9 justices currently serving on the Texas Supreme Court have raised $12 million in campaign contributions. The race for a seat on the Pennsylvania Supreme Court last year was the most expensive judicial race in the country, with more than $4.5 million dollars spent by the Democrats and Republicans.

And there is always a general concern over impartiality of judges. We all know that judges are supposed to recuse themselves if they have a conflict of interest that might impair their impartiality. Frequently, however, they simply ignore conflicts, some of them patent and some of them latent. Take for example the ruling by District Court Judge Martin Feldman which lifted the six-month deep water drilling ban imposed by the Administration. It just so happens that Judge Feldman has and has had for years sizable stock holdings in many petroleum-related companies, including a drilling rig operator whose business has been severely diminished by the drilling ban and several funds with huge ownership interests in BP. His decision could be overturned on that basis alone, without the appellate court even having to rule on the merits. Incidentally, one quite interesting piece of judicial history in this context is worth noting. Supreme Court Justice Samuel Alito, due to his ownership of several thousand shares of ExxonMobil stock, felt compelled to recuse himself from hearing the 2008 appeal by Exxon that the amount of punitive damages ($2.5 billion) which had been assessed against it as a result of the *Exxon Valdez* oil spill was excessive. Nevertheless, the Court ultimately decided that the amount was indeed excessive under maritime common law and remanded the case to the trial court for reconsideration.

Before we leave the subject of the judiciary, we should address the widely held (and correct) view that easy access to this branch of government has made America the most litigious country in the world by a wide margin. America spends twice as much on tort litigation as Germany and three times as much as Britain or France. Last year, more than 20 million civil cases were filed - that's a filing every one and a half seconds, one civil case filed for every 15 people in the country. The annual direct cost of American tort litigation exceeds $250 billion, just shy of 2% of our GDP. The total tab for our out-of-control legal system is about $1,200 per person per year. The cost of the U.S. legal system has been growing at better than four times the rate of our economy. According to a Gallup survey, one out of every five small businesses decides not to introduce a new product or improve an existing one because of fear of litigation. No wonder when you consider the costs of defense -- e.g., The National Floor Safety Institute estimates that the average cost to defend against a simple slip-and-fall lawsuit is $50,000 and the average judgment awarded in such cases that go to trial is $100,000.

And we hate to say it, but the attorneys are the only winners in all of this and they are big winners at that. Otherwise, we would not have the largest number of attorneys, 1,180, 386 at last count, and the largest per capita, 1 for every 260 people, in the world. Tort lawyers last year raked in more than $43 billion in fees.

And how does the public feel about all of this? Not so good. According to a survey conducted by Harris Interactive, 76% of those surveyed feel that fear of frivolous lawsuits discourages people from performing normal activities. Further:

❖ A mere 16% of people trust the legal system to defend them against frivolous lawsuits.

❖ 54 % do not trust the legal system at all.

❖ 67% strongly agree (and 27% somewhat agree) that there is an increasing tendency for people to threaten legal action when something goes wrong.

❖ 83% feel that the legal system makes it too easy to make invalid claims.

❖ 56% think that there are fundamental changes needed to make the civil justice system work better.

Perhaps most revealing of all, most Americans surveyed (55%) strongly agreed (and another 32% somewhat agreed) that the justice system is used by many as a lottery, to start a lawsuit and see just how much they can win.

We have to change the system. We know this in our hearts and in our minds. The losing party, as in most other countries, should have to pay the legal fees of the prevailing party. Alternative dispute resolution mechanisms, such as mediation and arbitration should be mandatory and binding in more cases. As compared with litigation, they are much faster and much less expensive processes. Additionally, contingency fee awards for trial lawyers should be capped at 25% of the judgment, not the 50% plus expenses that is customary today. And state and federal rules for assessing damages against attorneys who prosecute frivolous lawsuits or put forth frivolous defenses to legitimate actions should be broadened and rigorously and regularly enforced. We are not looking for a utopian judicial system because we know that any system devised by the mind of man cannot be made perfect. But we also know that we can do better than the current judicial system which is broken and in need of extensive repair. In this case, it is far better to try and fail than never to try at all!

CHAPTER 18

CAMPAIGN FINANCE
'Nothing Money Can't Buy'

"Enough. It's time to strike a decisive blow against the anything-goes fundraising and spending by both political parties. Looking beyond the current headlines regarding the source of these funds, the massive amount of money spent is astonishing and serves only to cement the commonly held belief that our elections are no more than auctions and that our politicians are for sale."
- Ernest "Fritz" Hollings, Democratic Senator from South Carolina from 1966-2005

"Money! It is money! Money! Money! Not ideas, nor principles, but money that reigns supreme in American politics.
- Late Robert Byrd, Democratic Senator from West Virginia from 1959 –2010

Now we begin to worry about the legacy we are leaving our children and grandchildren on our methodology for electing candidates for federal office. A pay to play or fee for favors mindset is pervasive in our electoral system. Almost as if to make the appearance of corruption and bias even more conspicuous, even though we use both public and private sources to finance our federal elections, the existing system has been built to effectively eliminate funding for third party candidates and render the two-party system politically bullet proof. The current system, created by and for the two major political parties in operation today, the Republican Party and the Democrat Party, purposely sought to exclude third parties from participating in federal campaigns by imposing rigid qualifying criteria in order to receive federal matching funds. This matter is discussed at some length in the chapter on Term Limits.

With the Supreme Court's decision in **Citizens United,** one could argue that the Supreme Court has opened the door to unlimited campaign financing for any candidate, including third-party candidates, however, in reality, the campaign funding will go much more profusely to the two major party candidates because the entrenched two-party system is in a far better position to offer the political paybacks required in order to attract the large sums of financing needed for election. 2008 set a new record for campaign funds as more than $5.3 billion was spent in the presidential and congressional races, according to the non-partisan Center for Responsive Politics. Almost half of this staggering sum was spent in the presidential race, including the primaries, 50% more than was spent in 2004 (and representing approximately $18 for each vote cast in the presidential election). In comparison, third party candidates combined raised only about $200 million (less than 5% of the amount raised by the two major parties). Moreover, how about the third parties in the presidential race? Absolutely pitiful. Independent Ralph Nader obtained only $4 million (of which 22% were from federal funds); Libertarian Bob Barr raised about $1.25 million (with no federal funds); Constitution Party candidate Chuck Baldwin raised $239,000 (with no federal funds) and Green Party candidate Cynthia McKinney had a paltry $188,000 (with only about $5,000 from the federal government).

No third party candidate qualified for full matching federal funds and the only third party candidate to have qualified for matching funds since the inception of the program in 1976 was Ross Perot and his Reform Party. The matching funds program also pays the cost of the two major parties' national conventions and, again, the Reform Party in 1996 and 2000 was the only third party convention to qualify for federal funding.

Do not forget that the sole reason Congress attempted to regulate the election business was an attempt to dispel the prominent public perception that federal elections were rigged. The 1960 presidential race between John F. Kennedy and Richard M. Nixon which many believed tainted by allegations of corruption by both parties, combined with the infamous Watergate Scandal of 1973, resulted in the Federal Election Campaign Act of 1974 and the birth of the Federal Elections Commission.

In addition, there have been other attempts by Congress to regulate the flow of money into federal elections with the stated purpose being to defuse the popular belief that elections are bought and paid by well-heeled donors. For example, in 2002, Congress again attempted to reign in campaign excesses by further limiting the use of hard money donations versus soft money donations, the objective being to control the amounts of money from groups such as unions and corporations that could be donated through the political action committees ("PACs"). However, with the **Citizens United** decision, virtually no limitations now remain as to the size of campaign donations that corporations, unions or other organizations may make.

In order, that the election process be considered unbiased and fair, changes in the way federal campaigns are financed are necessary. As noted above, more than $2 billion was spent in the 2008 presidential election. With the expenditure of such huge sums on a single election, one may think (and rightly so) that some contributors donated money in order to gain political influence with the winning candidate. Republicans like to tar Obama with the brush that has him beholden to labor unions and trial lawyers (his two biggest campaign contributors). Democrats levy charges against Republicans that they are deeply indebted to the American Medical Association, National Auto Dealers Association and the National Rifle Association. In addition, both parties received hefty contributions from the agricultural, banking and insurance industries. The truth is plain to see - Republicans and Democrats are equally obligated to their campaign benefactors, and each side represents vigorously the interests of its commercial constituencies.

For example, consider the heated debate regarding health care reform. Democrats are attempting to improve the health care choices for the folks who voted them into office whereas Republicans mounted a brutally aggressive negative campaign in order to protect their physician, pharmaceutical, and insurance compatriots. Strangely, as we have previously discussed, at the party level, it is less about who is winning the debate and more about how much money is collected in order to keep the debate going strong.

Unquestionably, the two major political parties control the political environment. Moreover, since they make the rules and their minions enforce the rules, there is not all that much concern on their part of being booted out. Yes, some incumbents may not be coming back after the November mid-term elections, but one of the two parties will still rule the congressional roost. In a major (and tragic) way, our political system is a cesspool of opportunity for a fortunate few. Moreover, even though some states have attempted to enact "clean election" legislation, such as Arizona and Maine, where the state treasury funds statewide elections, success has been marginal at best because the programs have failed to meet the intended objectives of placing more women and minorities into elected positions and capping the amount of money spent on elections. The primary reason for the failure is the ability of a candidate to opt out of the government-sponsored program and spend as much as allowed by state campaign financing laws. Take for example, California, where politicians and their patrons have run amuck, spending over $150 million on the most recent gubernatorial election. That is a boatload of money for a job that pays $212,179 annually!

So, where does all the above lead us? Most of the electorate firmly believes that contributors who donate huge sums to political campaigns expect payback in kind. To think otherwise is being naïve or foolish. This is particularly so, given that the two political parties regularly reward their large dollar contributors with plum political jobs, ambassadorships and consular appointments, cabinet and other high-level executive positions, judicial appointments, etc., or choice government contracts. In addition, it does not require the proverbial rocket science degree to enable one to realize that the reason an industry or company receives special tax treatment is for payback. There is a bill pending in both houses right now, sponsored by Democrats, which would give contingency fee trial lawyers a $1.6 billion tax break, but we are sure that it is just coincidence that the sponsors have received enormous campaign contributions from various trial lawyer groups.

The Internal Revenue Code is replete with special exemptions for select organizations and corporations. For example, the oil industry receives special tax consideration in return for their years of sizable contributions to candidates. It is akin to the Wild West, only in politics it is not the one who can draw the fastest gun who prevails but the one who can draw the fattest check.

And, as we discussed earlier, once an elected official becomes a former official, either by his choice or that of the electorate, he still continues with political paydays by becoming a bag man (lobbyist) for the well-heeled political patrons.

Then what is a registered voter to do? That which follows provides suggestions to improve upon the system now in place:

❖ change election rules to allow all qualified candidates on the ballot for federally elected positions

❖ eliminate the election of a party replaced by the election of a candidate

❖ fund election campaigns by taxpayers (Treasury) since elected officials represent the national interest when serving in Congress as does the president or vice-president

❖ establish spending limits for federal campaigns based upon population

❖ equalize the sums spent by each candidate predicated on the population of the state or locality represented

❖ eliminate private campaign donations in toto; further, eliminate non-profit and for-profit organizations who attempt to influence the outcome of federal elections

❖ do away with political action committees

❖ establish new, rigorous standards for news organizations who present political commentary

❖ classify commentators who fail to meet journalist qualifications as entertainers and require appropriate disclaimers before and after commentary to alert audiences that the information presented is the entertainer's opinion, and not that of the network or necessarily the sponsors

❖ rewrite federal election laws incorporating the precepts of clean elections

As it stands now, none of these suggested changes would be adopted because neither political party wants change, especially the type of change we are advocating. The reason? Both parties desire the certainty, stability and preservation attributes accorded by the status quo -- in short, they neither want nor seek far-reaching change, not even minimal ("pocket") change. Think about it. In the world of politics, they are the "Boss Hoggs" (the fictional nemesis of the stars in the popular television series *The Dukes of Hazard* who epitomized greed and unethical behavior). In fact, as inverted and distorted as can be, the world answers to them, not they to the world.

Both parties have created huge Orwellian-like monoliths, built, like the Pyramids, to last a thousand generations. The existing campaign finance rules were created to shield them against competition and the courts, to date, have seen fit to reinforce their mechanisms for maintaining control. The bottom line: the two parties are the only game in town and both work feverishly to ensure everything stays this way. Simply stated, both the Democratic Party and the Republican Party have total control of federal campaign finance laws. The only group who can change this bi-gopoly (to coin a word) of power is the group of voters. .

Not that the framers of the Constitution were advocates for a limited political system, for they were not. In fact, they were far more concerned with the candidate than the party. However, shortly after convening the first Congress it was apparent that two countervailing political viewpoints had taken center stage. The first, known as the Federalists, advocated a powerful central government and was led by Alexander Hamilton and John Adams (and early on James Madison, but he later switched positions). The anti-Federalists were led by Samuel Adams, Patrick Henry and later Thomas Jefferson, all of whom championed the cause of a limited central government, countered them. Nevertheless, the differences were based on political theory, ideology, not political parties. Today, differences are based on constructs and beliefs, with elected officials serving as party mouthpieces. All in all, the elected official's primary purpose is to preserve the sanctity of the party as if the party is a living, breathing, legally created person (well, given this Supreme Court's predilection for finding corporations are people too, the party stalwarts just might be on to something by embracing this point of view).

We have turned the founders' viewpoint on its head and made today's elections far more about political parties than the individual office seeker. Of course, the Constitution does not mention political parties, only political candidates. In this case, the whole (the party) has become much larger than the sum of the parts (the candidates and party members). The phrase "tow the party line" now has real meaning and real teeth with which to bite those who get out of that "line."

We have gone from establishing laws regarding liberty and freedom of choice and the pursuit of happiness for individuals to crafting legislation and creating commissions to protect and shelter artificial entities known as political parties, just as the Chinese officials have done to protect the communist party. So in our country, the time when political candidates were seen as elevated beyond the status of any political party (to rise above petty party politics, as it were) has long since past. For some time now, candidates, even incumbents, have been considered replaceable (fungible), whereas political parties have been accepted as irreplaceable (not to mention irredeemable). And so the cry continues, "Long Live the Party! And (unfortunately) so say all of us!"

Now, maybe, just maybe, there is a glimmer, a small glimmer, of hope, of change we together can believe in and, more importantly, participate in. If we adopt some or all of the abovementioned suggestions in the near future, our children and grandchildren may be able to bear witness that we awoke from our self-induced miasma and not only thought of them, but acted for them, *for a change*! If not, we envision years of contemptuous finger-pointing and pervasive (and deserved) criticisms of our inertia and lack of courage which rendered us weak and ineffectual. We do not want to be characterized as political impotents, a "do nothing" (or, maybe even worse, "do nothing good") generation. Tom Brokaw wrote a best-seller about our fathers, mothers, grandfathers and grandmothers called *The Greatest Generation.* Heaven help us if one of Tom Brokaw's three daughters should write a book about us entitled *The Weakest Generation*!

CHAPTER 19

TALKING HEADS
'Smiling Faces Tell Lies'

"It's hard to believe that in the greatest democracy in the world, we need legislation to prevent the government from writing and paying for the news."
- John Kerry, Democratic Senator from Massachusetts

"Americans have no trouble believing that an individual may and should do everything within his power (and the law) to affect public discussion and shape public policy; that is his right as a citizen, as a participant in sovereignty, and thus as a source of legitimacy. But the mass media are not citizens or sovereigns. They are corporate entities, creatures of the state; they are elected by no one and are answerable only to themselves. Yet they possess far more power over our public life than does any individual. Their temptation is to claim that they exercise no political power ... But any such claim would be met with utter disbelief. Hard as it has been for social science to measure the full range of media effects, the fact remains that the media, at least as selectors of information, possess a subtle but massive power to define the terms, issues, and especially the priorities of public discussion."
- Dr. Paul H. Weaver, political activist, author

We are nearing the end of our exhaustive and exhausting journey, our self-charted foray into topics of public interest. There will be other excursions into new territories in the near future, but this one has to end not with a whimper, we think, but a bang. This is the next to the last chapter in our first foray into publishable (at least we like to think so) political and economic narrative. And, as we wind down our thoughts and reflect on our quest to better understand the economic black hole which has swallowed so many of our jobs and homes and so much of our life savings, we have to come to the stark (and dark) realization that what we have watched unfold for the past three years is a story about greed and ambition not so different from an episode of the old 1970s television drama, *Dallas*. Only this is not a prime time scripted out soap opera, but a reality show with real people, us, forced into really dangerous situations with no stunt doubles and no retakes and no being brought back to life after being "killed off," unlike J.R. Ewing and his uncanny ability to escape all but certain death time at season's end. Yes, the same themes -- absolute power corrupting absolutely and money being at the root of much mischief -- were at work in both, but we could turn off the television show in the case of *Dallas* and return to "real life." We don't have that option with respect to the reality show that has been playing out over the past three years and has many of us in its throes (death throes, financially speaking). No, for us today, this is as real as it gets.

Speaking of a reality show, what we have been put through is more akin to *Survivor* or maybe *Fear Factor.* Or possibly it bears a greater resemblance to *The Truman Show* (a motion picture about a 24/7 television show featuring the life of Truman Burbank, played brilliantly by Jim Carrey, who lived his entire life in front of thousands of hidden cameras for the show, though he himself was unaware of this fact), only Truman ultimately wised up and was able to escape from the show presumably to lead a normal life, whereas we are stuck in the drama, and for many it has turned to tragedy.

Now that we are on the subject of real life vs. television life (life imitating art, as it were), it is a good time to examine the role of the media spin-doctors who take real life events and reshape them to suit their predispositions and promote their political points of view. What you typically hear on their daily "newscasts" is advice, most of it worthless and all of it self-serving, on how one party or the other is at fault for this or that or Wall Street is the good guy or the bad guy or why certain lawmakers are working for us or against us or how certain administration appointees are either helping or hindering our economic progress.

Never forget that the commentators who so vaingloriously present their views and suggestions each afternoon and evening have jobs and homes and health insurance and retirement and expense accounts. They are the "haves" and they have little empathy for the "have-nots" and they really don't care how the "have-nots" came to be "have-nots." In their view, the "have-nots" have fallen from financial grace and, as such, are to be viewed as the country's economic "pariahs" or "untouchables." Unemployment, foreclosure and bankruptcy are, to them, badges of dishonor, warranting banishment to some economic ghetto, some financial leper colony to be kept apart from "decent" (creditworthy), "hard-working" (having full-time jobs) Americans.

If you stop and think about it, we are not orders of magnitude (maybe not even one order of magnitude) better off today than before the passage of the Thirteenth Amendment when slavery and indentured servitude were banned. The main difference today is most do not go to jail for failing to pay their debts (debtor's prison), but Wall Street's credit masters still keep millions in fiscal servitude, just as the "slave master" kept his slaves in physical and mental servitude. Additionally, if you fail to toe the line and pay on time, you will be punished like any other servant who gets out of line, only in this case by beating down your credit score, which in turn can preclude you from finding a job, buying a house, leasing an apartment, buying or leasing a car, or paying tuition. More than 80% of the states specifically allow employers to use credit reports in making employment decisions. It's tantamount to being blacklisted through no fault of your own.

Anyway, back to the media masters. The hate mongers, such as Fox News political commentators Glenn Beck, Sean Hannity and Bill O'Reilly, along with their usual guest talking pit vipers Laura Ingram, Ann Coulter, Michelle Malkin, Dick Morris and Karl

Rove among others, attempt to influence viewers by cautioning them that the Democratic Party, especially Obama, is out to destroy their future and turn the sacred word "free" into a profane four-letter word. This "Obamaphobia" works like a charm for the Beck, Hannity and O'Reilly (and of course Rush Limbaugh) audiences because it provides them an easy target to blame for the viewers' and listeners' discontent. Further, since a disproportionately large segment of their audience is white, middle-aged and middle-class, this group believes they have the most to lose and are most threatened by a black man being president (Limbaugh once played on his national radio show a racially offensive song entitled *Barack the Magic Negro*, sung to the tune of *Puff the Magic Dragon*) and a fiscally-irresponsible Democratic-controlled Congress (conveniently forgetting that a Republican President and Republican Congress put the pedal to the metal when it came to deficit spending).

Of course, these are exactly the thoughts these commentators want their particular viewers to eagerly embrace since it makes their job of selling fear, anxiety, and enmity that much easier. They are the merchants of misery and mistrust and business is booming - - O'Reilly reportedly made about $15 million last year, Beck more than $25 million, Hannity over $30 million and Limbaugh topped a whopping $40 million. Lifting a page from famed Nazi propagandist Joseph Goebbels, they too believe if you *"tell a lie often enough, people will believe it"* and *"the bigger the lie, the more believable it becomes."* Television commentators like Beck and Hannity remind us more of television exhibitionist personalities like Jerry Springer or Maury Povich and radio commentators like Limbaugh bring to mind more vulgarly flamboyant personalities like Howard Stern. All of them are in the entertainment business only the latter do not pretend to hold to any modicum of broadcast ethics or integrity.

Do the former present the news or are they thinly veiled spokesmen for the Republican Party (or the right wing of the Republicans)? CNN's Larry King said this about Fox News in an interview with the Chicago Sun-Times in 2007: *"They're a Republican brand. They're an extension of the Republican Party with some exceptions."*

Writing for the *Los Angeles Times*, Republican and conservative columnist Jonah Goldberg pointed out that Fox leans to the right: *"Look, I think liberals have reasonable gripes with Fox News. It does lean to the right, primarily in its opinion programming, but also in its story selection, which is fine by me and elsewhere."*

While promoting his memoir, *What Happened,* Scott McClellan, former White House Press Secretary (2003-2006) for President George W. Bush, stated in 2008 that the Bush White House routinely gave talking points to Fox News commentators, but not journalists, in order to influence discourse and content. He noted that these were not given to provide the public with news, but to provide Fox News broadcasters with issues and perspectives favorable to the White House and the Republican Party. And Fox ate the talking points up.

Progressive media watchdog groups such as Fairness and Accuracy in Reporting (FAIR) and Media Matters for America contend that Fox News reporting regularly contains conservative, Republican-slanted editorializing within news stories. Others have referred to the network as *"Faux News," "GOP TV," "Fox Noise Channel," "Fox Nothing Channel," "Fixed News," "Cluster Fox,"* and *"the Most Biased name in News."* FAIR also claimed that in a study of a 19-week period, the ratio of conservative guests to liberals on *Special Report with Brit Hume* was 50:6 and obtained similar results from other Fox programs.

Compare the Fox approach to the chatty Kathy's from MSNBC who present the more liberal, Democratic Party line, most notably through broadcasters (and leftist activists) Keith Olbermann, Rachel Maddow and Chris Matthews. It appears that both Fox and MSNBC violate the Federal Election Campaign Act by acting as unregulated Political Action Committees (PACs) when they present diatribe after diatribe seeking to encourage (sometimes directly but repeatedly by implication) the election of one party over the other or one ideology over all others, and worse yet, without fear of regulatory intervention. Unquestionably, most of the commentators employed by these cable news organizations use (and abuse) political rhetoric to influence you to vote for the party of their choice. And their sponsors provide many millions of advertising dollars to support this media masquerade.

Think about it - Sean Hannity makes no bones about the fact that he is a card-carrying Republican (so was Bill O'Reilly until he learned a week before *The Washington Post* was going to publish an article revealing his registrations) who works tirelessly (although his message has grown somewhat tiresome with repetition) to hammer the Republican talking points across to his viewers. *The World According to Hannity* would have us believe that any and every negative political event which has occurred since Obama was elected as President is the fault of Obama (don't get us wrong, we find a lot at fault with the current administration, but it is not the complete and utter bane of our existence, at least not yet). In other words, the Hannitys of the world are able to throw all the stones they want since they are without blame (if you don't believe it, just ask them), but Obama and the Democrats are always guilty as charged.

Now, it would take the three wise monkeys (you remember them, the ones who see no evil, hear no evil, and speak no evil) to believe that not one elected official or political party is ever at fault. Not so with Hannity and Company of the "my way or the highway" mentality. They are right 100% of the time and their detractors and adversaries are just flat wrong and misguided 100% of the time. More importantly, however, you must ask yourself, how can such devious drivel, such broadcast blather, be considered anything other than propaganda? Is it news? No way. Is it even good entertainment? Not really. Well, maybe it is, if you like Vince McMahon's **WWE** (World Wrestling Entertainment).

And the powers behind the broadcasters would have it so. Consider the Fox bosses, Roger Ailes and Rupert Murdoch, the consummate "puppet masters." It appears these two do it more for the money, whereas their marionettes perform for the money, but also the power and influence. The bosses want to be rich -- the broadcasters, rich and famous.

One way they might make some more money would be to commission one of the toy companies to manufacture and market bobble head dolls of the big-name talking heads or better yet, produce look-alike dolls with strings the buyer can pull and the dolls will say "blah, blah, blah, yadda, yadda, yadda, yeah, yeah, yeah" or "look at me, listen to me, love me."

All good fun, to be sure, but the issue is serious -- whether Hannity's propaganda, in particular, crosses the line of opinion in violation of the Federal Election Commission rules and regulations as it relates to PACs. And Beck, an extremist of the highest order (or New World), like Hannity, but even more so, attempts to brand Obama as a communist, a freedom filcher, a defiler of democracy, a diabolical Debbsite (a closet follower of Eugene V. Debs, presidential candidate of the Socialist Party of America in 1904, 1908, 1912, and 1920). Neocons such as Beck, Hannity, Limbaugh, Neil Boortz, and O'Reilly preach from their political pulpits that the nation is headed for perdition if we do not derail the Obama Express. Alas, even the most extensive and detailed X-rays would reveal not one objective bone in any of their bodies. That being the case, is it not fair to say that what they present is not news, only political propaganda? And that being so doesn't their promotional pandering, at least on occasion, violate federal election campaign laws?

Those at Fox are of course sanctioned by the powers behind the broadcast booths, primarily Ailes and Murdoch, but also John Moody. Murdoch is the founder, Chairman and CEO of News Corporation, the owner of Fox News Channel. He is also the publisher of the **New York Post**, to which he brought the sensationalism "tabloid journalism" style, replete with lurid headlines, popular in Britain and Australia when he bought the paper in 1976. Murdoch also publishes *The Weekly Standard*, a neoconservative opinion magazine published 48 times a year, which *Economist Magazine* referred to in 2005 as "the neo-con Bible." In 2007, News Corporation acquired Dow Jones & Company, giving Murdoch effective control of the *Wall Street Journal*. Since that time, the paper's editorial pages have taken a decidedly more conservative bent. This is consistent with the Murdoch way of doing business. By way of illustration, during the buildup to the 2003 invasion of Iraq, all 175 Murdoch-owned newspapers worldwide, without exception, editorialized in favor of the war because Murdoch was very outspoken in his support of U.S. involvement.

Ailes is the President of Fox News Channel and Chairman of the Fox Television Stations Group. And the only way he could only display greater allegiance to the Republican Party would be if he donned fake tusks and a trunk. Ailes was hired by Murdoch to create the Fox News Channel for News Corporation and currently serves as Fox News CEO. For decades he was one of the savviest and feistiest Washington operatives for the Republican Party. He served as a media/image consultant for Richard Nixon, Ronald Reagan, and George H. W. Bush. Controversy ensued in the aftermath of the 911 attacks when it came to light that Ailes was sending political advice via "back channel messages" to the Bush administration through its chief political aide, Karl Rove. Ailes has a hand in all aspects of Fox News programming. His biases are so prevalent and so egregious that they have even raised the ire of members of the Murdoch dynasty. In January of this year, Matthew Freund, Murdoch's son-in-law, stated that he and other members of the Murdoch family are "ashamed and sickened" by the overtly right-wing leanings of Fox News. He specifically named Roger Ailes and accused him of engaging in "a horrendous and sustained disregard for journalist standards." Rupert Murdoch responded by saying he did not share these views and instead was "proud of Roger Ailes and Fox News." We would expect nothing less from the conservative commandant than a staunch defense of his aide-de-camp.

John Moody is CEO of Fox NewsCore, the internal wire service for News Corporation and former Vice President of News for Fox. Former Fox News employees have stated that Moody instructed them on the approach to be taken on particular stories, mostly with a conservative bias. The Washington Post quoted Larry Johnson, a former part-time Fox News commentator as describing the Moody memos as "talking points instructing us what the themes are supposed to be, and God help you if you stray."

Former Fox News producer Charlie Reina had this to say: "The roots of Fox News Channel's day-to-day on-air bias are actual and direct. They come in the form of an executive memo distributed electronically each morning, addressing what stories will be covered and, often, suggesting how they should be covered. To the newsroom personnel responsible for the channel's daytime programming, The Memo is the Bible. If, on any given day, you notice that Fox anchors seem to be trying to drive a particular point home, you can bet The Memo is behind it."

It would come as no surprise to us if we were to learn one day that the Fox News commentators received written broadcasting instructions along the following lines:

"Propaganda must always address itself to the broad masses of the people. All propaganda must be presented in a popular form and must fix its intellectual level so as not to be above the heads of the least intellectual of those to whom it is directed. The art of propaganda consists precisely in being able to awaken the imagination of the public through an appeal to their feelings, in finding the appropriate psychological form that will arrest the attention and appeal to the hearts of the national masses.

Propaganda must not investigate the truth objectively and, in so far as it is favorable to the other side, present it according to the theoretical rules of justice; yet it must present only that aspect of the truth which is favorable to its own side. The receptive powers of the masses are very restricted, and their understanding is feeble. On the other hand, they quickly forget. Such being the case, all effective propaganda must be confined to a few bare essentials and those must be expressed as far as possible in stereotyped formulas. These slogans should be persistently repeated until the very last individual has come to grasp the idea that has been put forward.

Always emphasize the same conclusion. The leading slogan may of course be illustrated in many ways and from several angles, but in the end the remarks must always be the slogan."

This sounds like it might have come straight out of a Fox newscaster orientation session hosted by Ailes or Moody. Only this is a passage from Adolf Hitler's **Mein Kampf** in which he begins to lay out his blueprint for Nazi propaganda.

Back to the broadcasters themselves. Together with Hannity and Beck, the narcissistic Bill O'Reilly rounds out Fox News' talking troika. He pretends, quite unsuccessfully, to seek the truth in his so-called "fair and balanced" broadcasts. But he bleeds Republican red and it takes only a few minutes of listening to him to realize that his shows are anything but fair or balanced. Understand that we find nothing wrong in having conservative beliefs, however, as a broadcaster purporting to stand for fair and balanced reporting, it is misleading and a travesty for him to use his show to crusade for conservative causes, which he does in more than 85% of his on air content. It makes a mockery of his slogan and costs him dearly in terms of journalistic credibility.

The difference between O'Reilly, on the one hand, and Hannity and Beck on the other is one of degree, not kind. O'Reilly is more subtle in the conveyance of his message, whereas Hannity and Beck rely on the direct "in your face" approach. O'Reilly poses as a political cleric, and gives more sophisticated sermons, whereas Hannity and Beck are the conservative charismatic, "on fire" for the cause, inviting their audiences to renounce the Satanic doctrine of liberalism and accept conservatism as America's only savior. This analogy gives new meaning to their brand of self-righteous "holier than thou" newspeak.

Seriously though, if one reads the federal election campaign laws or the Federal Communications Act relating to the broadcast of political commentary, commentators are supposed to be prohibited from influencing the vote of the electorate with their commentaries. In other words, commentators may be found to have violated federal law if their program is all about promoting a candidate or a party for election. The commentary presented by Hannity, Beck, and O'Reilly is so clearly one-sided that they should be required to announce before and at the end of each segment that the Republican National Committee sponsors their programs. At least inform the viewer that the commentary is only their opinion and not to be considered news! Such a disclaimer should be printed in bold letters along the bottom of the screen from time to time during their broadcasts.

There is obviously something rotten in America when a supposedly reputable news organization allows its commentators to present their biased opinions under its news umbrella. We wonder (and worry) about the number of viewers who are mistakenly led to believe that these commentators are reporting facts rather than just giving their opinions and conjectures. Even some of the commentators have admitted they practice on occasion "advocacy journalism" (well, they got it half right, and we bet you can guess which half).

Nevertheless, we are not advocating the reintroduction of the FCC's Fairness Doctrine which dictated that broadcasters had to provide equal time for opposing views (the doctrine was repealed during the Reagan years). Rather, we advocate that the public airwaves not be used for the singular purpose of serving as a broadcast beacon for any political party. Additionally, we would be better served as viewers by the following: (i) if the broadcast consists wholly or mainly of opinion, tell the viewers so; (ii) disassociate the political views of the ownership from those of the broadcasters; (iii) provide the viewers the qualifications of the commentators (and if, as is the case with Hannity and Beck, there are none, say so); (iv) inform the viewers of the commentator's political slant, if any, and the amount of money being paid for sponsoring a particular point of view; and (v) require full disclosure by commentators of party affiliation, past and present, political plans, if any (Beck for example is contemplating running as a Tea Party candidate), and political ties, past and present.

Consider the following for purposes of illustration: if O'Reilly has a segment on sexual misconduct, he ought to disclose that he, personally, was involved in a sexual misconduct legal case brought against him by a former female staffer claiming sexual harassment which he decided to settle out of court reportedly for millions of dollars. Alternatively, consider Beck, who forces his audiences to endure theatrics, sprinkled occasionally with crying and sobbing (crocodile tears, no doubt) -- he should disclose that he is a recovering alcoholic and drug addict, has no college training (he took one course in college and then dropped out), has sought professional treatment for mental disorders, has "training" restricted to performing on the airwaves as a radio disc jockey, is not a trained political journalist, is a Mormon, and has pre-existing relationships with the Republican Party and most of his guests and sponsors.

Or Hannity, who should disclose that he too lacks a college education, has no training as a political journalist (his job experience consists of working as a carpenter and bar tender), had his first talk show program canceled after one week for making scandalous homophobic slurs about gays and lesbians, and has pre-existing ties to the Republican Party and most of his guests, and sponsors. It is worth noting that, at one time, Hannity was a sponsor of now disgraced banker Allan Stanford and even encouraged his viewers to buy Stanford Financial Group's investment products. Surely this touting of Stanford did not turn out well for those of Hannity's viewers who took the bait, but Hannity quickly swept this negative information under the rug.

And Ailes and Murdoch went along with this without comment. In fact, rumor has it they weighed in with "gag orders" on the other Fox announcers regarding Hannity's "indiscretions." Only when full disclosure is provided can viewers and listeners decide the level of credibility and veracity they are willing to attribute to the messenger and the message. These broadcasters talk incessantly about the need for their audiences to be "informed." Let them live by those words, then. Right now, we are treated to broadcasts filled with bias, shows replete with spin, in which the Hannitys and Becks are allowed (often encouraged) to say whatever they deem fit for the airwaves, with nary a thought given to election campaign or broadcast communications rule or regulations. We have come a full 180 degrees from the days of responsible broadcast journalism evinced by Murrow, Cronkite, Brokaw, Huntley and Brinkley, Jennings, and Russert.

Nevertheless, Beck and Hannity are essentially commodities, and once Ailes or Murdoch tires of their shtick, or their ratings fall and sponsors drop out or someone takes them to task for violations of federal law, they will be dismissed without fanfare. Remember, when all is said and done, it is all about the money. When enough people get sick and tired of the histrionics of hate, people like Hannity and Beck and Limbaugh and Boortz and O'Reilly and so on and so forth will be out of a job. But that is unlikely to happen anytime soon, we are sad to say. Look at the attack ads in political races which have grown by leaps and bounds. People say in public opinion polls that they do not like them, are even disgusted with them. But yet the candidates keep running them because they work.

To be fair and balanced ourselves, let us take a brief look at the other cable news networks. As mentioned earlier, MSNBC is the cable channel that supports the Democratic Party position and liberalism and it comes across much like the political party it represents: wimpy, whimpering and whining. Even though they often present affective counterpoints to their arch-nemesis, Fox News, they tend to lack the fervor and forcefulness of the Fox propagandists. They are simply less adept at getting "down and dirty." When they go to toe to toe with Fox, it is as if they have come to a gun fight armed with a knife (and a dull one at that). Moreover, it is generally easier to play the role of the underdog than the role of the incumbent. Therefore, MSNBC is constantly on the defensive, and they consistently get their butts kicked by Fox in the ratings wars.

For the most part, CNBC caters to Wall Street in a big way. Half their time is spent in allowing corporate executives, analysts, fund managers, and other financial community spokespersons to pitch their securities. Watch closely and you will even see the commentators' body language and tone shift with the movement of the market. They are upbeat and relaxed when the stock market is going up and downbeat and tense when the market is falling. We could put the television on mute and still tell how the market is faring just be watching the facial expressions (are they smiling or scowling, grinning or grimacing) and body movements, they are so "in tune" with the movement of the Dow Jones, the S & P, and the NASDAQ.

These guys are all about the money and they toady to the "haves" and denigrate the "have–nots." And if you really want to witness some serious bowing and scraping, some unreal groveling, just let them get close to one of the big boys from the Street, Jamie Diamond (head of J.P. Morgan Chase), Lloyd Blankfein (head of Goldman Sachs), Warren Buffett (head of Berkshire Hathaway) or Vikram Pandit (head of Citigroup). Just make sure that you don't eat before you watch one of these nauseating moony eyed encounters. The **CNBC** commentators steadfastly refuse to seek accountability in their interviews and invariably throw the interviewees low arc softball questions they can crank out of the park. They give new meaning to the phrase "treat them with kid gloves" when it comes to interviewing big name bankers and their ilk. And CNN attempts to play it down the political middle but leans liberal. All in all, they do the best job of the cable babble set in presenting political opinion as they do attempt to present both sides of the argument.

The broadcast networks such as CBS, NBC, and ABC tend to shy away from "editorialized newscasts" by limiting political opinion and highlighting news analysis and accompanying commentary. Even though all three networks tend to lean left in their reporting, in no way do they come close to the "yellow journalism" standards adhered to by Fox News. Again, our major beef with the cable guys and gals is that they fail to disclose their political agendas in possible contravention of federal election campaign laws and the rules imposed on political sponsorship by the Federal Communications Commission. If you are a cable news network with a political agenda, disclose such and do not seek to hide behind the protections (in their case, façade) of news journalism when the commentary is, in essence, little or nothing more than talking points for a particular political party.

And what's the deal with Larry King, whose *Larry King Live* show has aired on CNN for 25 years? Now, maybe he shouldn't be mentioned in this chapter since he sometimes is more like the *"walking dead"* than a *"talking head."* All right, that wasn't nice or fair, we admit it and we freely apologize to all Larry King fans. But, seriously, has he ever asked a guest a really tough question? We don't think so. Just once (or maybe twice) we would like to see Larry take on just a tiny bit of the "in your face," "pull no punches" persona of a Mike Wallace, Dan Rather, Morley Safer, Ed Bradley or Lesley Stahl. We would be overjoyed (not to mention, astounded) to see Larry King throw a guest a fastball or a sweeping curve every now and then, rather than feeding them one low arc softball after another that no one ever has any difficulty hitting (answering), often right out of the park. Is it too much to ask for him to lean a smidgeon less to the entertainment side and a wee bit more to the investigative side? We know his claim to fame is making guests feel comfortable and creating a low anxiety setting, but he is so easygoing he often puts interviewees practically to sleep (not to mention the audience). It would appear that even Larry King has had enough of Larry King as he has announced his retirement this year.

Is the network going to see the light and bring in a hard-hitting investigative type journalist as King's replacement? Hardly. Quite to the contrary, it now appears the replacement will be none other than Priers Morgan whose main claim to fame is serving as one of the judges on *America's Got Talent*. Talk about making it all about entertainment instead of news. Maybe they can hire Paula Abdul as a co-host with Morgan. After all, she has 7 years experience as an *American Idol* judge and is currently available. And they can change their name from the **Cable News Network** to the **Comedy News Network**. That way they can still keep the **CNN** brand.

While we're in our mood of bashing cable entertainment masquerading as news, particularly the so-called business and finance channels, isn't it remarkable how obviously most of those channels pay attention to "eye candy" with their female broadcasters, but noticeably do not accord equal weight to "guy candy" when it comes to their male counterparts.

An additional point on this topic deserves mention -- even though we have not conveyed our personal political leanings throughout this journey we believe it is important for the reader to understand that we truly have no "dog in the hunt" when it comes to political association. Even though we admire Barack Obama for becoming the first Afro-American to win the presidency, we are disappointed in him and his administration because he has already been effectively "assimilated" by the Washington Borg and is becoming another "me too" politico. We find both the Republican and Democratic Parties to be seriously corrupt and controlling. When you get right down to it, neither one has truly genuine concern for the well-being of the people who voted their proxies into office. In fact we dare say those votes were cast, for the most part, under false pretenses perpetrated by the candidates through their misrepresentations of standing for honesty, integrity, justice, liberty, and responsible and accountable governance. If their performance reflects their true vision of those honorable qualities, we would hate to speculate what it would take for them to find irresponsibility and dishonesty in office -- maybe the current regimes in Myanmar or Somalia or the Politburo in Stalinist Russia.

All of the politicians drape themselves in the Stars and Stripes and proclaim their undying love for their country and fellow citizens, but they rarely, if ever, practice what they preach. There is an old saying passed down from our English forebears that the proof of the pudding is in the taste -- well, that being the case, the taste left in our mouths from the current political system and the current slew of politicians is foul indeed and has left us with a bad case of indigestion. It would appear their love for money and power eclipses their love of country.

Now, we should not expect any lawmaker, especially those who have served several terms in office, to be honest in expressing the real reasons they hold public office. And again, we question why an otherwise sane individual would seek a position that pays $160,000 a year, if it costs millions of dollars to be elected and most of their time is spent in raising money and campaigning rather than doing the job for which they were elected in the first place. Certainly the feeling of power is intoxicating, as many former officials have stated. And some start out with wanting to change Washington to make it more responsive and responsible to the electorate (remember "change we can believe in"). However, they usually become just another cog in the Washington wheel of fortune or they are ground under by the party machinery or they become disillusioned and do not seek reelection or they are co-opted by the lobbyists and the influence peddlers (sell their political souls, as it were) or they retire and go to work for the "money masters" who bought them while they served. Very few happy endings and, for the most part, none for us as voters and taxpayers.

Simply stated, from 1835 forward, the people of this great Nation have elected to office lawmakers and presidents who have amassed a national debt in excess of $14 trillion (of which 70% has been created since 2001), created an un-funded liability in excess of $55 trillion, saved a corrupt and contemptible Wall Street from itself, put millions of people out of work and left them without homes or savings or retirements, grown the annual federal budget to $2.5 trillion dollars of which $1.5 trillion is un-funded, and indebted each and every one of us to the tune of $45,000, and all of this predicated on change. But they fail to add "for the worse." This is hardly the kind of change in which we want to believe, but rather change we want to leave -- far behind. What we are experiencing is actually the converse -- we are being treated to more of the same. They keep rerunning the same movie and we are deathly tired of watching it. Changing the position of the deck chairs on the **RMS Titanic** is not the kind of change that will keep us from sinking. As for the kind of change we have been getting of late, we say *"keep the change."* Changing the spark plugs and the oil occasionally can only keep your car running for so long. At some point, if you want to keep driving, you have to let a skilled mechanic perform a complete engine overhaul or buy a new car. And that's where we are today.

The time has come for us, the electorate, to take back our airwaves, our political system, and our financial well being. Let us put ourselves in charge for a better America for our children and theirs. What we have seen and experienced for the past ten years especially has been both disheartening and eye opening. The two-party political system works for a handful but not for the vast majority. Wall Street is all about greed. As for government, more is less, as in the more we have of government, the less we have of liberty and freedom. It is now time to eliminate the two-party political system, make Wall Street pay us back for all they stole, and drastically reduce the size of government.

We're tired of all the "talking heads" telling us what we need to survive and how corrupt and sinister the other side is. We especially are tired of the hate mongering. We do not want to hear any longer the end product of Ailes' and Murdoch's minions and others who preach hate alone and who seek to divide this great country of ours for their personal pecuniary benefit. We have been doing the listening for far too long. Now we are going to do the talking. And we are going to speak straight from our hearts and also from the ballot box. And we will be heard, on that you can depend.

If we want our country back, we have to take it back and we can start by taking on the "talking heads"! We're game and hope you are too.

CHAPTER 20

THE FUTURE
'As Ye Sow, So Shall Ye Reap'

"The very best way to predict the future is to invent it."
- Immanuel Kant

"We are called to be architects of the future, not its victims."
- R. Buckminster Fuller

*"It is not enough to understand, or to see clearly. The future will
be shaped in the arena of human activity, by those willing to
commit their minds and their bodies to the task."*
- Robert F. Kennedy

Well, we have finally arrived at the final chapter and we hope
we have saved the best for last. We must agree that not being a part
of the solution makes us a part of the problem. Many have
delineated the problems and difficulties facing us, some in more
articulate fashion than we. But far fewer have provided a
comprehensive and organized plan to tackle them. Some have
taken a piecemeal approach and posited one or two solutions to
one or two problems. We have tried to do more, to wrap our arms
(and minds) around a host of concerns and deal with them at their
core.

We certainly do not want to be viewed as mere acolytes of
Eeyore, Winnie the Pooh's ever dismal and forlorn friend who
lived in an area in the 100 Acre Wood called "Eeyore's Gloomy
Place: Rather Boggy and Sad." On the other hand, maybe all of us
were a little too hasty in rudely scoffing at ***Chicken Little's*** dire

predictions (he who is now known in some circles as *Professor Little* or *Dr.* Little for his Ph.D. in the science of prognostication). And maybe we should not been so dismissive of the young boy *who cried wolf.* With 20-20 hindsight we can see how he might have been fooled (just as we were) by the wolves being cleverly clad in sheep's clothing – only this sheep's clothing was the three-piece kind of the highest grade wool, perfectly tailored, and bearing exotic names like Armani, Gucci, Yves Saint Laurent, Valentino and Hugo Boss (the hairy, large-toothed predator in *Little Red Riding Hood* could have learned a thing or two from these masters of disguise, as could the "blowhard" in the *Three Little Pigs*). And these lupine-like carnivores fearlessly roam the halls of Congress and state legislatures, corporate board rooms, the inner sanctum of the Federal Reserve Board of Governors, and countless bureaus, agencies, departments, and committee rooms licking their chops at the sight of all that money, our money.

Well we got that off our chests and we feel better for the first time since embarking on our odyssey into the tempestuous, sometimes treacherous, seas of government, politics, and economics. During our venturesome voyage, we have looked with trepidation upon the Leviathan called the Federal Government, sailed dangerously near the Scylla of the Federal Reserve and the Charybdis of Freddie and Fannie, watched many fall prey to the talking heads of the Hydras, heard the eerie, alluring calls of the Sirens of Wall Street, K Street and Pennsylvania Avenue, tacked frightfully close to the economic and governmental Kraken and watched in horror as they drowned millions of people, glimpsed the wicked faces of the "entitlement" Grindylows, gazed in horrid fascination upon the deadly Maelstrom of debt and deficits, and sighted the Loch Ness Monsters of politicos feeding up and down the Potomac. But we have a plan to bring these monsters and perils to bay and this is the reason we are feeling strong glimmers of hope.

We have had our moments of pessimism, to be sure, and we have shared a number of them with you. We find ourselves very disappointed in our generation for neither recognizing the infirmities plaguing our political system nor attempting to administer cures. We, like many before us, have passively accepted the political status quo, almost as if it was ordained by a higher power or sprang full-blown, like Hercules, from the head of Zeus. We, the many, have failed to challenge the few who decide that spending our money with reckless and feckless abandon and saddling us with insurmountable debt is acceptable.

We have failed to challenge and hold accountable Wall Street for putting millions of us in harm's way (economically speaking) and refused to hold the politicians and the lobbyists who feed them and feed on them accountable -- instead we have allowed them to believe they are endowed with an inalienable right to manipulate and exploit us. But we have a duty to protect ourselves and our families from such manipulation as did the Founding Fathers. To blame others for our misfortune is not going to bring about change. And just changing the guard every so often does nothing to change the system. Look at President Obama -- despite all the bellyaching about his being too liberal and too radical for America, he is proving himself and his Administration to be little more than another "me too" politician. In many ways he resembles George Bush a heck of a lot more than George Washington.

The one ideal of which we must never lose sight is that we, as a Nation, have the power to eliminate this abuse, to cease our masochistic ways whenever we so choose -- all it takes is the courage to do so.

However, to make matters more troubling, we allow media commentators to fool us into believing they are the only legitimate truth sayers and soothsayers, and no one need listen to anyone else. And should you question or worse, criticize them, you will be branded a heretic and blasphemer and denied political salvation. In reality, of course, they do not know the way to the Promised Land. What they do know is the way to the bank where they go daily to deposit the stacks of cash they make from selling their miracle elixirs. Most are entertainers who act more like circus performers than political journalists.

Sadly, though, we allow this deceit to be foisted upon us, but fail to challenge the hate speech, race-baiting, fabrications, innuendo and endless propaganda being substituted for news. These commentators are proud of their Nielsen ratings. However, once viewers are presented with the facts about their background and affiliations and the number of times they have had to "fess up" to distortions, half-truths and lies, a fall from ratings grace just might be forthcoming. Once the audience is made to understand that the views being expressed by various commentators are largely, if not totally, for entertainment value and not investigative reporting, fact-based news or authentic political commentary, most will become disinterested and cease watching and listening. If we just want to be entertained, we can all watch "commentators" like John Stewart and Stephen Colbert on cable television's Comedy Central. We cannot forget that we, the citizens, own the airwaves not Fox News or MSNBC or CNBC! And we can reclaim them.

During the last many weeks of introspection and reflection on the issues we now face as a Nation, and will continue to face unless and until we change direction, we have spent considerable time trying to better understand how we, the electorate, can take back the election process from the professional politicians and their benefactors. Most importantly, to determine how we can provide a better future for our children and grandchildren free from the political and economic tyranny we now endure. If the "American Dream" has always been to be able to give our children and grandchildren more opportunity, more prosperity and more freedom than we had, then we are witnessing the development of the "American Nightmare." We want to do something to awaken from the nightmare and get it far behind us.

Accordingly, we developed a plan entitled *A Plan for a Better America: Our Call for Action.* This, then, is our contribution to our countrymen in order to preserve and improve a Nation founded on enduring beliefs where we seek personal liberty over autocracy and plutocracy, hope over despair, independence over intrusion, and freedom of choice over the dictates of a few.

If we truly desire a better future, let us come together and find the courage and energy to change what is wrong with the American political system and never again allow lawmakers or political parties to dominate our lives. The lawmakers work for us. They are hired by us and they can be fired by us.

Let us learn from the recent economic destruction imposed upon us and promise ourselves never to allow lawmakers or their cronies to obligate or indebt us without our express approval.

And yes, what we are proposing will require citizens to be fully engaged and active in the political process in the future. But when our jobs, homes, health, transportation, security, liberty, retirement, and savings are at stake, isn't it worth our time and effort to be fully engaged and actively involved? Allowing a few "higher echelon" individuals total control over our lives is an open invitation to political and economic totalitarianism, which is where we are heading, no joke.

We believe the citizens of this great land are far better than the ones we have allowed ourselves to become -- complacent and largely hopeless. We challenge each and every citizen to stand up and take a stand, to walk the talk, just as our Founding Fathers did more than 250 years ago and the Greatest Generation did 70 years ago -- they gave their all so we could be free and prosperous. Good isn't good enough. We have to be at our best. We have a long and proud heritage to live up to. We cannot let our ancestors, but more importantly our descendants down. After all, there is a good reason the term "onus" (burden) is spelled as it is – because the obligation is truly *on us*. And we wouldn't have it any other way.

So let us answer the Call for Action! And let us do so today! We must do it right, to be sure, but equally important we must do it right now.

"Thou, too, sail on, O Ship of State! Sail on, O Union, strong and great! Humanity wit all its fears, With all the hopes of future years, Is hanging breathless on the fate!"

- Henry Wadsworth Longfellow

"I find the great thing in this world is not so much where we stand as in what direction we are moving: To reach the port of heaven we must sail sometimes with the wind and sometimes against it - but we must sail, and not drift, nor lie at anchor."

-   Oliver Wendell Holmes

A PLAN FOR A BETTER AMERICA

A CALL FOR ACTION

'Seize the Day'

1. Create Jobs

We demand that Congress establish a National Jobs Policy mandating jobs as our Nation's number one domestic priority. Jobs for all citizens who want work shall be the goal of the legislation. We have had a War on Drugs, a War on Crime, a War on Terrorism, and a War on Poverty. Why not a War on Unemployment? Ford Motor Company used to say "Quality is Job 1." We say "Jobs are Job 1" -- jobs for every person in America who wants to work. If we could put a man on the moon, can't we find a way to put people to work?

Under our plan, the federal government shall assist small companies in their formation, capitalization, hiring, training, marketing, financial controls, and regulatory compliance. Business owners shall be provided interest-free loans to create new jobs. The more jobs added the more capital provided the business owner. The loans become grants once a certain number of jobs are created provided the employer establishes and maintains approved retention policies. Congress shall act to encourage the creation and continuation of small farms, ranches, and aquatic businesses and provide financing for the purchase of equipment, land, and operating capital in conjunction with the Farm Credit Association.

Further, Congress shall help establish and create a new manufacturing base for the nation whereby business owners are provided real incentives to manufacturer products domestically. We must, as a matter of policy and practice, rec as a manufacturing center and reemerge as one of the world's leaders in the manufacturing of goods. Companies shall be provided currency adjustments in order to compete with countries such as China who artificially deflate their currencies in order to make their export goods cheaper than those we can produce at home due to our higher standard of living and higher wage base.

Incentives shall be provided to larger companies to repatriate jobs that were shipped overseas for perceived economic advantage and for refusing to jump on the outsourcing bandwagon. Our national policy shall clearly mandate the retention of existing manufacturing jobs. Trade policy and trade agreements shall be modified to include language encouraging the manufacture of products stateside. "Made in America" should once again have meaning.

We agree with Andy Grove, renowned co-founder of Intel Corporation, when he proposed earlier this year financial incentives to recharge American manufacturing, including an extra tax on products manufactured by offshore labor, and the use of the proceeds from the tax to support domestic-based manufacturing operations. Some will object strenuously that such a system would engender a trade war. Grove had a ready response to that contention: *"If the result is a trade war, treat it like other wars – fight to win."* And we cannot help but admire Mr. Grove's passion emanating from his personal experience and our historical experience when he observed:

> *I fled Hungary as a young man in 1956 to come to the U.S. Growing up in the Soviet bloc, I witnessed first-hand the perils of both government overreach and a stratified population. Most Americans probably aren't aware that there was a time in this country when tanks and cavalry were massed on Pennsylvania Avenue to chase away the*

unemployed. It was 1932; thousands of jobless veterans were demonstrating outside the White House. Soldiers with fixed bayonets and live ammunition moved in on them, and herded them away from the White House. In America! Unemployment is corrosive. If what I'm suggesting sounds protectionist, so be it.

We also demand for Congress to establish, in coordination with the states, a job policy for young people whereby community service activities such as assisting in hospitals, daycare and hospices, and cleaning roadsides, rivers, and public parks shall be provided to any young person who is in need of employment. The young employee shall receive fair compensation and school credit vouchers in order to attend college or job training facilities. This policy will be entitled the Full Employment Act for the Youth of America. We must make the elimination of the high unemployment rate among our young folks (above 25% for teenagers, the highest in over 60 years) a national priority and policy.

We must do the same for those over 55 who have also seen their unemployment surge by 331% over the last decade, from under 500,000 to well over 2,000,000). Replacing seasoned, higher-paid workers with less experienced, lower-waged recruits must be stopped. Age discrimination claims have reached record highs, but resort to litigation should not be necessary if our national policies are reoriented to promote jobs for the baby boomers who want (and more importantly, now need) to keep working and avoid "forced retirement." The over 55 job base is an incredibly valuable national resource and should be treated as such.

Further, Congress shall act to eliminate employment bias due to credit scores or the manner in which an applicant pays his or her debt obligations. No employer may access an applicant's credit file. At the very least a credit score holiday should be declared for the next ten years and then we can revisit the matter.

Congress shall encourage private equity firms to invest in start-up companies by rewarding these firms through the elimination or substantial reduction of corporate income taxes or other taxes such as excise and employment taxes. Further, if approved, private equity firms will be allowed to access capital through the Fed's discount window in order to supply capital to business start-ups.

Congress shall provide existing companies tax credits and a waiver on employment taxes for the hiring of all new employees who stay employed for not less than six months. Credits and tax waivers shall be paid for by the assessment of an entertainment fee assessed to sporting events, concerts, theater, movies, plays, and the like.

Monies needed to pay for the National Jobs Policy shall be supplied from the disgorgement of Wall Street profits earned from either the subprime collapse or credit bubble. Wall Street firms shall not be allowed to keep the profits earned from the taxpayers' bailout of these firms, including the profits generated from actions taken by the Fed's intervention under the "too big to fail" policy.

2. Require a Balanced Budget

We demand a balanced budget. Congress shall vote to present a constitutional amendment to the states requiring Congress to balance the federal budget on an annual basis. While no balanced budget amendment has ever passed at the national level, every state except Vermont has a balanced budget requirement. Until passage by the required number of states, Congress shall enact legislation whereby it does not either obligate or spend more money than it collects in any fiscal year and shall be prohibited from borrowing monies to fund new projects without providing the means to pay for any new spending. And no more gimmickry and trickery to circumvent this rule will be permitted, ever. Pay-as-you-go budget (PAYGO) rules (Congress can only spend a dollar if it saves a dollar elsewhere) shall become the *binding* fiscal policy of Congress, no exceptions except in times of national emergency and then only with the approval of two-thirds of both houses and the President.

In addition, Congress shall grant the President line item veto authority in spending matters that is crated to overcome judicial challenge. Further, Congress shall eliminate all spending known as "earmarks" -- period. Furthermore, Congress shall cease the practice of borrowing from the Social Security and Medicare Trust Funds to pay annual budget items (the only way Bill Clinton was able to make his false claim of a budget surplus). In times of defense-related or other declared emergencies, Congress shall enact necessary and fixed term (i.e., finite), single-purpose tax measures to pay for such expenditures (and solely such expenditures).

3. Institute Term Limits

We demand federal term limits. Congress shall present to the states a constitutional amendment requiring term limits for Congressmen and Senators. No elected Senator shall serve more than two 6-year terms and no elected Representative shall serve more than six 2-year terms. Current office holders shall be excluded from the new term limit legislation. The terms for either office may be held consecutively or non-consecutively. Congress shall pass legislation eliminating federal retirement benefits for lawmakers newly elected unless newly elected lawmakers have prior federal service. In that case time served as an elected office holder under the term limit provision shall be added to the member's retirement account.

Congress shall also present legislation which will provide a single-term appointment of 18 years for all federal judges, including the Supreme Court Justices. If it is determined that this proposal cannot survive constitutional challenge as an act of Congress, then Congress shall include this proposal in the constitutional amendment to be submitted to the states for ratification.

4. Eliminate the National Debt

We demand the elimination of the national debt. Congress shall pass legislation for the elimination of the national debt. The enabling legislation shall require that Congress eliminate the debt in not more than 10 years from the date of enactment. Further, Congress shall be required to reduce the debt in an amount not less than 10% annually until the debt has been fully repaid. In addition, Congress, with the aid of the Congressional Budget Office and the General Accounting Office, shall identify and quantify the unfunded liability. Further, Congress shall fully disclose to the taxpayers the amount of unfunded liabilities in line item fashion by department and use, and shall establish the means and methods to fund these obligations without increasing the deficit.

5. Reform Federal Tax Policy:

We demand a radical change in federal tax policy. Taxes shall be determined annually by the requirements of the federal budget. Further, there shall be a flat tax imposed on individual and business income to meet the funding requirements of the federal budget. Individual taxes shall not exceed 10% of income, earned or unearned, with the first $40,000 of income, earned or unearned, exempt from taxation. The exemption amount shall be annually indexed for inflation. There shall be no tax deductions, exemptions, or credits for individuals. Monies used to fund retirement accounts shall not be included in income, up to $50,000 annually, increasing by $10,000 annually up to a maximum of $100,000 annually, thereafter indexed for inflation. Capital gains, estate, gift, and alternative minimum taxes shall be repealed. Business income to include for-profit and not-for-profit entities and shall be taxed at a rate not less than 4% of net collected revenue. There shall be no business deductions, exemptions, credits, adjustments for losses, or deferrals. The size of the IRS shall be reduced commensurate with the simplified income tax system.

6. Phase Down Social Security:

We demand the phase-down of Social Security. In order for Social Security to be solvent for future generations Congress shall limit the number of Social Security claimants by encouraging the use of self-funded private retirement accounts. Congress shall exempt from taxation annually the first $100,000 of individual retirement self funding. Once the individual's retirement account equals or exceeds his Social Security retirement contributions, Social Security shall return the contributions to the payer and the payer shall not be eligible to participant in the Social Security Retirement System. Further, once the payer has been removed from the Social Security Retirement System neither the payer nor the employer shall be required to contribute via payroll taxes for Social Security taxes. Medicare tax collected as a payroll tax shall continue. Further, there shall be no limitation on the amount of income at which either Social Security or Medicare taxes shall be levied. The tax for Social Security shall continue to be 6.2 percent of payroll and 1.4 percent for Medicare with an equal amount of tax paid by the employer. In addition, to insure against the individual's catastrophic loss of retirement account principal, the FDIC shall insure account holders up to $1,000,000 indexed for inflation. Private insurance shall be made available for amounts greater than the FDIC insurance to be paid by the account holder.

7. Hold a National Referendum on Health Care, Limit Medical Malpractice Claims, Establish a Medical Health Corp and Proscribe Drug Company Advertising :

We demand a national referendum to let the electorate decide on health care reforms. In the interim, we demand the repeal of the *Patient Protection and Affordable Health Care Act*. A commission of experts and lay persons, at least 50% of the members of which must be non-partisan, shall be formed and shall develop and present to the American people for a vote not more than three nor fewer than two proposals for national health care reform. In order to be adopted, a proposal must be approved by an affirmative vote of not less than 40% of those voting. All persons eligible to vote in a presidential election shall be entitled to vote in this national referendum. We fully expect one of the proposals to be universal health care for all citizens, with health care coverage to be phased in as the national debt is phased down. We would expect this proposal to provide for private health insurers to manage and operate the program. We would also anticipate this proposal to require the federal government to wind down and phase out its Medicare operations and transfer the Medicare program to private insurers over a transition period not to exceed 8 years from the commencement date. It would be our recommendation that each state be responsible for the oversight of and regulatory compliance by the private insurers. Under this type of reform, as we envision it, Congress would establish general policies, procedures, rules, and regulations, to be administrated by the states which would include, at a minimum, the following provisions: (i) no exclusion for pre-existing conditions; (ii) policy portability; (iii) coverage cannot be terminated or rates increased due to the insured's health conditions; (iv) promotion of insurer competition with negotiated rates; (v) no lifetime cap on policy coverage; (vi) universal enrollment required; (vii) additional coverage available to those who desire a more comprehensive health plan and can afford to pay the higher premiums; (viii) all plans shall be individual plans requiring no employer paid plans; (ix) cash or other incentives for healthy enrollees; and (x) preventive health measures for all enrollees.

We would also expect and recommend that a plan along the lines of the highly successful hybrid public-private (mostly private) health care system of Singapore should receive serious consideration to see if parts of it at least can be adapted to America.

As an interim measure, we demand that: insurers be prohibited from excluding from coverage persons with pre-existing medical conditions, insurance premiums be capped pending the referendum, insurers be permitted to compete across state lines, and the antitrust exemption for insurance companies be eliminated. Congress shall act to ensure that no citizen shall be left behind when it comes to the availability of health care. Additionally, the administrative process for handling medical claims shall be standardized and streamlined so as to drastically reduce claims processing errors which, according to the AMA, results in more than $15 billion in unnecessary administrative costs and mishandling of more than 20% of all insurance claims by health insurers.

In addition, we demand that damage claims against medical providers be capped at $1,000,000 per incident, with the cap indexed annually for inflation.

Further, Congress shall enact legislation for the establishment of a Medical Health Corp whereby qualified students are recruited to be trained as physicians, nurses, administrators, support personnel, etc. The program's objective shall be to relieve a possible shortage of medical personnel due to the increase in the number of covered enrollees. The Medical Health Corp shall be part of the federal Department of Health and Human Services.

The United States Food and Drug Administration shall act to prohibit direct-to-consumer advertising of prescription drugs by pharmaceutical companies. The United States and New Zealand are the only countries in the world which allow such advertising and advertising in New Zealand is more limited. As we are all painfully aware, the result of permitting such advertising in the U.S. is a daily avalanche of drug advertisements. How many *Viagra, Levitra, Cialis, Lipitor* and *Crestor* commercials do we have to see every hour we watch television? Big Pharma spends more than $20 billion annually in the United States advertising their products. These advertising costs drive up the cost of prescription drugs and siphon money away from research and development for better and more effective new drugs. Major pharmaceutical companies spend 25% of their budgets on advertising, while only 13% on searching for new drugs. Also, by urging patients to "ask your doctor about our wonderful drug," the industry pressures the medical profession to prescribe drugs patients may not need.

We believe additional funding for a universal health plan, Medicare and the Medical Health Corp could be raised as follows: (i) a universal health plan could be funded by a 3% value added tax (VAT), excepting gasoline, medication and food; (ii) Medicare could continue to be funded by a payroll tax of 1.4% levied on all earned income; and (iii) the Medical Health Corp could be funded by a transaction fee of not less than one quarter of one percent (.0025) for each and every market transaction transacted on the listed or electronic exchanges including commodities, futures, and currency exchanges.

A footnote on the idea of using a special VAT: should the commission determine a national sales tax would be more beneficial than a VAT, then a national sales tax could be proposed at such rate as the commission shall recommend. By way of comparison, it is worth noting that Value Added Taxes have replaced sales taxes in most of the world's developed and developing countries and have, by and large, proven easier to collect since businesses rather than governments are responsible for most of the tax collection activities and generally have resulted in a reduction in tax fraud and evasion. VAT rates in the European Union range from 15% to 25%. Australia has a 10% VAT, New Zealand 12.5%, Canada 5%, South Africa 14%, the Middle East 10% to 16%, Southeast Asia 7% to 10%, Japan 5%, Singapore 7%, India 0% to12.5%, Pakistan 16%, the Peoples' Republic of China 3% to 17%, Mexico 16%, Brazil 0% to 25%, and other Latin American countries 5% to 22%. And the United Kingdom has just proposed increasing its VAT from 17.5% to 20% effective January 2011.

8. Reduce the Size of the Federal Government:

We demand an immediate and substantial reduction in the size of the federal government. Congress shall take immediate steps to eliminate federal departments to include Commerce, Energy, Education, and Housing and Urban Development. The data gathering segments of each department shall be transferred either to the Department of Labor or to the Department of the Interior. The Department of Defense shall combine its purchasing component under each branch to a central purchasing component for all branches. Military bases shall be grouped by geographic region and the branches consolidated whereby the Navy, Army, and Air Force will occupy the same training area where practical to do so. The Military shall curtail its expenditures on large-scale fighting systems, which were developed to fight large land armies such as the Soviet Union (and have become anachronistic) and, instead, change its war strategy to fight unconventional, small-scale conflicts. And there shall be an immediate reduction in the number of military bases and installations outside the United States (from the 830 installations in 150 countries) and the military and support personnel manning them. Surely the United States does not need to maintain a military presence in virtually every country in the world as our days of playing policeman to the world should be brought to an abrupt end.

We also must privatize the U.S. Post Office within the next five years. The Post Office lost $3.8 billion last year and is projected to lose $7 billion next year. That is simply unacceptable. Private industry will trim expenses, modernize the system and make mail delivery profitable and more efficient. Many "experts" have said privatization of the Post Office will never work. They are some of the same "experts" who also claimed privatization would never work for prisons and jails, but those naysayers have been proven wrong as privatization has been quite successful in the incarceration "industry".

Further, the three branches of the federal government shall eliminate, within 36 months of legislative enactment, 40% of all executive committees, federal boards, corporations, commissions, quasi-governmental agencies, and other non-appointed governmental positions. Thereafter, the three branches shall maintain appointed and non-appointed committees, commissions, boards, etc., at a level not greater than 25% of the amount authorized in the 2010 federal budget for such activities, indexed for inflation. If obesity has become a health crisis for our population (and it has), then the obscene obesity of our federal government has become an even "larger" crisis, in terms of financial burden and deprivation of liberty. We are well past the stage of dieting. We need governmental gastric bypass surgery and we need it now.

9. Control and Limit Lobbyists:

We demand that the role of lobbyists be strictly limited. All lobbyist meetings conducted with either lawmakers or administrative officials shall be recorded when conducted. It shall be a criminal offense for lawmakers to take monies in any manner, including gifts, travel, entertainment, event tickets, contributions, barter arrangements, trade or payment in kind from lobbyists or from those who employ lobbyists. No lawmaker or official, whether elected or appointed, shall be permitted to work for or as a lobbyist until the elapse of 5 years from the last day of the last position held in the federal government. Lobbyists and those who engage their services shall register with a designated official from both houses of Congress and maintain and submit accurate and complete records of all meetings, telephone calls and electronic communications with members of the House or the Senate and other governmental officials.

Lawmakers shall not accept funding in any manner from lobbyists especially with the advent of campaign financing to be paid for by the taxpayer. *See Point 13 below.*

Additionally, lawmakers shall be subjected to ethics rules regarding conflicts of interest comparable to those imposed upon the judicial and executive branches of government. Accordingly, members of Congress will be required to divest themselves of, or place in a blind trust, assets which are related to industries for which they have oversight responsibilities or else they must abstain from voting on all matters pertaining to such industries.

10. Reform Our Monetary Policy:

We demand a change in the way monetary policy is established and controlled. Congress shall repeal legislation authorizing that the Federal Reserve is the sole entity responsible for federal monetary policy. Instead, Congress itself shall become responsible for establishing and maintaining monetary policy and shall receive advice from a non-partisan commission composed of representatives from small business, big business, the academic community, and "think tank" representatives. This commission will also be demographically and geographically diverse in composition. Further, Congress shall be responsible for the oversight of the Federal Reserve to include full audit by the GAO and supervision of all aspects of the central bank's operations, without exception. The Chairman of the Federal Reserve shall continue to be appointed by the President, but his confirmation will require confirmation by both the House and Senate (today only the Senate has to confirm the appointment). The maximum term of office for a Fed Chairman shall be reduced from 14 years to 10 years.

11. Reform Our Dollar Policy:

We demand a change in our dollar policy. Congress shall reinstate a hard asset standard to serve as collateral for our money supply. In addition to its gold reserve, the government shall hold a basket of other precious metals, including, but not limited to, silver, platinum, copper, and palladium in addition to oil, gas, and coal. The reserve of metals shall equal not less than 40% of our money supply. Congress shall support and maintain a strong currency policy backed by a reserve of hard assets.

12. **Reform Our Energy Policy:**

We demand a change in our energy policy. Congress shall enact legislation establishing an in-depth, functional federal energy policy. Imports of foreign oil shall be limited to 20% of domestic production, with oil importation from Canada and Mexico exempted. In addition, Congress shall create an alternative fuels program for the replacement of the importation of foreign oil. The alternative fuels program shall be operational within 7 years of enactment. Reliance shall be placed primarily on the production and use of natural gas, which we have in abundance in this country, and there shall be a renewed emphasis on the rapid expansion of wind power to generate electricity. T. Boone Pickens, if in agreement, shall be appointed as Special Energy Advisor to Congress and shall assist in the drafting and implementation of the new energy policy. Restrictions regarding the domestic search or production of oil and gas exploration shall be reduced dramatically. Revenue derived from all new sources of oil and gas exploration shall be exempt from taxation for a period of time, provided such revenue shall be used to create an effective and efficient fossil fuel alternative energy replacement program.

The House bill introduced this year to extend corn-based ethanol tax credits for another five years, to 2015, shall be rejected and the ethanol tax set to expire on December 31, 2010 should be allowed to expire as scheduled. If extended, the tax credits would provide the conventional ethanol industry with $30 billion over five years. The bill is being vigorously opposed by the food industry and consumer groups for contributing to higher food prices by diverting food products to energy, by environmentalists because ethanol production is actually more detrimental to the environment than gasoline and no cheaper, and budget hawks because the credit will add to the federal deficit.

We also demand that Congress act to lift the tariff on the importation of ethanol, particularly from Brazil which uses sugar cane and we demand the government expedite the process for approving the use of nuclear energy, which is now one of the safest, most efficient and cleanest energy sources available. And the raw fuel for which is one this country has in abundance in several of the Western states. The ghosts and fears of the past when nuclear power had safety, containment and disposal issues have long been banished with new technology.

13. Reform Federal Campaign Laws:

We demand a change in the way we pay for our national elections. The Treasury shall pay the cost of our national elections. Congress shall repeal laws which allow for political contributions of any type from any individual or entity. Congress shall enact a National Election Campaign Act whereby a multi-party system is encouraged and supported. All qualified political parties shall be treated equally regarding national debates, spending on elections, and media coverage. Congress shall repeal laws which allow external sources to advertise or solicit the vote for a particular candidate or political party. Congress shall repeal tax laws which provide tax exemptions for political action committees (PACs) and non-profit organizations qualified under Internal Revenue Code Section 501(c)(3) that attempt to influence the outcome of federal elections. Congress shall allocate an approved amount for all federal elections. The current Commission on Presidential Debates shall be abolished and replaced with a commission established by Congress whose members must be non-partisan and will be appointed for staggered terms of office.

14. Eliminate the Electoral College:

We demand the elimination of the Electoral College. It is now anachronistic. Congress shall send to the states an amendment to repeal the 12th Amendment to the Constitution. Candidates for federal office or Congress shall be elected by the plurality of the vote, provided, however, some minimum percentage, perhaps 40%, shall be required and if no candidate receives the minimum, a run-off election between the top two candidates shall be held.

15. **Reform the Federal Judiciary:**

We demand the elimination of lifetime appointments for federal judges. Congress shall seek to amend Article III, Section 1 of the Constitution whereby federal judges shall be appointed to a judgeship for a period not to exceed 18 years.

16. **Mandate Disgorgement of Profits:**

We demand the recovery of profits from TARP-assisted institutions as "ill-gotten gains". Congress shall enact legislation mandating that any Wall Street entity that was a recipient of TARP funds and participated in either the subprime housing implosion or the credit bubble shall be required to return to the Treasury all profits earned from such involvement, including profits derived from the use of Fed funds, loans, or guarantees. Profit amounts shall be identified within 90 days of enactment of the enabling legislation and returned to the Treasury within 180 days of identification. Payment shall include interest on the profits at the statutory rate for civil judgments in federal court as provided by 28 U.S.C.A. § 1961.

17. **Bring Back Glass-Steagall:**

Named for its Congressional sponsors, Glass-Steagall was enacted in 1933 during the Great Depression to separate the "mundane" commercial banking from the "exciting" investment banking that took risk to new and dizzying heights during the "go-go" years of the 1920s, leading up to the stock market crash and leaving millions destitute. In 1999, Congress overturned Glass-Steagall amidst cries that the old law had become *"obsolete," "outdated," "archaic," "out of step with the modern, sophisticated financial systems in the world,"* a *"throwback to the Depression era,"* and a *"relic of bygone days"* that *"needed to be jettisoned"* so our banks could move into the *"twentieth century."* Proponents of the legislation to do away with the wall between commercial and investment banking contended that the *"new and improved"* financial markets and their highly skilled Wall Street custodians had *"grown up"* since the bad old days of the Great Depression and could now be trusted with our money and our support. And then along came 2008 and all that trust was dissipated almost overnight and was suddenly and dramatically shown to have been sorely misplaced. Maybe it's high time to go *"back to the future."* We agree with Nobel laureate economist Joseph Stiglitz that the repeal of Glass-Steagall played a major role in bringing about the financial calamity of 2008 and we second the motion of renowned economist and financial prognosticator Nouriel Roubini to reenact Glass-Steagall. Even former Fed Chairman Paul Volcker has called for the reinstatement of many aspects of Glass-Steagall (although Roubini does not believe Volcker goes far enough and refers to his proposals as *"Glass-Steagall Lite"*).

18. Regulate Trading of Derivatives, Municipal Bonds and Credit-Rating Agencies:

We demand that all derivatives, including those outstanding (which the new financial reform legislation does not touch) be subjected to SEC regulation and any future trades should be required to clear through a regulated exchange. Regulation of derivatives (particularly the now infamous credit default swaps) is imperative given the almost incomprehensible size of (and thus enormous inherent risk associated with) the market -- currently believed to total somewhere between $600 trillion and a quadrillion dollars in gross nominal value (nobody knows or really can know for certain because of their highly opaque, virtually unregulated and largely decentralized nature), or 10 to 15 times the estimated value of the entire world economy and 40 to 70 times the size of the American economy. And, need we remind you that the perils of the unregulated credit default swap market were instrumental in the collapse of Lehman Brothers, AIG and Bear Sterns and the financial carnage that ensued there from.

Additionally, we agree with SEC head Mary Schapiro that the

municipal bond market, which also operates deep in the shadows, certainly as compared with other debt securities, should be subjected to SEC regulation. The so-called "munis" represent no small potatoes market -- over $2.8 trillion of municipal bonds are currently outstanding and over $4 trillion traded last year, plus tens of billions more in derivatives based on them. According to Schapiro and many others, lack of regulatory oversight puts taxpayers at risk. How much risk? According to Pennsylvania's Auditor General, the lack of regulation has resulted in many municipal bond authorities being sold a bill of goods by Wall Street bankers in the form of derivatives called interest rate swaps that could end up costing taxpayers hundreds of millions of dollars in his state alone.

We also propose that the credit-rating agencies be regulated much more rigorously in order to end their business model which permits and even rewards activities fraught with conflicts of interest. We also demand that the SEC withdraw its regulations which currently exempt the credit-rating agencies from potential federal securities liability in connection with offers and sales of securities (leading some commentators to label the agencies *"untouchable"* or *"Teflon-coated"*). New regulations should be issued bringing the rating agencies into the fold of other parties who can be sued for misstatements in connection with securities offerings, including underwriters, sellers, issuers and "experts" (accountants, attorneys, and the like). There should be no more "free passes" for multi-billion dollar firms like Moody's, Standard & Poor's and Fitch's who are paid exorbitant fees for their "expertise," but suffer no adverse legal consequences when their ratings prove to be false and misleading, grossly negligent or careless or made with reckless disregard to the underlying facts and circumstances.

19. Reject the "Too Big to Fail" Policy:

We demand that Congress adopt resolutions, to be ratified by the President, that serve to reject and disallow actions precipitated on the *"too big to fail"* Policy. No financial or other institution shall be able to avail itself of such a policy in order to avoid liquidation, conservatorship or reorganization. Any institution deemed to be *"too big to fail"* and deemed to part of an oligopoly that has operated to unfairly suppress or stifle competition may be broken up as were Standard Oil in 1911 and AT&T in 1984. Additionally, no industry shall be exempt from the application of federal antitrust laws.

20. Reform Public Discourse:

We demand the separation of news journalism from opinion commentary in radio and television presentations. Congress shall enact legislation creating a firewall between political opinion commentaries in broadcast media versus political news. Further, the enabling legislation shall require that commentators of political opinion disclose their professional credentials; membership in political parties and other political organizations over the past 10 years; political aspirations; affiliations with political figures over the past 10 years; political positions, whether elected or appointed, and lobbying positions held during the past 10 years; amount of payments for opinions and identity of payers; and sponsors. In addition, commentators shall disclose that they are political and broadcast entertainers and not professional news journalists or reporters and that the content of their broadcasts should be viewed accordingly. Appropriate written and oral disclaimers shall be provided to the viewing audience before, during and after each presentation. Commentators shall be required to disclose if either a candidate or party or governmental official has supplied information to the commentator used in the commentary. Congress shall provide for criminal penalties for the failure of broadcasters and commentators and their employers to abide by these rules.

And so we come to the close of this work and what better place to end than to pick up on where we began, some 20 chapters ago, in the *Introduction*. You will recall we shared with you the inside story of the fall of Humpty Dumpty, that spectacle which has for so long been shrouded in secrecy. You will all be pleased to know that the people eventually erected a monument on the site of Mr. Dumpty's dramatic demise, and it bears this inscription:

Humpty Dumpty sat on the wall,

Humpty Dumpty had a great fall,

All the King's horses and all the King's men

Couldn't put Humpty together again.

But the American people,

The Constitution their glue,

Put Humpty together,

Yet better than new.

And they tore down the wall,

Tore it down to the ground,

And they knew then and there,

Their future they'd found.

Now that's change we can truly believe in!

ABOUT THE AUTHORS

Steven A. Cunningham was born in Austin, Texas and grew up in Enterprise, Alabama. Steve is an accomplished attorney and business advisor who has practiced securities and corporate law for the past 33 years. He has been a partner with some of the most prestigious law firms in Atlanta, Georgia, where he currently resides with his wife of 39 years, Betty, and his son, Austin. Steve graduated cum laude from Harvard Law School in 1977 with a Doctorate of Jurisprudence. He received his undergraduate degree from the University of Alabama in 1974, with majors in Political Science and Psychology, graduating summa cum laude and as salutatorian of the College of Arts & Sciences. Steve was also a  member of *Phi Beta Kappa*, the nation's oldest and most recognized academic honor societiy. He was awarded a national scholarship for academic merit and personal achievement by the United States Army Aviation Association of America (his father having been a long-time member of this highly respected organization during his distinguished career as an Army and federal civil service helicopter pilot and instructor at Fort Rucker, Alabama).

Steve graduated salutatorian from Enterprise High School, Enterprise, Alabama, in 1970. He was a champion high school debater, winning the State of Alabama Debate Tournament as a junior and a senior and placing at the National Debate Tournament as a junior. He also won several speaking and essay awards in the *Voice of Democracy* competition sponsored by the VFW.

Steve is an avid tennis player, reader, cook (more so, eater), and sports spectator. He has traveled widely during his career. He is a member of the Episcopal Church and is proud to consider himself part of the worldwide Anglican Communion. He is currently working on a book on dogs, which he is dedicating to his two "best friends", Scooter and Suzie Spot, who died earlier this year, leaving a permanent hole in his heart.

Steve and Leigh have been close friends and business associates for many years and Steve considers Leigh a passionate and articulate spokesperson for the positions and themes presented in this book.

P. Leigh Thomason was born in Dade City, Florida and grew up in Lakeland, Florida. He graduated from Mercer University/Atlanta with under-graduate degrees in history and economics. He won both the Department of History Award in 1972 and Department of Eco-nomics Award in 1974 for Outstanding Academic Student. In 1977 Leigh graduated from Columbus State University (f/k/a Columbus College) with a Master of Business  Administration (MBA) and later attended Thomas Cooley School of Law in Lansing, Michigan. Leigh has also attended Central Michigan University and Troy University.

Leigh has worked both in the public and private sectors, having first worked in the public sector for the Internal Revenue Service and later the Department of Army. In the private sector, Leigh has started several private financial management consulting companies specializing in tax, corporate governance, merger and acquisitions, and capital formation for over 40 business start-ups. In addition,

Leigh has extensive knowledge of the commercial and residential lending industry, having owned both a commercial lending company as well as a residential mortgage lender.

Leigh is married and currently lives in North Atlanta. He considers Steve a very good friend, as well as an astute and insightful political observer, remarkable researcher and excellent writer.